Health Improvement and Well-being

Health Improvement and Well-being: Strategies for Action

Frances Wilson, Mzwandile Andi Mabhala and Alan Massey

JET LIBRARY

Open University Press

Open University Press
McGraw-Hill Education
McGraw-Hill House
Shoppenhangers Road
Maidenhead
Berkshire
England
SL6 2QL

email: enquiries@openup.co.uk
world wide web: www.openup.co.uk

and Two Penn Plaza, New York, NY 10121-2289, USA

First published 2015

A catalogue record of this book is available from the British Library

ISBN-13: 978-0-33-524495-9 (pb)
ISBN-10: 0-33-524495-5 (pb)
eISBN: 978-0-33-524496-6

Library of Congress Cataloging-in-Publication Data
CIP data applied for

Typesetting and e-book compilations by
RefineCatch Limited, Bungay, Suffolk

Dedication

The authors would like to dedicate this book to all those who contributed to it including our fellow professionals, students and not least our families for their support and encouragement.

Contents

Figures

Tables

About the authors

Frances Wilson is a senior lecturer in Health Improvement and Well-being at the University of Chester.

Dr Mzwandile (Andi) Mabhala is a senior lecturer in Public Health at the University of Chester.

Alan Massey is a senior lecturer in Professional Nursing at the University of Chester.

Donna Hart is a principal lecturer at Isle of Man Government, Department of Health and Social Care Education and Training.

Moyra Baldwin is a retired senior lecturer at the University of Chester and Clatterbridge Centre for Oncology.

Dr Janine Talley is a staff tutor at the Open University.

Allison Thorpe is an independent public health specialist.

Foreword

We live in an age where the enjoyment of good health and longevity has for many people become a normal expectation. However, even as medical research and its applications advance, there are still areas of our health and well-being that remain deeply troubling. Defeating some of the cruellest and most obstinate diseases remains a challenge; ill health and distress are often hidden, and frequently caused by the pace, pressure and isolation of our modern lives.

Writing in Chester, I compare the challenges presented to our authors with those of Chester's most famous public health physician, Dr. John Haygarth, who 240 years ago was faced with problems more apparent. The people of Chester had succumbed to an outbreak of typhus and smallpox, and Haygarth was determined not only to understand and to treat his patients, but to inform his esteemed colleagues about the outbreak. He wrote an article, 'Observations on the Population and Diseases of Chester, in the year 1774', and delivered his findings to the Royal Society. It remains one of the most influential papers in public health history.

The centuries may be divided by a chasm of different expectations of health and illness, yet for the clinician and the writer there are challenges that remain remarkably similar. In this text the authors have presented a series of significant, relevant and substantial debates. Some of them, such as inequalities in health, are established but topical. Others, for example health at work, are taking on a new poignancy as the boundaries between our home and professional lives become more blurred.

The construction of each chapter is user friendly and creative, and the 'Thinking point' sections engage those ready to participate and hopefully prompt interactive discussion with colleagues and fellow students from a wide range of health and social care disciplines. Likewise, the case studies bring a textured reality to the book, which will inevitably support practice and students studying at undergraduate and postgraduate levels.

Wilson, Mabhala and Massey (and fellow authors), for their commitment to dissecting the multiple health issues of 2014, have earned their place at the 1774 dinner table of Dr. John Haygarth. I wish I could be a fly on the wall!

Elizabeth Mason-Whitehead, Professor of Health and Social Care
University of Chester, August 2014

Acknowledgements

This book is based on several programmes of study at the University of Chester. All staff involved in the development and delivery of these programmes are thanked for their efforts. Special thanks go to Roger Whiteley for administrative and pastoral support.

Overview of the book

Introduction

As the practice of public health embeds itself in holistic approaches to addressing the complex determinants of health, theorists and practitioners require greater awareness of factors that improve health and well-being. In seeking to advance the elements which create subjective and objective health and well-being, practitioners need to engage with health improvement and well-being as a specific set of public health skills. This book provides global as well as local (UK) perspectives on health improvement and well-being via exploration of the key concepts, particularly those such as social and health inequalities, social justice, political influences, and commissioning, funding and delivery of services that can be translated into interventions to improve health and well-being.

Structure of the book

Each chapter adopts a similar structure. This commences with an introduction to the scope of and rationale for each chapter. Definitions and an outline of theoretical perspectives relevant to each topic allow the reader to gauge the accepted wisdom in each of the fields under discussion. Case studies are utilized to illustrate local and global perspectives. Questions are included to encourage students to think and reflect on the key points of each chapter and apply theory to practice by reviewing the skills required.

Chapter outlines

Chapter 1 – Making sense of health improvement and well-being

The concepts and definitions of health, health improvement and well-being are explored in a universal context. These are deconstructed and critiqued in the context of underpinning theory and evidence of the individual, community and population approaches to health improvement and well-being.

Chapter 2 – The social and health inequalities agenda

Building on the definitions and theories analysed in the previous chapter, exploration of the evidence of the impact of the social determinants of health on health and well-being are undertaken. Political and policy perspectives are outlined, with specific emphasis on the economic implications of health. Finally, theories to address health inequalities are explored.

Chapter 3 – Lifespan transitions and health

This chapter focuses on lifespan transitions between birth and old age. Age and disease profiles are also a feature as are how different strategies for improving health and well-being are required, for example, in an ageing population. Countries with younger age profiles are contrasted. Life expectancy and life point transitions in different parts of the world are explored, considering the major influencing factors resulting in inequalities using case studies of differing approaches to improving health and well-being.

Chapter 4 – Lifestyle and health

The chapter aims to promote understanding of lifestyle factors and choices people make that may improve or impair health. This will include specific health issues resulting from affluence and poverty from UK and wider global perspectives, and practical approaches to improving health and well-being.

Chapter 5 – Behavioural approaches to health and well-being

Person-centred and population approaches to health improvement and well-being are explored focusing on case studies to illustrate effective and successful behaviour change with examples from the lifespan continuum.

Chapter 6 – Social justice and global perspectives on health improvement and well-being

'The way in which people live, and their consequent chances of illness and their risk of premature death, relates to fairness in society' (Marmot 2010). Policy-making and socio-economic factors are explored from a global and UK perspective.

Chapter 7 – Environmental and external influences on health and well-being

The chapter will consider the wider determinants of health including the natural and built environment and other external factors influencing the health and well-being of individuals, communities and populations. The settings in which people live, work and play are explored in order to understand the factors needed to address environmental influences on health and well-being.

Chapter 8 – Commissioning for health improvement and well-being

How governments and local health and social care organizations commission for health improvement and well-being is fundamental to services provided and the type of intervention or local initiative undertaken. Systems of commissioning health and social care provision are explored and compared with those in the UK.

Chapter 9 – Evaluating outcomes following health improvement and well-being interventions

Measuring and evaluating health and well-being outcomes following an intervention is fundamental to demonstrating if the intervention has been successful by reducing inequalities in health and achieving short- and long-term health gains. This chapter explores the various methods of evaluating success.

Chapter 10 – Skills and activities for improving health and well-being

This chapter focuses on the skills required by the range of people working in health improvement and public health sectors of the UK and beyond, with examples of national and international requirements. Some skills are generic and universal while others are very specific professional skills requiring extensive training and education. Throughout the chapter these are linked with activities for improving health and well-being.

Reference

Marmot, M. (2010) *Fair Society, Healthy Lives* (The Marmot Review). Available at www.marmot review.org/AssetLibrary/pdfs/Reports/FairSocietyHealthyLives.pdf (accessed 28 June 2011).

1 | Making sense of health improvement and well-being

Frances Wilson, Alan Massey and Dr Mzwandile (Andi) Mabhala

Introduction

This chapter explores concepts and definitions of health, health improvement, and well-being. These concepts will be deconstructed and critiqued in the context of underpinning theory and evidence of the individual, community and population approaches to health improvement and well-being.

This is undertaken to allow the reader to appreciate the differences and similarities of these concepts. It will allow the reader to appreciate the contribution of these concepts to providing health care, public health and the promotion of health improvement and well-being. The use of case studies will facilitate the integration of these concepts with practice in the fields of health, improvement, and well-being.

The chapter includes the following sections:

- Health, including definitions and explorations of medical, sociological and environmental constructs of this concept.
- Health improvement, including discussion of this concept from a United Kingdom policy perspective.
- Well-being, including measuring well-being and enhancing individual and population well-being.

Definitions and concepts of health

Defining health has interested academics, practitioners, policy makers and lay people for a number of years, and to date no consensus has been reached on how to define and utilize the concept. According to Tones and Green (2010), health is a contested concept and often conceptualized from polar positions – for example, professional perspectives versus lay perspectives, or positive perspectives of health versus negative perspectives of illness. What is clear according to these authors is that, although health as a concept is disputed, the search for its meaning should continue. The rationale for this approach is that without clear aims and objectives then services that provide for health and well-being would lack direction. Without an understanding of health from differing perspectives, providing effective strategies to improve health is beyond our grasp. Although there have been voices contesting this point of view, arguing that a strict definition of health would stifle debate and research, it is generally accepted that defining health and reaching consensus on this concept is a useful if challenging undertaking.

Perspectives on health

Traditional definitions of health adopted a sociological, environmental, biological and cultural focus, and considered the balance of man, his environment, and the agents of disease. For example, the word 'health' comes from the old English word *hale*, meaning wholeness. Hippocrates (*circa* 377 BC) indicated health was the delicate balance of the four essential fluids. Traditional Chinese definitions of health outline health as harmony and balance between man and his environment. These sentiments are echoed in traditional Latin, Native American and Polynesian definitions of health. All these incorporate awareness of the holistic balance of people and their environment, including the spiritual, cultural and social environments (Üstün and Jakob 2005). According to the same authors, there are additional traditional definitions of health worth considering, based on religious teachings. Buddhism and Hinduism, for example, both outline the necessity for man to live in harmony and to undertake health behaviours conducive to a fruitful life.

The traditional holistic definitions indicating harmony and balance have been replaced in relatively recent times by medical perspectives of health. The medical model of health came to dominate the late nineteenth and early twentieth centuries. Definitions within this model were based on the premise that health was the absence of disease, and that all disease had a specific cause; it was assumed that the medical model could identify, treat and prevent all diseases (Wylie 1970). Within the medical/scientific models, most research into experiences of health and well-being focused on disease and the causes, process and outcomes of disease. As such, professional definitions of health have been located in the medical model of health since this time. It could be argued that, despite growing awareness that the causes of disease are multifactorial, this model still dominates care provision.

Historically, the medical perspective of disease has been useful as definitions of disease are the first steps in the measurement and prevention process. The disease process is therefore easier to measure and to protect against, than the nebulous concept of promoting health and harmony/well-being. Measuring health and well-being are difficult because they are culturally and subjectively defined.

In 1948, the World Health Organization (WHO) defined health as, 'a complete state of physical, mental and social well-being, and not merely the absence of disease or infirmity'. Following the end of the Second World War this definition reflected the mood of its time, namely, that health is a basic human right, that health should strive for equity and empowerment, and that health should be aspi-rational. The concept of wellness emerges within the definition, signalling a return to awareness of the wider sociological, environmental and cultural factors that determine our health (Tones and Green 2010).

The re-emergence of public health and growing awareness of the limits of the medical model have meant there has been a shift of emphasis towards under-standing factors that promote health. Policy makers since the Lalonde report (1974) have sought to shift the focus of health provision from the medical model to the sociological model of health, in an attempt to gain deeper understanding of factors, in conjunction with biology, that influence or determine our health (Scriven 2010). Similarly, there has been a growing awareness of the role psychology plays in health and health behaviours. Maslow's hierarchy of needs and models such as Antonovsky's sense of coherence have been instrumental in better understanding that health and disease are interpreted by individuals on a continuum of experience, and not as juxtaposed positions of the same concept. Out of this growing awareness, the well-being agenda has arisen (Tones and Green 2010).

Thinking point

In your opinion, should we seek to understand health via a holistic under-standing of all the factors which may shape our health? Or is disease the obvious indication of health and as such holistic understanding is unnecessary?

The role of the WHO in developing approaches to addressing health

The Ottawa Charter 1986 was instrumental in directing the efforts of policy makers and governments towards creating environments conducive to health, based on current awareness of the factors that determine a person's health. The Charter was also influential in seeking to move definitions of health towards a holistic or wellness approach to health, with the intention of health improvement across the globe. These approaches are evidenced within the Millennium goals. The move to progress definitions of health to better suit modern lived experiences of health and disease is required as patterns of disease have changed. However, the WHO's definition of health still dominates attempts to address health improve-ment. This definition has been widely criticized and Huber *et al.* (2011) indicate that its continued use by the WHO is counterproductive as it embeds the medicali-zation of health into care provision.

Modern qualitative exploration of what is health (Bishop and Yardley 2010) indi-cates that health is a search for wholeness. This view is supported by Polakoff and Gregory (2002) who indicate that non-medical theorists seek to develop care based on the integration of the mind, body and spirit. The search for harmony and balance in human health mirrors its historical definitions. Researchers into lay definitions of health indicate that an understanding of health is not solely focused on biological definitions and measurements. Rather, they are concerned with the presence of health (to be health), the ability to function and carry out roles (to do health) and health as a positive attitude (to have health) (Bishop and Yardley 2010).

Individual, community and population approaches to assessing and measuring health improvement and well-being

Beattie (1991) offers a useful framework which outlines the distinctions between approaches to assessing health (Figure 1.1).

In seeking to explore health from these perspectives, the following mechanisms are commonly utilized:

- Qualitative individual self-assessment of health status.
- Quantitative service utilization data.
- Quantitative health surveillance data.
- Quantitative epidemiological data (demographics, morbidity and mortality).
- Qualitative and quantitative risk assessment data.
- Qualitative and quantitative health needs assessments.
- Qualitative and quantitative health impact assessments.

The purposes of these streams of enquiry are to systematically analyse the health problems facing an individual, community or population, so that analysis of

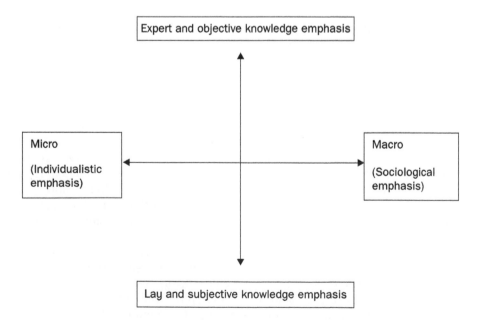

Figure 1.1 Beattie's model of health promotion (1991): a framework for assessing health

the health threats and determinants of health faced can be understood, and priorities for interventions ascertained (Tones and Green 2010).

On an individual level, this is usually undertaken via a health assessment and focused on the health issues facing that individual. There is no universally accepted health assessment tool. This is owing to theorists' interpretation of the key concepts, which shape health assessment tools. Specifically, what shapes health are interpretations of the concepts of health, the role of the individual, the role of the environment and the focus of interventions. This form of assessment is predominantly reactive in nature, and generally occurs once an individual has presented with a health problem or following a form of screening.

In seeking to take an upstream approach, the concepts of community and population health assessments have been developed. In highlighting the control of the medical model, it should be noted that until relatively recently this process has been dominated by epidemiological investigation. Disquiet with the medical model has developed owing to its focus on disease. This same criticism is levelled at epidemiology, and to redress this balance, population-based health assessments now incorporate lay opinions of health needs alongside the epidemiological data, in addition to analysis of the factors which determine health. Factors which determine health were encapsulated by the Lalonde health field concept (1974) (Figure 1.2).

In addition to upstream thinking, the concepts of partnership, empowerment, health inequalities and choice are embedded within needs assessments. This is owing to the requirement for qualitative and quantitative research into people's health needs, and the policy directive to address provision where needs are identified. This process is seen as the best mechanism for engaging all local

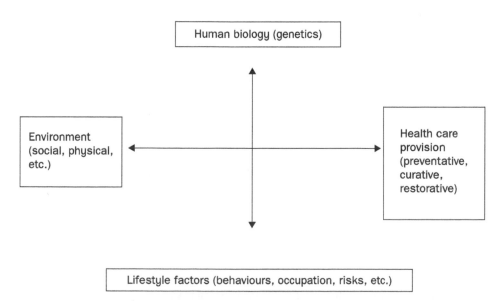

Figure 1.2 The Lalonde field concept (1974)

stakeholders in decisions about their health and for creating strong partnerships
to implement effective interventions. Figure 1.3 shows the Joint Strategic Needs
Assessment (JSNA) framework from the Department of Health (DH) in England
(2007a).

According to Glasby and Ellins (2008), these joint needs assessments are seen
as the glue which will bind together the different voices of what health is and

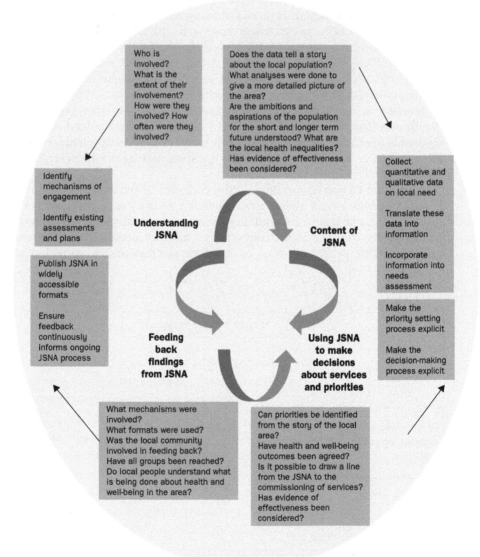

Figure 1.3 Joint Strategic Needs Assessment framework
Source: DH (2007a).

what health can be via partnerships and joint working. This allows competing views of health to be debated and for agreed priorities for action to be taken. However, partnership working is fraught with problems as best illustrated by the work of Sherry Arnstein (1969). Arnstein indicates that a pluralistic approach to health planning is always open to differing interpretations of power and how power should be exercised. For successful partnership to occur, power should be shared equally by all concerned. The effectiveness of the needs assessment approach is open to debate, and Marks *et al.* (2011) make a powerful argument as to why guidance on what counts as success in public health is required before debates on particular elements of this public health mechanism can be concluded.

Marmot (2010), Wilkinson and Pickett (2010) and Rowlingson (2011) indicate that the links between the determinants of health, particularly inequalities, do lead to differences in health outcomes and that addressing the social determinants of health is essential. Rowlingson within her report on income inequalities indicates that research into the role of status anxiety is emerging. This is a state of stress caused by the self-knowledge of one's place in society. This has echoes with the work of Antonovsky (1987) who indicated that whatever approach is used to identify factors that determine health, be it disease based or sociologically based, researchers tend to adopt a pathogenic approach focused on the causes of disease. Antonovsky advocated focusing on salutogenesis in addition to pathogenesis. Salutogenesis is the term he used to describe focusing on factors which are health enhancing. Antonovsky indicated that the debates surrounding how best to deal with health should accept that health is constantly challenged, and it is how individuals cope with the challenges they face that lead to health outcomes. By focusing on how individuals cope, we can best focus on health and health enhancing activities.

In summary health is a contested concept. Individuals and professional bodies interpret the concept of health in different ways. People's subjective experience will shape their view of what health is, as such, what is healthy for one individual may be considered unhealthy for another. This may be at odds with you as a professional or with other professional bodies.

It is clear that global efforts are required to not only deal with the outcomes of ill health, but that steps are required to improve health. The following section is an in-depth analysis of health improvement from a United Kingdom (UK) perspective.

Population and community approaches to health improvement

Understanding of health improvement concerns matters that are essential to sustain human existence across the whole lifespan. The concept of health improvement was first made prominent in UK public health policy by the publication of *The New NHS: Modern and Dependable* (DH 1997), in which the Labour government outlined their commitment to social justice principles, and provided an overview of their public health strategy to reduce inequalities in health. In this policy paper, specialized public health organizations were to be set up to tackle the problems of health inequalities, ill health, deprivation and poor or fragmented services. The justification for establishing these new specialized bodies – led by local authorities, but working in partnership with a wide range of organizations, including the National Health Service (NHS) – was that the fragmented NHS had been poorly placed to tackle crucial issues that required better integration across health and social care.

The concept of health improvement lacking a stable and bounded definition leaves it open to multiple interpretations and debates. Some debates hinge around whether health improvement is primarily about health, health care or the wider socio-economic determinants of health inequalities; others ask where the responsibility for carrying out health improvement resides – is it with health care or with social care? In the UK, the lack of a single definition has made the concept malleable, suitable for use by proponents of contrasting interventionist and non-interventionist strategies. Interventionists' views of health improvement generally refer to upstream population-based activities associated with tackling the core determinants of health inequalities. Non-interventionists refer to activities associated with encouraging individuals to make healthier choices and take responsibility for their own health.

Within that context, it was proposed that the principles and values that underpin health improvement are social justice, equality, fairness, integration, partnership, and cooperation between NHS bodies and local authorities, and that the previous internal market with its emphasis on competitive values was at odds with the ethos of fairness intrinsic to the public health discipline (Mabhala 2012). Health improvement programmes would create an environment where competitive values would be replaced with cooperation and integration, and which would facilitate equitable access to health and social services at local levels, as well as tackling other shortcomings (DH 1997). These objectives were strengthened through new legislation – the Health Act 1999, sections 27–31 – which made provision for local authorities and health authorities to prepare a plan setting out a strategy for improving the health of the people for whom they are responsible (HM Government 1999).

During the early years of the New Labour administration, health improvement was considered to be a concept that encompassed many fundamental health determinants, including those residing outside the NHS and health-care jurisdictions. The specialized health improvement programmes were seen as a direct response to the *Independent Inquiry into Inequalities in Health Report* (DH 1998) which proposed that tackling wider determinants of inequalities in health required genuine joint working between health and social policy makers. Mackenbach and Bakker (2003) provided an explanation of the need for joint working, noting that health policy makers do not usually make decisions about the economic, social and environmental well-being of their areas, while social policy makers may not always be certain how their economic, social and environmental policies affect the health of their population.

Since the publication of *The New NHS: Modern and Dependable* (DH 1997) the public health community has recognized health improvement as one of their domains. The public health model that first recognized this was presented in *The Review of the Public Health Function in Northern Ireland* (Health, Social Services and Public Safety 2004) which explored how the activities and functions of public health were organized. This consultation proposed a model of public health practice organized around three domains: health improvement, health protection and service development. This model has been adapted by several public health bodies, political organizations and researchers (Griffiths *et al.* 2005; Thorpe *et al.* 2008): for example, Sian Griffiths (then the president of the UK Faculty of Public Health) and colleagues used teenage pregnancy as a case study to demonstrate the practical application of these three domains, proposing that in this context the health improvement domain required links at policy level with education, schools, youth services, and Connexions (a youth employment/training/careers advisory service) (Griffiths *et al.* 2005). Several public health reports concur with their position; they, too, propose that health improvement is characterized by activities focusing on addressing the determinants of health (causes of causes) and the root causes of ill health, such as poverty, education, income, inequalities, education and housing, as well as activities aimed at promoting positive health and well-being, such as smoking prevention, tackling obesity and screening programmes (DH 1997, 1999; Health, Social Services and Public Safety 2004; Griffiths *et al.* 2005; Thorpe *et al.* 2008; Faculty of Public Health 2010). Thorpe *et al.* (2008) assert that this model provides a comprehensive framework for the development of skills and competencies in the context of practice within the public health workforce.

Individual approaches to health improvement

After 2004 there was a noticeable change in the interpretation of health improvement, moving from its original emphasis on the upstream population and the wider social determinants of health, to a focus on downstream individual lifestyle and behaviour approaches. This reflects changes in the definition of public health from the one published in *Independent Inquiry into Inequalities in Health Report* (DH 1998) – also known as the Acheson Report – and in Faculty of Public Health (2010), both of which defined it as the 'science and art of promoting and protecting health and well-being, preventing ill-health and prolonging life through *the organised efforts of society*' [emphasis added]. Contrast this with the definition used in *Securing Good Health for the Whole Population* (HM Treasury 2004) – also known as the Wanless Report – in which public health was defined as the 'science and art of preventing disease, prolonging life and promoting health through the organized efforts and *informed choices of society*, organizations public and *private*, communities and *individuals*' [emphasis added].

This change in the definition of public health fuelled a debate about whether health improvement is the responsibility of individuals, state, private organizations or society. The Wanless Report concluded that ultimately individuals were responsible for their own and their children's health, and that it was the aggregate actions of individuals which would determine if the optimistic 'fully engaged' scenario unfolded. It went on to assert that people needed more active support to make better decisions about their own health and welfare, arguing the need for policies that enable individuals to access enough information to consider fully the wider social costs of their behaviours, as well as ingrained social attitudes not conducive to individuals pursuing healthy lifestyles. The greatest emphasis in this review was on supporting individuals to change behaviour and make healthier choices, and it identified three areas where health-related policy intervention might be needed – minimum income, work and stress, and environment. This emphasis on individual responsibility and individual choice resonates with the libertarian vision of civil society: collective well-being is best achieved through the exercise of individual free will and self-responsibility (Almgren 2007). Libertarians are concerned solely with limiting the adverse effect of governmental interference upon individuals' ability to exercise control over their own lives (Powers and Faden 2006; Almgren 2007), and argue that because illness, unemployment and even old age are risks intrinsic to human social existence, it is the role and responsibility of individuals in a free and civil society to self-protect through mechanisms of insurance and savings (Almgren 2007).

Subsequent policy papers continued this shift to a downstream approach. For example, the principles that underpinned successive papers on public health (DH 2004a, 2004b, 2006, 2010b) were primarily about personal responsibility, working together and informed choice, all delivered through a process of contestability, commissioning and giving people a choice (DH 2004a; UKPHA 2005).

Several health professional bodies, including the British Medical Association (BMA), Royal College of Nursing (RCN), and United Kingdom Public Health Association (UKPHA), expressed major concerns about this emphasis on downstream behavioural interventions (Raine *et al.* 2004; UKPHA 2005). For example Raine *et al.* (2004) argued that changing behaviour would require the implementation of comprehensive structural, environmental and economic interventions, while UKPHA (2005) asserted that choice was an irrelevant concept in public health, and that health education would have a negligible, or possibly a detrimental, effect on health status and inequality. Both UK Health Watch (2005) and UKPHA (2005) reminded us that many individuals could not choose whether they had sufficient income to live in warm and safe housing and eat healthy food.

The public health community favoured the model of health improvement outlined in the earlier *Saving Lives: Our Healthier Nation* (DH 1999), for its commitment to social justice principles and upstream public health interventions (Evans 2003; Hunter and Sengupta 2004; UKPHA 2005). This view sees health improvement as giving people a better education; creating employment so that people can achieve greater prosperity; building social capital by increasing social cohesion; reducing social stress by regenerating neighbourhoods and communities; and tackling aspects of the workplace which are damaging to health (DH 1999) – in short, tackling the fundamental determinants of health inequalities.

Change in the political landscape

When the Conservative-led coalition government came into power in 2010 the concept of health improvement was high on their agenda, and their first policy paper, *Equity and Excellence: Liberating the NHS* (DH 2010a), outlined their

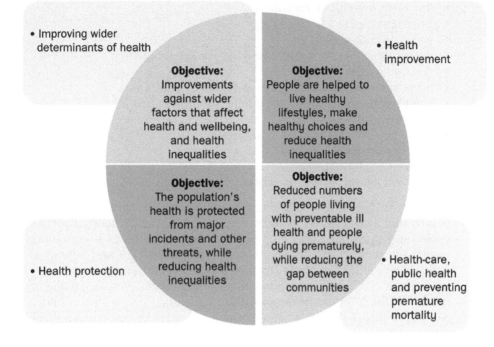

Figure 1.4 Domains of public health

Source: adapted from public health framework (DH 2012).

plans to deliver local health improvement. These included transfer of responsibility to deliver health improvement programmes from the primary health-care
trusts to local authorities, and aimed to establish new statutory arrangements
within local authorities' 'health and well-being boards' to take on the function of
joining up the commissioning of local NHS services, social care and health
improvement (DH 2010a). These health and well-being boards were intended
to allow local authorities to take a strategic approach and promote integration
across health and adult social care, children's services (including safeguarding),
and the wider local authority agenda. The first coalition government policy paper
on public health *Healthy Lives, Healthy People* (DH 2010b) outlined how health
improvement would be delivered through local authorities, proposing a public
health outcomes framework, and introducing a premium intended to incentivize
local government and communities to improve health and reduce inequalities.
The public health framework (Figure 1.4), published in *Improving Outcomes
and Supporting Transparency* (DH 2012), consisted of four domains of public
health.

According to the framework, the health improvement domain focuses on actions
to help people make healthy choices and lead healthy lifestyles. Health improvement indicators include:

- low birth weight of term babies
- breastfeeding
- under 18 conceptions
- excess weight in the 4–5 and 10–11 years age groups
- diet and excess weight
- proportion of physically active and inactive adults
- smoking prevalence amongst adults (over 18s)
- recorded diabetes
- alcohol-related admissions to hospital
- cancer screening coverage
- self-reported well-being
- falls and injuries in people over 65.

Seeing health improvement as primarily about individual lifestyle change was one of the main differences between recent and earlier policy documents. The coalition government apparently had a strong commitment to promoting health improvement. However, its emphasis on individual care and individual choice within the context of public health policy arguably reflects the libertarian views of those on the political right who, as the UK Education Secretary explained in his speech to the National Society for the Prevention of Cruelty to Children on 12 November 2013, believe that intervention is bound to be costly and is rarely if ever effective (Department for Education 2013). This view rejects the social theory analysis which identifies manifestations of health inequalities – such as substance abuse and domestic violence – as being socially caused; instead it advocates reducing health (and indeed other) inequalities by working with individuals to get them to recognize their wrong choices and harmful patterns of behaviour, and to improve their own lives (Department for Education 2013).

Thinking point

In your opinion, which of the two approaches debated above, upstream or downstream, are best suited to improve the health of your local community?

What are the advantages of adopting an upstream approach to health improvement? What limitations does a downstream approach place on health improvement programmes? In utilizing downstream approaches do you feel that holistic factors which improve health, such as well-being programmes, need further consideration?

Definitions and concepts of well-being

Our Health and Wellbeing Today (DH 2010c) declares well-being is an important part of our health. England's population has average well-being when compared internationally, but there are likely to be wide variations within the country.

Figure 1.5 Definitions of well-being
Source: Dodge *et al.* (2012).

Well-being as a concept has a variety of definitions and applications which will be explored at individual, community and population levels.

Defining well-being has been attempted by many academics and organizations. The Department for Environment, Food and Rural Affairs suggests a broad definition which includes physical, social and emotional dimensions of well-being: Well-being is

> a positive physical, social and mental state; it is not just the absence of pain, discomfort and incapacity. It requires that basic needs are met, that individuals have a sense of purpose, that they feel able to achieve important personal goals and participate in society. It is enhanced by conditions that include supportive personal relationships, strong and inclusive communities, good health, financial and personal security, rewarding employment, and a healthy and attractive environment. (DEFRA 2010: 13)

Well-being can be described as a balance between the challenges in life and the ability to mobilize individual resources to meet those challenges, thus maintaining a state of equilibrium or stability. These resources and challenges may have psychological, social and physical manifestations. When the challenges outweigh the resources, then well-being may decline or vice versa (see Figure 1.5; Dodge *et al.* 2012).

Enhancing well-being

Evidence suggests that positive mental health is a vital factor in enhancing well-being and it is influenced by actions we take and the way we think[1] (Foresight Mental Capital and Well-being Project 2008). Actions may be taken in several ways to address the psychological, mental, social, physical and economic aspects of well-being (see Table 1.1). It should be noted that all aspects of well-being are interlinked and capable of contributing to the mental health and well-being of an individual. A sense of community and the natural environment also contributes to social and mental well-being.

Table 1.1 Enhancing well-being

Mental well-being	Evidence suggests that physical, social, psychological and economic well-being links to mental well-being. Connecting with people, being active, learning new skills, giving and sharing with others, and being aware of your environment comprise the five steps to mental well-being
Physical well-being	Keep active through increasing your usual amount of daily or weekly activity. Examples include walking, cycling, running, sport, gardening, dancing or taking the stairs. Joining a leisure centre or gym are options. Maintain a healthy diet and health awareness
Social well-being	Develops and maintains social contact and good relationships with friends, neighbours and family. Interpersonal skills. Engagement with the community and shared activities – a sense of belonging. Social capital. Does not engage in antisocial behaviour, or is socially excluded.
Psychological well-being	Giving to others such as volunteering, being helpful, building new social networks, managing own emotions, being resilient.
Economic well-being	Household and individual income from employment or pensions. Benefits payments. Consumption, expenditure and wealth. Making ends meet.

Source: Information distilled from DH (2007b); NHS (2013); NICE (2013); OECD (2013a).

Measuring well-being

How well-being is assessed and measured is an area for wide debate as there are many influencing factors to consider. An evolving mass of evidence links well-being in general terms to positive mental well-being. However, recent surveys of well-being support a framework approach to common determinants or 'domains' of well-being (Office for National Statistics 2013), which will be adopted as a baseline for this book as they are supported by a growing body of research evidence.

Figure 1.6 contextualizes individual well-being within a framework of factors that impact either directly or indirectly on it. Each individual will be affected differently by these key factors and as such will influence analysis and policy development in ways that may be unanticipated. Each of these factors feature in the domains of national well-being.

Domains of national well-being

These were developed following a public consultation and national debate in England in 2011. The intention is to provide annual reports which indicate well-being in relation to the economy, people and the environment, and aim to provide an overview of 'how society is doing'. A first report called *Measuring National Well-being, Health, 2012* was published in July 2012 and reflects a snapshot of

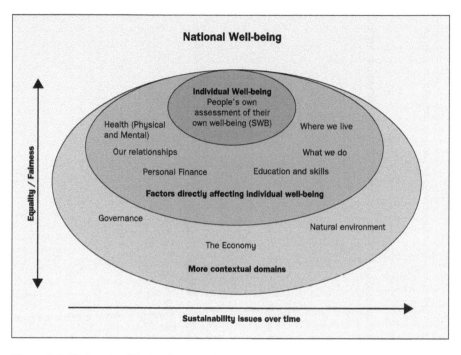

Figure 1.6 National well-being framework

Source: Beaumont (2011).

well-being in the UK at that time (Beaumont and Thomas 2012). The key areas measured in each domain are a combination of self-rated and statistical measures. Other data such as unemployment, crime and satisfaction with life is also considered.

Measures of national well-being are based on the domains and measures shown in Table 1.2.

The table contains the ten domains of well-being, examples from the 38 key measurement areas that have been developed following research by the ONS and a breakdown of the questions asked in the annual survey. A visit to the interactive website will provide results for the years 2011 to 2013 (ONS Interactive site 2014). The analysis of such data is complex, and it should be read in context.

Well-being and life satisfaction

What is the point of measuring well-being? Measuring some aspects of personal well-being can be subjective, such as allocating a score to how you are feeling – for example, by reflecting on the previous week. However, life satisfaction asks people to evaluate their lives as a whole, taking into account the long-term view and resulting in a more balanced perspective.

The survey revealed that personal well-being improved in the UK between

Table 1.2 Domains of well-being and areas of measurement

Domain of well-being	Examples of how well-being can be measured
Personal well-being	Satisfaction with personal life; activities felt to be worthwhile; rated happiness or anxiety; population mental well-being
	Sources: ONS; UKLHS
Our relationships	Satisfaction with family and social life; having a close person to rely on e.g. spouse, family member or friend
	Sources: EUQLS; UKLHS
Health	Life expectancy at birth
	Reported long-term illness and disability
	Levels of satisfaction with their health
	Evidence of probable psychological or mental ill health
	Sources: ONS; UKLHS
What we do	Unemployment rate
	Level of satisfaction with their job and amount of leisure time
	Volunteered or engaged/participated in arts or cultural activity in last year
	Adult participation in 30 minutes of moderate intensity sport each week
	Sources: ONS; UKLHS; SE
Where we live	Crimes against the person
	Feeling safe walking alone after dark (men/women)
	Access to natural environment at least 1 time per week
	Belonging to their neighbourhood
	Good transport access to key services or work
	Fairly/very satisfied with accommodation
	Sources: ONS; NE; UKLHS; DT

Personal finance	Levels of satisfaction with the income of their household
	Report finding it quite or very difficult to get by financially
	Sources: DWP; UKLHS
Economy	Income per head
	UK public sector debt as a percentage of GDP
	Inflation rate as measured by CPI
	Source: ONS
Education and skills	Five or more GCSEs A* to C including English and Mathematics
	UK residents aged 16 to 64 with no qualifications
	Sources: ONS; DEd
Governance	Registered voters who voted
	Trust in government
	Sources: IIDEA; E
Natural environment	Total greenhouse gas emissions
	Protected areas in UK
	Energy consumed within the UK from renewable sources
	Recycled household waste
	Sources: DECC; DEFRA

Key: UK Household Longtudinal Study (UKLHS); Office for National Statistics (ONS); European Quality of Life Survey (EUQLS); Sport England (SE); Natural England (NE); International Institute for Democracy and Electoral Assistance (IIDEA); Eurobarometer (E); Department of Transport (DT); Department of Work and Pensions (DWP); Department of Education, Wales, Scotland, N. Ireland (DEd); Department of Energy and Climate Change (DECC); Department for Environment, Food and Rural Affairs (DEFRA)

Source: based on the ONS (2013).

2011/12 and 2012/13. A greater proportion of people in Northern Ireland rated their life satisfaction, happiness and feeling that life was worthwhile as very high (9 or 10 out of 10) than in any other country. Among the English regions, the South West and the South East had some of the highest levels of average life satisfaction and worthwhile ratings in 2012/13. The South West also had proportionately more people than any other region rating life satisfaction, feeling that life was worthwhile and happiness as 9 or 10 out of 10.

The relationship between personal well-being and local circumstances is complex and the reasons why different areas of the UK have different levels of personal well-being are not yet fully understood. The Office for National Statistics (ONS) plans to publish further analysis looking in detail at how different aspects of where we live contribute to personal well-being.

Clearly measuring well-being is more than simply measuring the growth in GDP. Both economic and social progress are essential measures that reflect the mood of the country, and can be measured over time as regular surveys are undertaken. This is not unique to England: the Organisation for Economic Co-operation and Development has a *How's Life* (OECD 2013b) life index which compares well-being across countries, based on 11 categories of well-being similar to those used by the ONS. In addition the OECD aims to measure inequalities between different groups in society including levels of income, education, health or general satisfaction with life; it also asks if gender makes a difference. This approach helps identify differences in well-being which can influence the policy-making agenda (OECD 2013a).

The OECD in 2007 requested that all countries produce such data so comparisons could then be made. There is evidence since the economic crisis in the first decade of the twenty-first century that there has been a measurable downturn in well-being in some countries. There is no doubt that individuals have been affected economically with higher levels of unemployment, increased personal debt and increased poverty. This can be observed, for example, in the societal changes evident in the UK with its proliferation of 'food banks'. However, this must be analysed in its broader context, and students should be aware that the impact of the economic crisis may only be evident in years to come.

Australia, Canada and the USA are also producing measures of well-being – the measures are linked to the social, economic and environmental progress of countries, and can be accessed via individual websites. Again, there are direct links between the poor state of a country's economy following the impact of recession and a decline in well-being. Interestingly, the Canadian Index of Well-being (CIW) shows less economic security and increased levels of unemployment, yet an increased feeling of belonging to a community. Canada's overall health has also improved very little, although there is increased life expectancy and it remains one of the highest in the world. Again these indicators must be viewed in the context of the whole report (CIW 2013).

Well-being and policy development

The measures of well-being also provide governments with evidence to target policy development to meet the needs and aspirations of the people, and measure

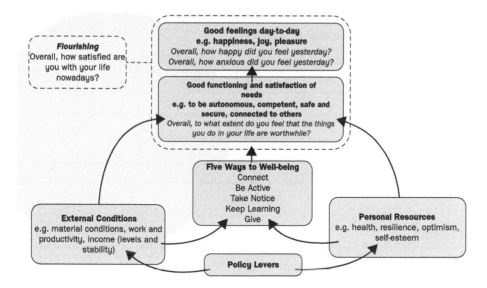

Figure 1.7 Policy influences the drivers of well-being

Source: Seaford (2011) cited in Maxwell *et al.* (2011).

the impact of policy in hindsight. Examples include targeting policy at groups in society that will benefit their health, increase job opportunities and improve education (Figure 1.7).

UK policies in recent years have been instrumental in promoting and improving well-being. In 2013 Public Health England was established with the remit to improve health and well-being and reduce health inequalities. Delivery of public health will now be led by local authorities and health and well-being boards (HWBs) through local partnerships. The Public Health Outcomes Framework for England specifically targets well-being, linking it directly to the ONS domains of well-being. The outcomes indicators for well-being will be measured annually. Other specific policies which are either new or being reviewed incorporate well-being objective measures, also linked to the ONS. Examples relating to policy and strategy development include Alcohol Strategy; Mental Health and Well-being; Well-being in the Workplace, Staff Well-being (in the DH); Young People's Well-being; Education; Troubled Families; Transport Systems; and The Built Environment. A similar approach is being taken in Scotland and Wales (DH 2013)

Thinking points

What are the main sources of data for measuring well-being in a population? How reliable are the research and statistics on which well-being data is based? How far does well-being data usefully inform policy making and government decision making? Is the data comparable with other countries in the UK, Europe and globally?

Well-being definition box

Please make notes and define well-being in the following contexts:

Well-being	Mental	Physical	Psychological	Social	Economic
Individual					
Community					
Population					

Conclusion

Within this chapter, we have identified that concepts such as health, health improvement and well-being are contested. When seeking to define a concept it is clear that a variety of theoretical perspectives exist. In translating these perspectives into action to address health and well-being, cultural and socially constructed meanings of health are influenced by factors such as ethical and moral acceptability, the dominance of medical and economic perspectives of health, and the need for evidence of effectiveness.

It is widely accepted that the biomedical model of health has dominated efforts to address health and well-being since the mid-nineteenth century. In recent years, alternative models of health have developed to address the inherent flaws of the biomedical approach (Tones and Green 2010), which does not take sufficient account of the psychosocial factors which influence health. Similarly, medicine is reactive rather than proactive, focusing on factors that prevent or treat disease, and therefore has limited appeal to those seeking to identify factors that improve or maintain health and well-being. Proactive models have been developed to do just that – the intention being not only to extend life, but also to gain greater understanding of factors that improve quality of life and add to subjective feelings of health and well-being. As such, the well-being agenda falls within positive definitions of health and has an aspirational element to it.

The rise of consumerism and the choice agenda has meant that individuals and society have clear aspirations towards a good lifestyle. The holistic nature of well-being and the promise to deal with mind, body and soul are appealing to many, and within the developed world people are much wealthier and healthier than before. However, in modern industrialized nations the increase in relative wealth has not been matched by an increase in subjective feelings of well-being; for example, the quality of family life is thought to have decreased. Finally, according to White (2010), well-being offers hope in its move from a reductionist perspective towards a holistic approach, via its emphasis on the subjective strengths of individuals and communities.

Note

1   Ways in which to improve and maintain mental well-being include getting and keeping active, social links with others, keeping learning, being aware of yourself and the world around you, and giving to others. NHS Choices provides a well-being self-assessment tool that individuals may find useful. It is based on a series of 14 questions such as being optimistic about the future, and being interested in yourself and other people (Foresight Mental Capital and Wellbeing Project 2008).

References

Almgren, G. (2007) *Health Care Politics, Policy and Services: A Social Justice Analysis.* New York: Springer.

Antonovsky, A. (1987) *Unraveling the Mystery of Health – How People Manage Stress and Stay Well.* San Francisco, CA: Jossey-Bass.

Arnstein, S.R. (1969) A ladder of citizen participation, *Journal of the American Institute of Planners,* 35(4): 216–24.

Beattie, A. (1991) Knowledge and control in health promotion: a test case for social policy and social theory, in J. Gabe, M. Calnan and M. Bury (eds) *Sociology of Health Services.* London: Routledge.

Beaumont, J. (2011) Measuring Wellbeing: A discussion paper on domains and measures. Office for National Statistics http://www.ons.gov.uk/ons/dcp171766_240726.pdf

Beaumont, J. and Thomas, J. (2012) *Measuring National Well-being, Health, 2012,* 24 July, Office for National Statistics. Available at www.ons.gov.uk/ons/dcp171766_271762.pdf (accessed 14 May 2014).

Bishop, F. and Yardley, L. (2010) The development and initial validation of a new measure of lay definitions of health: the wellness beliefs scale. *Psychology and Health,* 25(3): 271–87.

Canadian Index of Well-being (CIW) (2013) *Canadian Index of Well-being.* Available at https://uwaterloo.ca/canadian-index-well-being/ (accessed Dec. 2013).

Department for Education (2013) *Michael Gove Speech to the NSPCC: Getting it Right for Children in Need.* London: HM Government. Available at www.gov.uk/government/speeches/getting-it-right-for-children-in-need-speech-to-the-nspcc (accessed Dec. 2013).

Department for Environment, Food and Rural Affairs (DEFRA) (2010) *Measuring Progress: Sustainable Development Indicators 2010.* Available at www.defra.gov.uk/sustainable/government/progress/documents/SDI2010_001.pdf (accessed Jan. 2014).

Department of Health (DH) (1997) *The New NHS: Modern and Dependable.* London: DH.

Department of Health (DH) (1998) *Independent Inquiry into Inequalities in Health Report* (Acheson Report). London: DH.

Department of Health (DH) (1999) *Saving Lives: Our Healthier Nation.* London: DH.

Department of Health (DH) (2004a) *Choosing Health: Making Healthy Choices Easier.* London: DH.

Department of Health (DH) (2004b) *The NHS Improvement Plan: Putting People at the Heart of Public Services.* London: DH.

Department of Health (DH) (2006) *Our Health, Our Care, Our Say: A New Direction for Community Services.* London: DH.

Department of Health (DH) (2007a) *Guidance on Joint Strategic Needs Assessment.* www.dh.gov.uk/prod_consum_dh/groups/dh_digitalassets/@dh/@en/documents/digitalasset/dh_081267.pdf (accessed Oct. 2010).

Department of Health (DH) (2007b) *Foresight – Tackling Obesities – Future Choices Project.* Available at www.gov.uk/government/collections/foresight-projects (accessed May 2014).

Department of Health (DH) (2010a) *Equity and Excellence: Liberating the NHS*. Available at www.
dh.gov.uk/prod_consum_dh/groups/dh_digitalassets/@dh/@en/@ps/documents/digitalasset/
dh_117794.pdf (accessed 15 Apr. 2011).

Department of Health (DH) (2010b) *Healthy Lives, Healthy People: Our Strategy for Public Health
in England*. London: DH.

Department of Health (DH) (2010c) *Our Health and Wellbeing Today*. Available at
www.gov.uk/government/uploads/system/uploads/attachment_data/file/215911/dh_122238.pdf
(accessed Nov. 2013).

Department of Health (DH) (2012) *Improving Outcomes and Supporting Transparency – Part 1:
A Public Health Outcomes Framework for England, 2013–2016*. London: DH.

Department of Health (DH) (2013) *Well-being Policy and Analysis. An Update of Well-being Work
across Whitehall*. Available at www.gov.uk/government/uploads/system/uploads/attachment_
data/file/224910/Well-being_Policy_and_Analysis_FINAL.PDF (accessed Mar. 2014).

Dodge, R., Daly, A., Huyton, J. and Sanders, L. (2012). The challenge of defining well-being,
International Journal of Well-being, 2(3): 222–35. Available at doi:10.5502/ijw.v2i3.4

Evans, D. (2003) Taking public health out of the ghetto: the policy and practice of multi-disciplinary
public health in the United Kingdom, *Social Science & Medicine*, 57(6): 959–67.

Faculty of Public Health (2010) *What is Public Health*. Available at www.fph.org.uk/what_is_
public_health (accessed 18 Apr. 2013).

Foresight Mental Capital and Well-being Project (2008). *Final Project Report – Executive Summary*.
London: Government Office for Science.

Glasby, J. and Ellins, J. (2008) *Implementing Joint Strategic Needs Assessment: Pitfalls,
Possibilities and Progress*. Birmingham: DH.

Griffiths, S., Jewell, T. and Donnelly, P. (2005) Public health in practice: the three domains of public
health. *Public Health*, 119(10): 907–13.

Health, Social Services and Public Safety. (2004) *The Review of the Public Health Function in
Northern Ireland*. Belfast: Health, Social Services and Public Safety.

HM Government (1999) *Health Act 1999*, c8 C.F.R. (1999). London: HMSO.

HM Treasury (2004) *Securing Good Health for the Whole Population* (Wanless Report). London,
Treasury Office.

Huber, M., Knottnerus, J.A., Green, L., *et al.* (2011) How should we define health? *British Medical
Journal*, 343: d4163.

Hunter, D.J. and Sengupta, S. (2004) Building multidisciplinary public health, *Critical Public
Health*, 14(1): 1–5.

Lalonde, M. (1974) *A New Perspective on the Health of Canadians. A Working Document*. Ottawa:
Government of Canada.

Mabhala, M. (2012) Embodying knowledge of teaching public health. Unpublished doctoral thesis,
Faculty of Education, University of Brighton.

Mackenbach, J.P. and Bakker, M. (2003) *Reducing Inequalities in Health: A European Perspective*.
London: Routledge.

Marks, L., Cave, S., Hunter, D.J., *et al.* (2011) *Public Health Governance and Primary Care Delivery:
A Triangulated Study* (Project Report). London: National Institute for Health Research.

Marmot, M. (2010) *Fair Society, Healthy Lives* (Marmot Review). Available at www.marmotreview.
org/AssetLibrary/pdfs/Reports/FairSocietyHealthyLives.pdf (accessed 28 June 2011).

Maxwell, S., Henderson, D., McCloy and Harper, G.(2011) *Social Impacts and Wellbeing: Multi-
Criteria Analysis Techniques for Integrating Nonmonetary Evidence in Valuation and Appraisal
a Discussion of Current Approaches and Opportunities*. London: Department for Environment,
Food and Rural Affairs. Available at www.gov.uk/government/uploads/system/uploads/attach-
ment_data/file/69481/pb13695-paper5-socialimpacts-wellbeing.pdf (accessed 5 Mar. 2014).

National Health Service (NHS) (2013) *2013/14 Choice Framework*. Available at www.nhs.uk/
choiceintheNHS/Rightsandpledges/NHSConstitution/Documents/2013/choice-framework-
2013-14.pdf (accessed 1 May 2014).

National Institute for Care and Clinical Excellence (NICE) (2013) *PH40 Social and Emotional Wellbeing – Early Years: Guidance*. Available at http://guidance.nice.org.uk/PH40/Guidance/pdf/English (accessed 1 May 2014).

Organisation for Economic Co-operation and Development (OECD) (2011) *Measuring National Well-being: A Discussion Paper on Domains and Measures*. Available at www.ons.gov.uk/ons/dcp171766_240726.pdf (accessed Dec. 2013).

Organisation for Economic Co-operation and Development (OECD) (2013a) *Measuring National Well-being – Review of Domains and Measures, 2013*. Available at www.ons.gov.uk/ons/dcp171766_308821.pdf (accessed Dec. 2013).

Organisation for Economic Co-operation and Development (OECD) (2013b) *How's Life? 2013: Measuring Well-being*. Paris: OECD Publishing. Available at doi.org/10.1787/9789264201392-en.

Office for National Statistics (ONS) (2013) *Office for National Statistics Interactive Map*. Available at www.neighbourhood.statistics.gov.uk/dissemination/LeadBoundaryViewer.do?xW=1280&xH=1024 (accessed 1 May 2014).

Office for National Statistics (ONS) (2014) *Office for National Statistics*. Available at www.ons.gov.uk/ (accessed 1 Dec. 2013).

ONS Interactive site (2014) *Measures of National Well-being: Measuring What Matters: Understanding the Nation's Well-being*. Available at www.ons.gov.uk/ons/interactive/well-being-wheel-of-measures/index.html (accessed 1 Dec. 2013).

Polakoff, E. and Gregory, D. (2002) Concepts of health: women's struggle for wholeness in the midst of poverty, *Health Care for Women International*, 23(8): 833–45.

Powers, M. and Faden, R. (2006) *Social Justice: The Foundations of Public Health and Health Policy*. Oxford: Oxford University Press.

Raine, R., Walt, G. and Basnett, I. (2004) The white paper on public health: is promising, but has some blind spots, which must be tackled, *British Medical Journal*, 329(7477): 247–8.

Rowlingson, K. (2011) *Does Income Inequality Cause Health and Social Care Problems?* York: Joseph Rowntree Foundation.

Scriven, A. (2010) *Promoting Health: A Practical Guide*, 6th edn. London: Bailliere Tindall.

Seaford, C. (2011) Well-being evidence and policy: making some links. Paper presented to University of Cambridge Well-being Institute and the Centre for Science and Policy (CSaP) panel discussion on Measuring National Well-being, Church House Conference Centre, London, 29 September.

Thorpe, A., Griffith, S., Jewell, T. and Adshead, F. (2008) The three domains of public health: an internationally relevant basis for public health education? *Journal of Royal Institute of Public Health*, 122(2): 201–10.

Tones, K. and Green, J. (2010) *Health Promotion: Planning and Strategies*, 2nd edn. London: Sage.

UK Health Watch. (2005) The Experience of Health in an Unequal Society. Available at www.pohg.org.uk/support/publications.html (accessed 23 Mar. 2006).

United Kingdom Public Health Association (UKPHA) (2005) *Choosing Health or Losing Health? A Response from the UKPHA to the White Paper Choosing Health*. London: UKPHA.

Üstün, B. and Jakob, R. (2005) Calling a spade a spade: meaningful definitions of health conditions, *Bulletin of the World Health Organization*, 83: 802.

White S.C. (2010) Analysing wellbeing: a framework for development practice, *Development in Practice*, 20(2): 158–72.

Wilkinson, R. and Pickett, K. (2010) *The Spirit Level: Why Equality is Better for Everyone*. London: Penguin.

World Health Organization (WHO) (1948) Preamble to the Constitution of the World Health Organization as adopted by the International Health Conference, New York, 19–22 June 1946, and entered into force on 7 April 1948.

Wylie, C.M. (1970) The definition and measurement of health and disease. *Public Health Reports*, 85(2): 100–1.

2 The social and health inequalities agenda

Dr Mzwandile (Andi) Mabhala

Introduction

How much the health and well-being of individuals and populations can be improved depends upon understanding the wider determinants of health and the social and health inequalities agenda. This chapter aims to build on the concepts introduced in Chapter 1 and to explore the differences in health outcomes globally and across the UK. This will be achieved through an examination of up-to-date policy and publications such as *Fair Society, Healthy Lives* (the Marmot Review – Marmot 2010), *The Commission Calls for Closing the Health Gap in a Generation* (WHO 2008b) and *The Impact of Inequality* (Wilkinson 2005). Health outcomes can be measured, but how can health inequalities be reduced and health and well-being improved? What are the economic implications of impaired health, and how can strategic planning improve health and reduce inequalities?

Definitions and concepts of health inequalities

The definitions of health inequalities that inform this chapter are uneven distributions of health benefits and disease burdens that are unjust, unfair and avoidable, or differences in health status that that are unjust, unfair and avoidable (Dahlgren and Whitehead 1991; Mackenbach and Bakker 2003). It is believed that tackling inequalities in health is a matter of social justice (Marmot 2009). Social justice and health inequalities are rooted in the common belief that inequalities in the distribution of 'primary social goods' are the fundamental cause of the uneven distribution of health and disease in our society. In this book 'primary social goods' refers to those socio-economic determinants known to influence inequalities in health (Beauchamp 1975; Powers and Faden 2006). In the UK these are often conceptualized as domains of indices of multiple deprivation, namely: income; employment; health and disability; education, skills and training; barriers to housing and other services; crime; and living environment (DCLG 2011). Of the seven domains, income, employment and education are universally recognized as factors that have the most impact on health inequalities (DCLG 2011; Wilkinson and Marmot 2003).

Scenario

Spend a day in a hospital Accident and Emergency department and you will learn that most patients are admitted for what could be considered lifestyle-determined causes, including smoking-related, obesity-related, alcohol-related and drug-related conditions. However, you rarely see diagnoses such as coronary heart disease secondary to smoking or obesity, or chronic obstructive pulmonary disease secondary to heavy smoking. Nor do you see death certificates that state the cause of death to be heart failure secondary to poverty, obesity or poor diet.

Dig deeper into their social background and you will find that most of the patients come from adverse social backgrounds including unemployment, low paid jobs, poor housing and fuel poverty. Imagine a scenario where every patient is given a medical as well as an epidemiological diagnosis – where the death certificate indicates the medical alongside the epidemiological causes of death. What do you think would be the public reaction? Would inequalities in health still be seen as an abstract concept? What would be the politician's response?

Conceptualization of the inequalities in health

In his doctoral thesis Mabhala (2012) argues that the common concern of all those who embody public health is the evidence that too many people die prematurely due to uneven distribution of the determinants of health. There is a plethora of evidence on how health inequalities are created and sustained. The question is, why are they not being eradicated? It could be argued that the lengthy chain of association between health and inequalities in health makes health inequalities an abstract concept understood only by academics and politically subversive groups. It thus lacks full support from the general public and particularly from policy makers, and those who are directly affected by health inequalities find them difficult to counter.

Mabhala argued that avoidable premature loss of life is more than a matter of statistical evidence; it is a moral and ethical concern. He argued that where it is possible to provide social goods essential for the support of health and well-being and these are not being provided, then that is a human rights issue (Mabhala 2012). He therefore proposed that inequalities in health can be conceptualized in three dimensions. Figure 2.1 illustrates a triad model of social justice to frame the argument about health inequalities.

Dimensions of inequalities in health

- Science dimension: this enables us to establish evidence of the association between disease and social environment, and explain the pattern and distribution of disease and health. It is through this knowledge that we can demonstrate that the distribution of disease follows a social class gradient, and to argue that socially produced diseases are avoidable.
- Ethical and moral dimension: this is the view that socially produced diseases are unfair and unjust, and that tackling them is the right thing to do.
- Human rights dimension: based on the Alma Ata declaration of health as a human right (WHO 1978), this is the affirmation of health as a human right, aimed at bringing concern for improving the health of the disadvantaged from the voluntary realm of charity to the realms of law and entitlement.

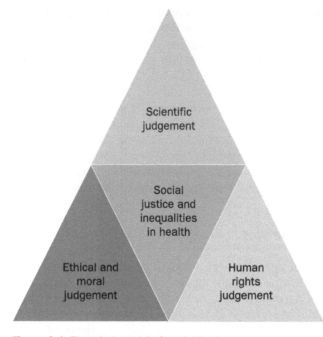

Figure 2.1 The triad model of social justice
Source: Adapted from Mabhala M. (2012)

Exploring the evidence for social determinants of health, and their impact on health and well-being within and between countries

In Britain, the scientific evidence which supported the argument that uneven distributions in primary social goods are major causes of inequalities in health benefits and disease burdens was established by a working group of scientists led by Sir Douglas Black (DHSS 1980). The Black Report made moral and ethical recommendations for a comprehensive anti-poverty programme. It proposed two elements to tackle health inequalities: a fair distribution of resources, and provision of the necessary educational and employment opportunities for active participation (DHSS 1980; Smith *et al.* 1998). These have since been shown to be aimed at tackling fundamental determinants of health and ameliorating social injustices (DH 1998a; Marmot 2010; Mackenbach 2011). Unfortunately, the political ideology at the time of publication of the report was underpinned by 'market justice', defined by Beauchamp as systems that 'emphasize individual responsibility, minimal collective action and freedom from collective obligation except to respect other person's fundamental rights' (Beauchamp 1975: 102–3). This stands in contrast to the social justice principles advocated by the Black Report. When the UK Labour government came into power in 1997, they introduced the Black Report's recommendations into the policy agenda in the form of the *Independent Inquiry into Inequalities in Health Report*, written by a working group led by Sir Donald Acheson (DH 1998a).

Since its publication, evidence from the Black Report has been tested by burgeoning volumes of research which built on rather than challenged it. For example, research studies that made significant contributions to the theory of socially produced disease include that of Wilkinson (1997), which suggested that differences in mortality in developed countries were affected more by relative than absolute living standards. It explained this by three pieces of evidence. First, mortality was related more closely to relative income within countries than to differences in absolute income between them. Second, national mortality rates tended to be lowest in countries that have smaller income differences and thus have lower levels of relative deprivation. Third, most of the long-term rise in life expectancy seemed unrelated to long-term economic growth rates, but was linked to the way economic benefits were distributed within society.

The conclusion drawn from this evidence is that inequalities in mortality were reduced in societies that are more egalitarian because the burden of relative deprivation was reduced (Wilkinson 1997). Wilkinson's findings identifying income differences as one of the most important factors responsible for uneven distribution of health and disease within and between countries are supported by several other studies (Kennedy et al. 1998; Mackenbach and Bakker 2003; Marmot 2005; Mackenbach 2009). For example, Kennedy et al. (1998) examined income inequalities to predict individual morbidity, as measured by self-rated health status. They found that the effects of income inequalities were most pronounced among low-income groups: those in this category had about a 30 per cent increase in the risk of fair or poor health in US states with the greatest inequalities in income.

Among the largest studies which examined the effect of income inequalities within and between countries was one commissioned by the WHO in 2005 (Marmot 2005, 2009). This found that low-income countries experienced a heavier burden of infant mortality and low life expectancy than high-income countries: for example, men in the high mortality countries of Europe had a more than 40 per cent probability of death between age 15 and 60 years, compared with a 25 per cent probability in Southeast Asia (Marmot 2005, 2009). Between countries, the differences were even more dramatic. The probability of a man dying between ages 15 and 60 years is 8.3 per cent in Sweden, 82.1 per cent in Zimbabwe and 90.2 per cent in Lesotho (Marmot 2005, 2009). The findings from this study could be erroneously interpreted as suggesting that living in a poor country means you will die earlier, and living in a rich country means you will live longer. This would be true only if one disregards Wilkinson's theory that it is relative rather than absolute living standards that have the most effect.

Furthermore, the study by Mackenbach and Bakker (2003) appears to confirm Wilkinson's conclusion. This investigated socio-economic inequalities in mortality in six Western European countries, and demonstrated that within the high-income countries the health benefits of economic prosperity were not equally shared across the high and low socio-economic groups, and this was reflected in the distribution of diseases. They came up with a new theory to explain the widening gap between the low and high socio-economic groups, proposing that the widening was mostly due to faster proportional mortality declines in the higher groups (Mackenbach and Bakker 2003): although absolute mortality decline was usually fast in lower socio-economic groups, relative mortality decline was usually faster in the upper groups. Marmot (2010) provided a theoretical explanation that took account of the differences in health, disease, mortality and life expectancy in both the developing and developed world, explaining that health follows a social gradient – the higher the position in the social hierarchy, the lower the risk of ill health – and suggested that this was irrespective of country. With so much evidence establishing the association between inequalities in health and inequalities in income, the question for health professionals is no longer whether there is a link between income differences and health; it is whether they accept as their moral, professional and humanitarian duty the need to address inequalities in health.

The key ethical argument for tackling health inequalities is based on three points: people valuing health; fairness; and protection of human life. The notion of people valuing having health was clearly articulated by Sir Michael Marmot in his address to the WHO, when he stated that the reason for taking action on health inequalities is a matter of social justice; the reason for doing it is because it is the right thing to do. This was based on evidence that people value having good health, not because it gets them a better job or lets them live in better neighbourhoods, but simply because they value health (Bolam 2004; Marmot 2009). That means where, in our judgement, these differences in health, these systematic inequalities in health, are avoidable and are not avoided, then they are unfair; putting them right is a matter of social justice (Marmot 2009). Arguably, judging tackling inequalities in health as being 'the right thing to do', 'avoidable' and 'unfair' implies the acceptance of moral, ethical and humanitarian responsibilities to tackle them.

The argument for tackling inequalities in health as a matter of justice and fairness has been supported by several prominent writers in the field of social justice and public health (Beauchamp 1975; Krieger and Birn 1998; Krieger 2001, 2007; Hofrichter 2003, 2006; Gostin and Powers 2006; Powers and Faden 2006), all of whom draw from Rawls's (1971) theory of justice and fairness. Krieger and Birn (1998) contend that fairness and equality are two key attributes of social justice. It has been argued that ethical and moral judgement is based upon recognition that all social groups are not treated equally in society (Gostin and Powers 2006; Powers and Faden 2006), thus the moral and ethical responsibility of social justice is to promote an equitable distribution of primary social goods, institutional resources and life opportunities (Hofrichter 2003). This was reaffirmed by Gostin and Powers (2006) who explained that the moral account of social justice stresses the fair disbursement of common advantages and the sharing of common burdens.

Reaffirming the argument about health professionals' moral and ethical responsibility to tackle inequalities in health, Gostin and Powers (2006) assert that the social justice view of public health is logically and ethically justified if one accepts the vision of public health as being the protection of all human life. Concurring, Beauchamp (1975, 2003) proposes that our moral responsibility to address inequalities is based on understanding that public health is ultimately and essentially an ethical enterprise committed to the notion that all persons are entitled to protection against the hazards of this world, and to the minimization of death and disability in society (Beauchamp 2003; Hofrichter 2003; Powers and Faden 2006). The notion of 'entitlement' implies that access to good health is not only ethically and morally right, but it is also a human right.

The promotion of health as a human right occurred at a WHO conference in London, where for the first time WHO (1946) declared that discrimination leading to differences in access to the resources and opportunities for health between groups was unfair. WHO (1946) also asserted that health is a human right, that is, everyone has a right to enjoy the highest attainable standards of health in their society. This declaration was repeated in 1978 in the Alma Ata declaration (WHO 1978), where countries were asked to commit to incorporating this in their national policy directives. Since then, several public health writers have made significant contributions to advancing this argument (Beauchamp 2003; Gostin and Powers 2006; Levy and Sidel 2006; Powers and Faden 2006; Bayer et al. 2007). The unifying view is that under social justice, all persons are equally entitled to the key outcomes of health protection or minimum standards of income (Beauchamp 1975, 2003; Hofrichter 2006; Bayer et al. 2007). That means it is a human right for all to have access to equal opportunities to be healthy, and that public health institutions have human rights obligations to remove barriers to individuals and groups which prevent them realizing their rights to health (Levy and Sidel 2006).

Arguably the fact that inequalities in health are still prominent in some societies, despite countries' commitment to the Alma Ata declaration, indicates that human rights standards and legal obligations relevant to social justice are not being fulfilled in many, perhaps most, places (Levy and Sidel 2006). However, it has been argued that human rights instruments provide a powerful contribution towards efforts to tackle public health issues of social justice, by removing concerns for improving the health of disadvantaged groups from the realm of voluntary charity to the realms of law and entitlement (Beauchamp 1975, 2003; Levy and Sidel 2006). For example, we now have international human rights instruments relevant to public health that are binding: they include the UN's Universal Declaration of Human Rights; the International Covenant on Economic, Social and Cultural Rights; the Convention against Torture and Other Cruel, Inhuman or Degrading Treatment or Punishment; the Convention on Elimination of all forms of Discrimination Against Women; and the Convention on the Rights of the Child (Donaldson and Banatvala 2007).

Furthermore, achieving a balance between respecting the rights of the individual and the population is crucial. This involves challenging the market justice norms which claim that poor people have poorer health because they engage in health-damaging behaviours such as smoking and eating less nutritious foods, implying that these behaviours are entirely freely chosen rather than being shaped by the conditions in which disadvantaged groups live because of their social position (Levy and Sidel 2006).

Socio-economic determinants of health inequalities

Socio-economic determinants of health (SEDH) refers to the conditions in which people are born, grow up, live, work and age that are known to influence their risk of illness, life expectancy and opportunity to be healthy (Milton et al. 2012). Several studies reported that social, economic and political institutions and the decisions that they take create, reinforce and perpetuate differences in economic and social status which fundamentally cause inequalities in health (DHSS 1980; Dahlgren and Whitehead 1991; DH 1998a; Marmot 2005; WHO 2008a).

Several public health theorists have developed models to explain the complexity of the interacting factors that determine inequalities in health; these models are all termed 'socio-economic determinants of health models'. The most prominent models include Dahlgren and Whitehead's (1991) model; the selection and causation model of van de Mheen *et al.* (1998); Wilkinson and Marmot's (2003) model; the WHO (2005) Equity Team's social determinants framework; and Rawls' (1971) fairness as justice model.

Although differing in degree of complexity and detail, these are all based on a common view that low socio-economic status leads to ill health (Dahlgren and Whitehead 1991; Mackenbach and Bakker 2003; Wilkinson and Marmot 2003; WHO 2005). The model that has been most extensively used in policy making, particularly in the UK (DH 1999) and in Europe (WHO 2005, 2008a), is the SEDH model by Dahlgren and Whitehead (1991). This model proposes five layers of influence that act either as risks for or protection against disease depending on one's socio-economic status. These include (a) biological variation including genetic makeup and sex; (b) individual lifestyle factors; (c) social and community influence; (d) living and working conditions; and e) general socio-economic, cultural and environmental conditions (Dahlgren and Whitehead 1991). Chapter 3 provides a detailed description of this model.

The general view among the SEDH theorists is that those health differences in the first layer, which arise as a result of biological variations such as sex (some disease is more prevalent in one gender than the other), age (elderly people are sicker than younger) and genetic factors (some groups have genetic predispositions to certain diseases) can be considered as fair and unavoidable (Whitehead 1990; Dahlgren and Whitehead 1991; Mackenbach and Bakker 2003), and therefore very little could be done to modify them. A large proportion of the global burden of disease can be attributed to the second layer, which results from health-damaging individual lifestyle-related factors, such as obesity, coronary heart disease and diabetes relating to physical inactivity; cancer and chronic obstructive pulmonary disease relating to smoking; liver cirrhosis and pancreatic cancer to excessive alcohol consumption; and mental illness to drug misuse. While it may appear that lifestyle alteration may lead to reduction of health differences, the evidence shows that such behaviours are concentrated in groups in adverse social conditions (Mackenbach and Bakker 2003; Cubbin *et al.* 2006; Krieger 2007; Kawakami *et al.* 2011).

The evidence suggests that individuals in disadvantaged circumstances including deprived neighbourhoods with low availability of health-promoting goods (third layer) face greater financial barriers to opting for a healthier lifestyle (Pearce *et al.* 2007; Macintyre *et al.* 2008; Kawakami *et al.* 2011). That means it is an individual's social position that determines exposure to health-damaging behaviours and poor health over time, not personal choice (Mackenbach and Backer 2003; Macintyre *et al.* 2008). Changing factors in the fourth and fifth layers – that is, structures of society that generate and distribute power, wealth and risk, such as the education system, labour policies, cultural norms and political institutions – therefore address the root causes of inequalities in health (Mackenbach and Backer 2003).

It is generally accepted that to reduce inequalities in health one needs greater understanding of SEDH, to make explicit the linkages among different types of determinant and to locate strategic entry points for policy action (WHO, 2005). Arguably all interventions to reduce health inequalities are linked to each layer of the SEDH model, and are broadly categorized as downstream (interventions that focus on biological and behavioural risk factors), midstream (interventions that focus on reducing the exposure to specific material working and living conditions such as pollution) and upstream (interventions that focus on societal intervention) (McKinlay 1974; Stronks and Mackenbach 2005; UK Health Watch 2005). There is widespread agreement that interventions that address the root causes of inequalities in health are those that focus on upstream solutions (Mackenbach and Bakker, 2003; Stronks and Mackenbach 2005; UK Health Watch 2005; Marmot 2010). However, the evidence has shown that too much effort and emphasis is being placed on downstream approaches (Raphael 2004; Mackenbach 2011). This propensity towards downstream approaches has been attributed to lack of research design to measure the effectiveness of the upstream approaches. As downstream projects are more amenable to experimental research design, it steers the research effort towards the more obvious lifestyle projects (Stronks and Mackenbach 2005; Mackenbach 2011).

Thinking point

As a health professional imagine a scenario where accurately diagnosing and treating a medical condition is given equal merit to accurately diagnosing and prescribing social intervention to eradicate the causes of the causes. Virchow's (1941) notion that 'politics is nothing more than medicine on a grand scale' would seem true as most of the prescriptions would go to the central government ministries.

How can health inequalities be addressed?

The literature distinguishes three levels of intervention to reduce inequalities: 1) reducing an unfair distribution of determinants of the inequalities in health; 2) reducing the unfair distribution of healthcare provision; and 3) assisting individuals in overcoming avoidable health inequalities. Many health policies focus on the latter two levels. These levels of intervention compare favourably with McKinlay's (1974) theory of 'focusing upstream' in which he categorized interventions to reduce the inequalities in health into downstream, midstream and upstream approaches.

There is a general consensus that upstream interventions to reduce health inequalities have more leverage than individual behavioural interventions in tackling the fundamental causes (McKinlay 1974; Mackenbach and Bakker 2003; Grumbach *et al.* 2004), but it is recognized that health professionals may make contributions at different levels. Mackenbach (2009) asserts that in their decision-making process about their role, health professionals may want to think of an imaginary 'ladder of political activism' with four rungs. The first or lowest rung is political passivism – that is, information on health risks and opportunities for health improvement are exchanged within the health sector only, and politicians are only informed if they ask for it. On the second rung, public health professionals actively disseminate relevant information among politicians, for example by addressing their reports to the government, by drawing the attention of the media, and by participating in advisory committees. On the third rung public health professionals may try to directly influence the political process, for example by lobbying and by actively engaging politicians of specific political parties. On the highest or fourth rung, public health professionals become politicians themselves, and make a direct contribution to policies aimed at reducing inequalities in health. The following section reviews policies that have had an impact on health inequalities in the UK.

Political and policy perspectives – the economic implications for health

Table 2.1 lists a selection of some of the key policy documents that shaped the UK public health agenda to reduce inequalities in health.

Table 2.1 Policies that informed the public health agenda to reduce health inequalities

Year	Policy
1997	The New NHS: Modern, Dependable
1999	Saving Lives: Our Healthier Nation
1999	Making a Difference: Strengthening the Nursing, Midwifery and Health Visiting Contribution to Health and Healthcare
2001	Shifting the Balance of Power within the NHS: Securing Delivery
2001	Annual Report of the Chief Medical Officer 2001
2001	Health and Social Care Act 2001
2001	Tackling Health Inequalities: Consultation on a Plan for Delivery
2002	Tackling Health Inequalities: the Results of the Consultation Exercise
2002	Tackling Health Inequalities 2002 Cross-cutting Review
2003	Tackling Health Inequalities: A Programme for Action
2003	Liberating the Public Health Talents of Community Practitioners and Health Visitors
2004	The NHS Improvement Plan: Putting People at the Heart of Public Services
2004	Choosing Health: Making Healthy Choices Easier
2005	Tackling Health Inequalities: Status Report on the Programme for Action
2005	Commissioning a Patient-led NHS
2006	Our Health, Our Care, Our Say: A New Direction for Community Services
2006	Modernising Nursing Careers: Setting the Direction
2008	Tackling Health Inequalities: 2007 Status Report on the Programme for Action
2009	Tackling Health Inequalities: 10 Years On
2010	Equity and Excellence: Liberating the NHS
2010	Healthy Lives, Healthy People: Our Strategy for Public Health in England

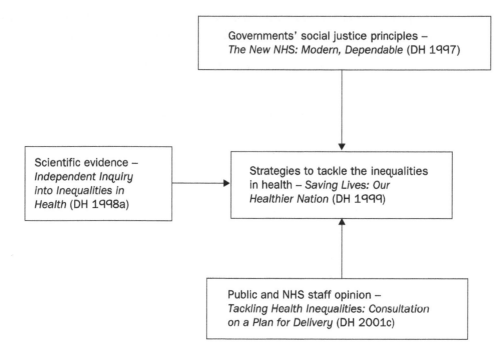

Figure 2.2 UK strategies to tackle inequalities in health

In the UK *The New NHS: Modern, Dependable* (DH 1997) set the foundation on which the agenda to reduce health inequalities was to be built. At the time it appeared to be an ideological change from market justice to social justice. This policy document offered a number of proposals, including providing a fairer health service, tackling inequalities in health and developing a new model of primary care delivery. It promised an NHS that does not just treat people when they are ill, but works with others to improve health and reduce inequalities. It identified the internal market justice principles as inconsistent with the NHS founding principles of free and fair health care for all, and set out how market justice principles would be replaced by social justice principles in the form of an 'integrated care' system, based on partnership and driven by performance. This policy document led to the replacement of the terms 'competition' and 'internal market' by 'co-operation' and 'collaboration' (Hennessy 2000; Ham 2004). Figure 2.2 illustrates the three policy drivers that shaped the UK foundation for the agenda to reduce inequalities in health.

As Figure 2.2 illustrates:

1 *The New NHS: Modern, Dependable* (DH 1997) set out the context and under-pinning principles.
2 *Independent Inquiry into Inequalities in Health Report* (DH 1998a), established by the UK Department of Health, provided a weight of scientific evidence in support of a connection between SEDH and health inequalities.

3   *Tackling Health Inequalities: Consultation on a Plan for Delivery* (DH 2001c)
    provided the government with insight into the opinions of NHS staff and the
    public on inequalities in health.
4   The consultation led to publication of the Green Paper *Our Healthier Nation*
    (DH 1998b).
5   Based on these investigations, the Department of Health published the first
    public health-specific policy document *Saving Lives: Our Healthier Nation*
    (DH 1999) which adopted most of the *Independent Inquiry* (DH 1998a)
    recommendations.

Saving Lives: Our Healthier Nation proposed three areas as crucial in reducing
inequalities in health:

• All policies likely to have an impact on health should be evaluated in terms of
  their impact on health inequalities.
• High priority should be given to the health of families with children.
• Further steps should be taken to reduce income inequalities and improve the
  living standards of poor households.

   Several public health writers acclaimed the proposals in *Saving Lives* as a
demonstration of the government's commitment to social justice principles and
upstream public health interventions (Evans 2003, 2009; Hunter and Sengupta
2003; UK Health Watch 2005). In particular, the government proposed to: give
more people better education; create employment so that people can achieve
greater prosperity; build social capital by increasing social cohesion; reduce social
stress by regenerating neighbourhoods and communities; and tackle aspects of
the workplace which are damaging to health (DH 1999). These proposals were
considered as tackling fundamental determinants of health inequalities
(Mackenbach and Bakker 2003; UK Health Watch 2005; WHO 2005, 2008b; Marmot
2011).
   The UK Labour government had made a promise that in their first two years in
office they would keep to the public spending set out by the previous Conservative
government. That meant that the delivery of their social justice strategy had to be
delayed until their next term. During the 2001 election campaign, Labour
announced a reform of the NHS, with social justice back on the agenda. This was
signified by the number of policy documents published that year that had a clear
focus on public health. These policies focused on three areas of public health
delivery:

• Structural reforms. *Shifting the Balance of Power Within the NHS: Securing
  Delivery (SBoP)* (DH 2001b) provided a clear infrastructural framework for the
  delivery of public health and the modernization agenda. It articulated details of
  the new relationship between the Department of Health and the NHS (DH
  2001b), and was intended to move power and control over budgets to front-line
  staff and patients. At the heart of the changes was the decision to establish
  primary care trusts (PCTs) throughout the NHS, shifting the focus of health-
  care delivery to public health, and reducing the number of health authorities.
  The aim was to give PCTs 75 per cent of the budget to strengthen the public
  health function (DH 2001b; McDonald and Harrison 2004). Each PCT was to

have a director of public health (DPH) and team who were to be 'the engines of public health delivery'.

- Public health workforce. The *Annual Report of the Chief Medical Officer 2001* (DH 2001a) provided a framework for the public health workforce to deliver the health agenda, and identified three major categories in the public health workforce: specialist, practitioner and wider workforce.
- Progress monitoring. This was to be followed by regular reviews to determine progress. The first of three reviews was published in 2003: *Tackling Health Inequalities: A Programme for Action* (DH 2003) suggested that there had been very little improvement in some indicators such as life expectancy since the Labour government came to power.

Competing pressures on the agenda

The government agenda to tackle inequalities in health was increasingly under pressure from within and outside the government. The pressure from within came from the internal debate between modernizers who were willing to embrace some of the market justice values versus traditionalists who wanted to replace all the traces of market justice with social justice principles.

The external pressures came from:

- public health experts who presented scientific evidence which indicated the most effective interventions to tackle health inequalities are those that focus on the fundamental socio-economic determinants
- the public who wanted short-term quantifiable outcomes such as reducing waiting lists
- NHS staff who wanted more doctors, more nurses, more therapists, fair pay, training, less bureaucracy, prevention and joined-up working (DH 2001c).

In response to these pressures the UK government published *Tackling Health Inequalities: A Programme for Action* (DH 2003), a strategy based on four themes that focused on downstream, midstream and upstream solutions to health inequalities. These were:

- supporting families, mothers and children
- engaging communities and individuals
- preventing illness and providing effective treatment and care
- addressing the underlying determinants of health.

From these four themes they developed a basket of indicators of inequalities in health (DH 2003), including:

- provide access to primary care
- reduce road accidents
- reduce child poverty
- promote diet (for example, 'Five a Day')
- improve educational attainment
- reduce homelessness
- improve housing

- increase the uptake of influenza vaccinations
- increase physical activity (PE) and school sport
- reducing smoking prevalence
- reduce teenage pregnancy
- reduce mortality from major killer diseases.

These became targets that NHS organizations were measured against, and were to be followed by regular reviews to determine progress.

The government's strategy to reduce inequalities in health was attracting the interest of the Treasury department: as the Department of Health was restructuring the tiers of the NHS, the Treasury was taking increasing interest in the financing and performance of the reformed health service. In March 2001 the Chancellor of the Exchequer commissioned a review of the long-term trends affecting the health service and of the resources required over the next two decades to deliver the public health agenda (Evans 2003). In 2002, the first of the two, Sir Derek Wanless's report *Securing Our Future Health: Taking a Long-Term View*, was published (HM Treasury 2002), and it concluded that (a) although the UK health system does many things very well, standards of health care have fallen behind people's expectations; and (b) UK health-care systems are not keeping up with the quality of service provided routinely in many other countries. It attributed these shortfalls to the combination of cumulative under-investment over at least 30 years, and organizational and delivery arrangements which are not designed to meet the challenges of providing health care in the twenty-first century.

The report presented three possible scenarios to model spending patterns, namely slow uptake, solid progress and fully engaged (HM Treasury 2002). The most desired scenario was 'fully engaged', which would result in high levels of public engagement with public health messages; increased life expectancy; dramatic improvement in health status; increased confidence in the health system; and increased demand for high-quality care. The health service would be responsive with high rates of technology uptake, particularly in relation to disease prevention. This report (HM Treasury, 2002) essentially supported the direction of government policy on social justice principles and the NHS, with a strong emphasis on public health action and recommendations for long-term sustained investment in public health delivery. The cross-governmental interest in social justice was formalized when the Treasury and DH jointly published the review on tackling inequalities in health (Department of Health and HM Treasury 2002).

In April 2003 the Prime Minister, the Chancellor and the Secretary of State for Health asked Wanless to provide an update of the challenges in implementing the fully engaged scenario set out in his report on long-term health trends. This review asked the profound question 'Who is responsible for tackling inequalities in health and what support is needed?' The report from the second review concluded that ultimately individuals were responsible for their own and their children's health, and it was the aggregate actions of individuals which would ultimately be responsible for whether the optimistic 'fully engaged' scenario unfolds (HM Treasury, 2004). It went on to assert that people needed to be supported more actively to make better decisions about their own health and welfare, because there were widespread, systematic failures that influenced the decisions individuals made. Failures identified included a lack of full information, the difficulty individuals had in considering fully the wider social costs of particular behaviours, engrained social attitudes not conducive to individuals pursuing healthy lifestyles, addictions, and inequalities related to individuals' poor lifestyles; these tended to be related to socio-economic and sometimes ethnic differences. The greatest emphasis in this document was on supporting individuals to change behaviour and make healthier choices, and it identified three areas where health-related policy intervention might be needed – minimum income, work and stress, and environment.

This policy document marked the turning point of policy direction in the UK. After the publication of *Securing Good Health for the Whole Population* (HM Treasury 2004), there was a shift downstream to supporting individuals to change behaviour rather than focusing on upstream determinants of health. Table 2.2 lists some of the policies that informed the agenda on reducing health inequalities following the Wanless Report. The common theme in all these is their emphasis on individual responsibility, working together and informed choice (DH 2004a, 2004b, 2010a, 2010b). They all proposed that those principles be delivered through a process of contestability, commissioning and choice (DH 2004b, 2005).

In November 2008, ten years after the *Independent Inquiry into Inequalities in Health*, Professor Sir Michael Marmot was asked by the then Secretary of State for Health to chair another independent review to propose the most effective evidence-based strategies for reducing health inequalities in England from 2010. The outcomes of the subsequent report compared favourably with those of *Independent Inquiry* (DH 1998a) and *Saving Lives* (DH 1999), proposing that reducing health inequalities would require action on six policy objectives:

- Give every child the best start in life.
- Enable all children, young people and adults to maximize their capabilities and have control over their lives.
- Create fair employment and good work for all.
- Ensure a healthy standard of living for all.
- Create and develop healthy and sustainable places and communities.
- Strengthen the role and impact of ill-health prevention.

This chapter has examined inequalities in health, which have been identified as a major public health problem. The analysis of SEDH models demonstrated that sustainable interventions to tackle health inequalities are those that address the causes of the causes. However, the literature showed the propensity of health

Table 2.2 Post-Wanless Report policies

2004	The NHS Improvement Plan: Putting People at the Heart of Public Services
2004	Choosing Health: Making Healthy Choices Easier
2005	Commissioning a Patient-led NHS
2006	Our Health, Our Care, Our Say: A New Direction for Community Services
2010	Equity and Excellence: Liberating the NHS
2010	Healthy Lives, Healthy People: Our Strategy for Public Health in England

professionals and policy makers to place greater emphasis on downstream approaches. Finally, this chapter critically examined a selection of policies that shaped the strategies to tackle health inequalities, and revealed the market justice forces that influenced them.

References

Bayer, R., Beauchamp, D.E., Gostin, L.O. and Jennings, B. (2007) *Public Health Ethics*. Oxford: Oxford University Press.

Beauchamp, D.E. (1975) Public health: alien ethics in a strange land? *American Journal of Public Health*, 65(12): 1338–9.

Beauchamp, D.E. (2003) Public health as social justice, in R. Hofrichter (ed.) *Health and Social Justice: Politics, Ideology and Ineqiality in the Distribution of Disease*. Washington, DC: Jossey-Bass.

Bolam, B. (2004) Public participation in tackling health inequalities: implications from recent qualitative research, *European Journal of Public Health*, 15(5): 447.

Cubbin, C., Sundquist, K., Ahlen, H., Johansson, S.E., Winkleby, M.A. and Sundquist, J. (2006) Neighbourhood deprivation and cardiovascular disease risk factors: protective and harmful effects, *Scandinavian Journal of Public Health*, 34(3): 228–37.

Dahlgren, G. and Whitehead, M. (1991) *Policies and Strategies to Promote Social Equity in Health*. Stockholm: Institute for Future Studies.

Department for Communities and Local Government (DCLG) (2011) *The English Indices of Deprivation 2010*. Available from www.gov.uk/government/uploads/system/uploads/attachment_data/file/6871/1871208.pdf (accessed 3 June 2013).

Department of Health (DH) (1997) *The New NHS: Modern, Dependable*. London: DH.

Department of Health (DH) (1998a) *Independent Inquiry into Inequalities in Health Report*. London: DH.

Department of Health (DH) (1998b) *Our Healthier Nation: A Contract for Health*. London: DH.

Department of Health (DH) (1999) *Saving Lives: Our Healthier Nation*. London: DH.

Department of Health (DH) (2001a) *Annual Report of the Chief Medical Officer 2001*. Available at www.dh.gov.uk/en/Publicationsandstatistics/Publications/AnnualReports/DH_4005607 (accessed 24 Feb. 2014).

Department of Health (DH) (2001b) *Shifting the Balance of Power Within the NHS: Securing Delivery*. London: DH.

Department of Health (DH) (2001c) *Tackling Health Inequalities: Consultation on a Plan for Delivery*. London: DH.

Department of Health (DH) (2003) *Tackling Health Inequalities: A Programme for Action*. London: DH.

Department of Health (DH) (2004a) *Choosing Health: Making Healthy Choice Easier*. London: DH.

Department of Health (DH) (2004b) *The NHS Improvement Plan: Putting People at the Heart of Public Services*. London: DH.

Department of Health (DH) (2005) *Commissioning a Patient-led NHS*. London: DH.

Department of Health (DH) (2010a) *Equity and Excellence: Liberating the NHS*. Available at www.dh.gov.uk/prod_consum_dh/groups/dh_digitalassets/@dh/@en/@ps/documents/digitalasset/dh_117794.pdf (accessed 15 Apr 2011).

Department of Health (DH) (2010b) *Healthy Lives, Healthy People White Paper: Our Strategy for Public Health in England*. Available at http://www.dh.gov.uk/prod_consum_dh/groups/dh_digitalassets/documents/digitalasset/dh_124040.pdf (accessed 31 Nov 2010).

Department of Health (DH) (2012) *Improving Outcomes and Supporting Transparency – Part 1: A Public Health Outcomes Framework for England, 2013–2016*. London: DH.

Department of Health and HM Treasury (2002) *Tackling Health Inequalities 2002 Cross-Cutting Review*. London: DH and HM Treasury.

Department of Health and Social Security (DHSS) (1980) *Inequalities in Health: Report of a Research Working Group* (Black Report). London: DHSS.

Donaldson, L. and Banatvala, N. (2007) Health is global: proposals for a UK Government-wide strategy, *Lancet*, 369(3): 857–61.

Evans, D. (2003) Taking public health out of the ghetto: the policy and practice of multi-disciplinary public health in the United Kingdom, *Social Science & Medicine*, 57(6): 959–67.

Evans, D. (2009) The role of schools of public health: Learning from history, looking to the future, *Journal of Public Health*, 31(3): 446–50.

Gostin, L.O. and Powers, M. (2006) What does social justice require for public's health? Public health ethics and policy imperatives, *Health Affairs*, 25(4): 1053–60.

Grumbach, K., Miller, J., Mertz, E. and Finocchio, L. (2004) How much public health in public health nursing practice? *Public Health Nursing*, 21(3): 266–76.

Ham, C. (2004) *Health Policy in Britain: The Political and Organisation of the National Health Service*. London: Palgrave Macmillan.

Hennessy, D. (2000) Health policy and the position of nursing leadership in the United Kingdom: a new perspective. *Policy, Politics & Nursing Practice*, 1(2): 107–15.

HM Treasury (2002) *Securing Our Future Health: Taking a Long-Term View*. Available at www. hm-treasury.gov.uk/consult_wanless_final.htm (accessed 23 Mar. 2010).

HM Treasury (2004) *Securing Good Health for the Whole Population*. London: Treasury Office.

Hofrichter, R. (2003) *Health and Social Justice: Politics, Ideology, and Inequity in the Distribution of Disease*. Washington, DC: Jossey-Bass.

Hofrichter, R. (ed.) (2006) *Tackling Health Inequities Through Public Health Practice: A Handbook for Action*. Battle Creek, MI: W.K. Kellogg Foundation.

Hunter, D.J. and Sengupta, S. (2003) Building multidisciplinary public health, *Critical Public Health*, 14(1): 1–5.

Kawakami, N., Li, X. and Sundquist, K. (2011) Health-promoting and health-damaging neighbourhood resources and coronary heart disease: a follow-up study of 2 165 000 people, *Journal of Epidemiology of Community Health*, 65(10): 866–72.

Kennedy, B., Kawachi, I., Glass, R. and Prothrow-Stith, D. (1998) Income distribution, socio-economic status, and self rated health in the United States: multilevel analysis, *British Medical Journal (BMJ)*, 317(3): 917–21.

Krieger, N. (2001) Theories for social epidemiology in the 21st century: an ecosocial perspective, *International Journl of Epidemiology*, 30(4): 668–77. Available from http://ije.oxfordjournals. org/cgi/reprint/30/4/668.pdf (accessed 24 Mar. 2010).

Krieger, N. (2007) Why epidemiologists cannot afford to ignore poverty, *Epidemiology*, 18(6): 658–63.

Krieger, N. and Birn, A.E. (1998) A vision of social justice as the foundation of public health: commemorating 150 years of the Spirit of 1848, *American Journal of Public Health*, 88(11): 1603–6.

Levy, B.S. and Sidel, V.W. (2006) The nature of social injustice and its impact on public health, in B.S. Levy and V.W. Sidel (eds) *Social Injustice and Public Health*. New York: Oxford University Press.

Mabhala, M. (2012) Embodying knowledge of teaching public health. Unpublished doctoral thesis, Faculty of Education, University of Brighton.

Macintyre, S., Macdonald, L. and Ellaway, A. (2008) Do poorer people have access to local resources and facilities? The distribution of local resources by area deprivation in Glasgow, Scotland, *Social Science Medicine*, 67(6): 900–14.

Mackenbach, J.P. (2009) Politics is nothing but medicine at a larger scale: reflections on public health's biggest idea, *Journal of Epidemiology and Community Health*, 63(3): 181–4.

Mackenbach, J.P. (2011) Can we reduce health inequalities? An analysis of the English strategy (1997–2010), *Journal of Epidemiology and Community Health*, 65(7): 568–75.

Mackenbach, J. P. and Bakker, M. (2003) *Reducing Inequalities in Health: A European Perspective.* London: Routledge.

Marmot, M. (2005) Social determinants of health inequalities, *Lancet*, 365(9464): 1099–104.

Marmot, M. (2009) Closing the health gap in a generation: the work of the Commission on Social Determinants of Health and its recommendations, *Global Health Promotion*, 16(23): 23–7.

Marmot, M. (2010) *Fair Society, Healthy Lives: Strategic Review of Health Inequalities in England post-2010.* Available at http://www.instituteofhealthequity.org/Content/FileManager/pdf/fair-societyhealthylives.pdf (accessed 12 Dec 2010).

Marmot, M. (2011) *Social Determinants of Health – What Doctors Can Do.* Available at www.google.co.uk/url?sa=t&rct=j&q=people%20do%20not%20want%20health%20because%20it%20gives%20them%20jobs%20they%20want%20health%2C%20marmot%20&source=web&cd=5&ved=0CEAQFjAE&url=http%3A%2F%2Fbma.org.uk%2F-%2Fmedia%2FFiles%2FPDFs%2FWorking%2520for%2520change%2FImproving%2520health%2Fsocialdeterminantshealth.pdf&ei=bn4LUoDhFsnKhAfwy4DADg&usg=AFQjCNFcEGJEywCN7nMo1OxrX9c0_maamA (accessed 14 Aug 2013).

McDonald, R. and Harrison, S. (2004) Autonomy and modernisation: the management of change in an English primary care trust, *Health and Social Care in the Community*, 12(3): 194–201.

McKinlay, J.B. (1974) *A Case for Refocussing Upstream: The Political Economy of Illness.* Seattle, WA: New York Free Press.

Milton, B., Moonan, M., Taylor-Robinson, D. and Whitehead, M. (2012) *How Can the Health Equity Impact of Universal Policies Be Evaluated? Insights into Approaches and Next Steps.* Geneva: WHO.

Pearce, J., Witten, K., Hiscock, R. and Blakely, T. (2007) Are socially disadvantaged neighbour-hoods deprived of health-related community resources? *International Journal of Epidemiology*, 36(2): 348–55.

Powers, M. and Faden, R. (2006) *Social Justice: The Foundations of Public Health and Health Policy.* Oxford: Oxford University Press.

Raphael, D. (2004) *Social Determinants of Health: Canadian Perspectives.* Toronto: Canadian Scholars Press.

Rawls, J. (1971) *A Theory of Justice.* Cambridge: Harvard University Press.

Smith, G.D., Morris, J. and Shaw, M. (1998) The Independent Inquiry into Inequalities in Health, *British Medical Journal (BMJ)*, 317(7171): 1465–6.

Stronks, K. and Mackenbach, J. P. (2005) Evaluating the effect of policies and interventions to address inequalities in health: lessons from a Dutch programme, *European Journal of Public Health*, 16(4): 346–53.

UK Health Watch. (2005) *The Experience of Health in an Unequal Society.* Available at www.pohg.org.uk/support/publications.html (accessed 23 Mar 2006).

Van de Mheen, H.D., Stronks, K. and Mackenbach, J.P. (1998) Sociology and ill-health, in C. Seale, J. Gabe, S. Wainwright and C. Williams (eds) *A Lifecourse Perspective on Socio-economic Inequalities in Health: The Influence of Childhood Socio-economic Conditions and Selection Processes (Vol. 20).* Chichester: Wiley.

Virchow, R. (1941) Die Medizinische Reform, in H.E. Sigerist (ed.) *Medicine and Human Welfare.* New Haven, CT: Yale University Press.

Whitehead, M. (1990) *The Concepts and Principles of Equality and Health.* Copenhagen: WHO.

Wilkinson, R.G. (1997) Health inequalities: relative or absolute material standards? *British Medical Journal (BMJ)*, 314(7080): 591–5.

Wilkinson, R.G. (2005) *The Impact of Inequality: How to Make Sick Societies Healthier.* London: Routledge.

Wilkinson, R.G. and Marmot, M. (2003) Social determinants of health: the solid facts, in R. Wilkinson and M. Marmot (eds) *Social Determinants of Health: The Solid Facts.* Available at http://books.google.co.uk/books?id=QDFzqNZZHLMC&printsec=copyright&source=gbs_pub_info_r#v=onepage&q&f=false (accessed 1 Oct. 2010).

World Health Organization (WHO) (1946) *Constitution of the World Health Organization*. London: WHO. Available at http://whqlibdoc.who.int/hist/official_records/constitution.pdf (accessed 5 Nov. 2010).

World Health Organization (WHO) (1978) *Alma Ata declaration*. Available at www.righttohealthcare. org/Docs/DocumentsC.htm (accessed 5 Nov. 2010).

World Health Organization (WHO) (2005) *All for Equity: World Conference on Social Determinants of Health*. Rio de Janeiro: WHO.

World Health Organization (WHO) (2008a) *Commission on Social Determinants of Health – Final Report*. Available at www.who.int/social_determinants/thecommission/finalreport/en/index.html (accessed 24 Nov. 2010).

World Health Organization (WHO) (2008b) *The Commission Calls for Closing the Health Gap in a Generation*. Geneva: WHO.

3 | Lifespan transitions and health

Frances Wilson

Introduction

Major changes to society and lifestyle in England have resulted in the emergence of different health challenges requiring new public health strategies. Different age ranges present distinct health and well-being opportunities for improvement – hence a 'one size fits all' approach to improving health and well-being is not an option.

The Department of Health published *Healthy Lives, Healthy People: Our Strategy for Public Health in England* (DH 2010a) and a complementary policy *Our Health and Well-being Today* (DH 2010b) in response to the Marmot review of public health (Marmot 2010). The overall aims of the government's public health strategy are to support people to live long and healthy lives by 'taking a coherent approach to different stages of life and key transitions, instead of tackling individual risk factors in isolation' (DH 2010b: 30).

This chapter reviews the life stages and transition points for people in England and similar high-income countries, and explores some of the health strategies in place that are tailored to address different life stages. A section of the chapter compares the points of transition between life stages with low-income countries and their emphasis on alternative strategies for improving health and well-being.

Life stages and transition

The Department of Health recognizes five distinct life stages: developing well; starting well; growing up well; living and working well; and ageing well. This raises the question, at what age does a person move between stages? The boundaries between stages are distinctly blurred and those with long-term and lifelong health conditions will experience these divisions as they transit from one stage to the next. This also has implications for the workforce and the roles of care professionals who are employed in health and social care services. In England, health services and the workforce are targeted at different age ranges and loosely focused on one or other of the life stages. The key health areas associated with each phase are summarized in Table 3.1.

Within these life stages there are distinct events occurring that are unique to each individual and to family life. Of course, not everyone will succeed in transitioning all of the life stages and life can be cut short at any point due to illness or

Table 3.1 The life stages and challenges

Starting well	Early on, the health of mothers before and during pregnancy and good parenting are crucial to getting the best start in life
Developing well	As children develop, it is important to encourage healthy habits and avoid the adoption of harmful patterns of behaviour
Growing up well	Childhood is also a critical time for identifying, treating and preventing mental health problems
Living and working well	Lifestyle choices in adulthood and employment can have profound impacts on an individual's longer-term health and well-being
Ageing well	As people age and become increasingly at risk of frailty there are challenges in supporting them to remain resilient to ill health by maintaining their social networks and by being physically active.
	Protecting vulnerable people, including the elderly, from preventable harms is also an important challenge for public health and includes falls prevention, protecting people from seasonal weather extremes and providing vaccinations such as the seasonal flu jab

Source: DH (2010b: 3–4)

accident. However, some or all of these events may occur, such as conception, birth, walking, talking, starting and leaving school, childhood, adolescence, entering higher education, entering the workforce, adulthood, marriage, divorce, single parenthood, becoming a parent or grandparent, middle age, retirement, illness or disability at any point, old age and death. These points in life will represent times of upheaval and change not just physically but socially and emotionally for the individual and others such as family members and associates. An overview of these stages and health implications is therefore taken with reference to life course theory approaches.

Theories of the life course and the potential impact of health improvement strategies

Life course approach theories suggest that there are many complex interrelated factors that influence health and illness at different stages in our lives. The life course health development framework (LHDF) (Halfon and Hochstein 2002) is based on wide-ranging research explaining how health patterns develop over an individual's lifetime. In essence, early life experiences, the presence of risk or protective factors, affect people's long-term health outcomes. By understanding this it may be possible to shift from treatment of later stages of disease to prevention and intervention strategies. This can also be likened to changing focus from downstream to upstream approaches to promoting health.

Sir Michael Marmot's latest *Review of Social Determinants and the Health Divide in the WHO European Region* (WHO 2013a) further emphasizes the life-course approach to health giving the highest priority to children ensuring they receive a good start in life through universal education and childcare systems. In tandem with this, tackling the social determinants of health to improve average health and reduce health inequities both within and between countries is essential in order to achieve better outcomes in all areas. The way in which health-care systems can achieve this is through better organization to achieve universal access to health services throughout Europe and policy development to drive change (WHO 2013a).

A representation of the life course is seen in Figure 3.1 emphasizing the accumulation of positive and negative effects on health and well-being over the life course.

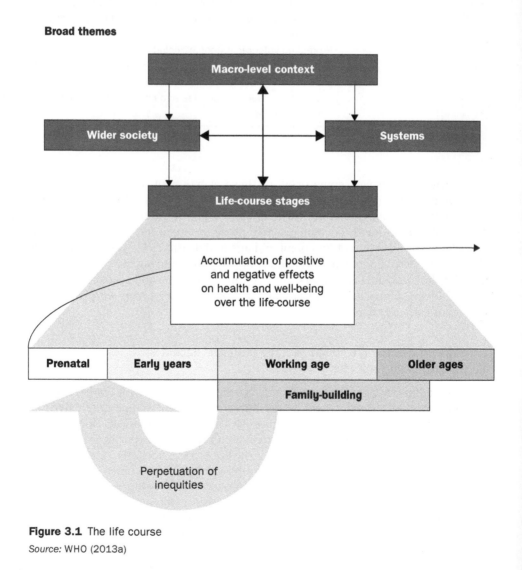

Figure 3.1 The life course

Source: WHO (2013a)

Conceptual models of the life course

The WHO (WHO and International Longevity Centre-UK 2000) promotes the training of health-care professionals in the life course approach and proposes four conceptual models:

- A critical period model
- A critical period with late effect modifiers
- Accumulation of risk with independent and uncorrelated insults
- Accumulation of risk with correlated insults (clustering chains or pathways of risk).

During growth and development phases from conception, foetal growth, early infancy and childhood through to adolescence there is evidence of 'critical periods of growth'. During these times environmental exposure to adverse influences may have lifelong effects not modified by later experiences (Detels *et al.* 2010). These influences may be the precursors of adult diseases such as coronary heart disease (CHD). In addition, there is also evidence of 'sensitive developmental stages' in childhood and adolescence when all aspects of learning and skills acquisition are more easily assimilated. Again these early experiences have implications for health in adult life and whether their impact may be negative or positive.

There is a plethora of research available that links low birth weight babies with chronic disease in later life. For example, research in the USA (Curhan *et al.* 1996) concludes that low birth weight babies have a higher risk of developing high blood pressure and diabetes mellitus, and high birth weight was associated with increased risk of obesity. The Caerphilly study (Frankel *et al.* 1996) also links low birth weight to CHD and body mass index (BMI) in middle-aged men.

The third model suggests an accumulation of risk over each stage of the life course, which is an area of ongoing research. Examples of the fourth model relate to children residing in poor socio-economic conditions, and chains of risk may be evident between, for example, passive smoking, asthma and adult respiratory disease. Social chains of risk are also associated with this example to school absence and low educational attainment. Many other examples can be found in the research for further exploration.

The life course perspective also suggests that lifespans may be interconnected and can be demonstrated through disease trends in a population over time (Detels *et al.* 2010).

Since the publication of *Health at Key Stages of Life – the Life Course Approach to Health* (WHO n.d.) the WHO has introduced four key health programmes into Europe that propose targeted intervention strategies: The Maternal and New-born Health programme; The Child and Adolescent Health programme; The Sexual and Reproductive Health programme; and The Healthy Ageing programme. Gender issues are addressed in each programme. The programmes support the WHO strategic objective 4 to: 'Reduce morbidity and mortality and improve health during key stages of life, including pregnancy, childbirth, the neonatal period, childhood and adolescence, and improve sexual and reproductive health and promote active and healthy ageing for all individuals.' (WHO n.d: 16)

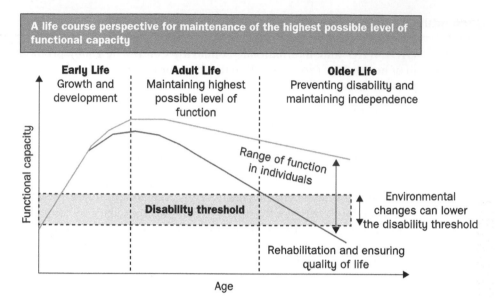

Figure 3.2 Functional capacity and the life course
Source: WHO (2000).

The process of ageing begins before birth. A person's functional capacity will develop and decline according to age, lifestyle choices, early life course influences (that may or may not be moderated) or degree of disability. Figure 3.2 encapsulates early, adult and later life in an average trajectory. To achieve maximum potential at any age adopting healthy lifestyle choices and behaviours, including regular exercise, a balanced diet and regular activity, should help to reduce decline. Conversely, unhealthy behaviours including smoking, excessive alcohol consumption, lack of physical exercise, poor diet, other health issues such as obesity and chronic health conditions may all contribute towards a steeper decline in function and increased risk of CHD or disability. Changing such behaviour can reverse or slow the decline with the support of health improvement and intervention strategies. Additionally, social determinants can adversely influence functional capacity and the ability of an individual to actively seek or adopt health enhancing behaviour.

For those with a disability or illness which may have been identified at or around birth or at a later life stage, early diagnosis, appropriate intervention, support and rehabilitation are essential to maintain function or delay decline, thus maximizing quality of life and well-being (WHO 2000).

Starting well

Maternal physical, social and mental health and well-being all have a bearing on the health of the child. Health and well-being of the mother is crucial to a developing child even before conception, during foetal growth and subsequent development of the newborn infant. Certain factors, if present, increase the risk of low birth weight, infant morbidity and mortality. Many of these factors can be moderated or eliminated to reduce the associated risks through promoting healthy strategies, such as: stopping smoking and excessive alcohol consumption; improved maternal nutrition and reduction in obesity; and the increased initiation of breast feeding (DH 2010b).

Various types of screening are undertaken in pregnancy designed to identify the health status of both mother and foetus. Examples include testing for the presence of infections, for example, sexually transmitted diseases which can be treated to prevent or reduce damage to the developing foetus.

Ultrasound scans are undertaken at predetermined stages in pregnancy to monitor foetal growth, identify any delays and detect abnormalities. Other tests can identify possible genetic problems before or shortly after birth, for example, Down's syndrome. Blood spot screening of the infant can detect conditions such as cystic fibrosis and sickle cell disease. Screening for hearing impairment is a recent advance in universal screening of the newborn.

Other factors influencing the first months and years of life are early emotional experiences. Positive parenting relationships can influence brain development and this can balance out some of the effects of poverty and deprivation that can have a negative effect on physical, social and intellectual development (Kiernan and Mensah 2010).

The following case studies represent two different types of intervention – the first to screen for hearing impairment and the second to promote the initiation of breast feeding.

Case study: Universal hearing screening

Universal hearing screening (UHS) of the newborn undertaken within a few weeks of birth is a recent medical and technological advance meaning that the majority of children with a congenital hearing impairment can be detected early. One or two babies in every 1000 are born with a degree of hearing loss each year in the UK. The implications of the UHS programme are revolutionary as it has considerably enhanced health outcomes for children by initiating alternative means of communication and appropriate therapies within weeks of birth, optimizing speech and language development. Before this advance, children were often not diagnosed until much later, consequently delaying development and commencement of intervention strategies.

Website

For further information see website http://hearing.screening.nhs.uk

Case study: Initiation of breastfeeding

The infant feeding survey is undertaken every five years by the NHS Information Centre and some of the results are as follows. In 2010 the proportion of babies breastfed at birth in the UK rose from 76 per cent to 81 per cent. Exclusive breast-feeding at 6 weeks was 24 per cent. However, this number drops significantly by 3 months to mothers breastfeeding exclusively to 17 per cent (up from 13 per cent in 2005) and at 4 months, 12 per cent (up from 7 per cent in 2005). However, exclusive breastfeeding at 6 months remains at around 1 per cent.

The *Healthy Child Programme* (DH 2009c) proposes that involvement of fathers will have a positive effect via education of the health benefits and encouraging their support for breastfeeding partners. Fathers have a key role in the successful initiation and continuation of breastfeeding (DH 2009c). Breastfeeding has long-term health benefits for mothers and their babies, can reduce inequalities and has the potential to save the NHS millions of pounds.

The initiative aims to:

- set up a breastfeeding support group for fathers
- improve breastfeeding rates
- improve health outcomes in the short and long term.

Websites

Unicef, The Baby Friendly initiative. UK Breastfeeding rates, www.unicef.org.uk/
    babyfriendly/about-baby-friendly/breastfeeding-in-the-uk/uk-breastfeeding-rates/
Healthy Child Programme (DH 2009), www.gov.uk

Case study written by Nichola Hayden, student, MSc Specialist Community Public Health Practice (Health Visitor), University of Chester 2013/14

Thinking points

There are many factors that contribute to children having a poor start in life. This section has provided a few examples from the maternal and child perspective. Summarize the examples given in this section and add more of your own. You may wish to explore the websites and literature further and the public health strategy for England (DH 2010a). Students should explore the websites and data about universal hearing screening and initiation of breastfeeding. Then answer the following questions:

- What are the societal benefits of implementing the UHS programme?
- How will early detection of hearing impairment improve health and well-being?
- Why is the initiation of breastfeeding important for the future life course?
- What health improvement strategies are employed by health visitors and midwives to promote breastfeeding?
- How do breastfeeding rates compare with other selected countries in Europe and low-income countries?

Developing well

The initial early stage of a child's life may influence the whole life course. Parental relationships throughout childhood into adulthood are vital for optimal physical, intellectual, emotional and social development. Poor parenting increases the risk of mental health problems in children and adolescents. In 2004, one in ten children and young people (10 per cent) aged 5–16 in Great Britain had a clinically diagnosed mental disorder (Green *et al.* 2005). This figure has remained constant. Of adults who experience mental illness, 50 per cent experienced symptoms before the age of 14 years and 75 per cent before approximately 25 years of age, indicating that promoting good parenting and prevention of mental illness in children is an area for increased investment. In 2011 the government published *Health Visitor Implementation Plan 2011–15. A Call to Action,* a strategy for the training of 4200 additional health visitors to support children and families (DH 2011).

Establishing healthy behaviours in childhood can influence the life course, therefore health promotion and improvement strategies should be targeted at such behaviours known to be problematic, such as smoking, alcohol consumption and eating healthily. There are many statistics related to the health of children but perhaps eating healthily and preventing the onset of obesity are one of the most important. Many obese children will become obese adults with associated health risks such as diabetes, CHD, some cancers and impaired functional capacity. It is estimated that by 2050 half of the UK population will be overweight (NHS Choices 2012).

The following case study outlines the National Child Measurement programme (NCMP) that aims to determine prevalence, raise awareness and improve understanding of childhood obesity and promote healthy lifestyles.

Case study: The National Child Measurement Programme (NCMP) – progress 2005–13

The NCMP was introduced in 2005 and data continues to be collected annually. The programme has become more embedded since its inception and provides a platform for promoting health improvement strategies to children and families The responsibility for delivering the programme shifted in 2013 from PCTs to local authorities (LAs) who now have responsibility for public health. The data will inform the Joint Strategic Needs Assessment (JSNA) and joint health and well-being strategies that will aim to reduce the prevalence of childhood obesity. The number of children overweight or obese is an indicator in the Public Health Outcomes framework (PHOF) data.

Children in England are weighed and measured annually in reception at the ages of 4–5 years and in Year 6 at ages 10–11 at state primary and middle schools and academies. The aim is for at least 85 per cent participation to produce reliable longitudinal data on the weight of children to determine the prevalence of childhood obesity. A child's individual measurements are shared with their parents, who have the right to withdraw their child from participation should they wish (HMSO 2008). Approximately 7 million children have been measured to date, contributing to a

(continued)

robust database for ongoing research. In time the accumulating data will be used to monitor health and obesity across the life course. The school nursing service has a key role in implementing the programme.

Over 1 million or 93 per cent of eligible children participated in 2011–12. Data revealed that 22.6 per cent of children in reception and 33.9 per cent of children in Year 6 were overweight or obese. The data also demonstrated a strong correlation between prevalence of obesity and deprivation. In addition socio-economic inequalities in obesity prevalence have widened since data collection began (PHE 2013a).

The latest data from the school year 2012–13 shows a very slight reduction in overweight and obese children in Reception and Year 6 from the previous year. This is the first time this trend has reversed since the programme began. It is interesting to note that some of the children in Year 6 may also have been measured in 2006–07 but at this time a link cannot be established (HSCIC and PHE 2013). Evaluation of the programme in future years should be followed through to identify trends and possible impact of health improvement strategies.

Websites

Students should explore the following websites:

www.noo.org.uk/NCMP
www.hscic.gov.uk/

Thinking points

Students should explore the websites and data about the NCMP. Then answer the following questions:

- What are the societal benefits of implementing this programme?
- How is data collected?
- How can accuracy of the data be confirmed?
- What health improvement strategies are employed in schools to promote good eating habits and why is this important for the future life course?
- What strategic measures can be undertaken to improve the population health?

Growing up well

This period of the life course generally refers to adolescence and young adulthood up to the mid-twenties. It is a time of rapid change and stress when young people are maturing physically, neurologically and emotionally, taking examinations, leaving school, leaving home, entering higher education or the world of work and forming new emotional attachments. It is also a time of new experiences and responsibilities. Smoking, alcohol consumption and sexual experimentation are commonly part of the repertoire. The main causes of morbidity and mortality also change. One of the highest causes of mortality in this age range is road traffic accidents often associated with alcohol consumption (DH 2010b).

Referring to the models of life-stages development, adolescence constitutes a 'sensitive development period' influenced by puberty and rapid brain development and a range of social factors leading to new behaviours. This stage lies between childhood and adult transitions, and experiences at this stage will influence health and well-being in adult life. As in earlier childhood, positive parenting and social and health equity will help to smooth the way to adulthood. Evidence of effective interventions in adolescence includes those targeted at improving access to education and employment (Viner *et al.* 2012).

Many mental health issues surface in adolescence or early adulthood and of most concern are the rising incidents of self-harm, suicidal thought and suicide. Poor sexual health is another area with increasing prevalence of sexually transmitted infections (STIs). However, teenage conceptions and pregnancy are the lowest since the mid-1990s but high when compared with other parts of Europe. Obesity is following the upward trend and poor dietary habits continue (DH 2010b).

The following case study outlines a proposal to improve young people's health and well-being aimed at adolescents who self-harm.

Case study: A proposal to initiate a training package to enable school nurses to competently assess and support adolescents who self-harm

Over the past ten years rates of self-harm in children and young people in the UK have increased and are among the highest in Europe (Nixon 2011). A targeted approach to prevention and education is proposed to address the causes and improve the outcomes for young people.

The aims of the initiative are to:

- provide specialized training for school nurses to increase their understanding of the underlying causes of self-harm and how to address associated stigma.
- facilitate health and well-being strategies which empower young people to make healthier choices, develop decision-making skills and increase self-confidence.
- reduce the incidence and severity of self-harm through early intervention strategies.

Adolescent mental and emotional health is an area of national importance as they are the adults of the future. It is important that young people receive age appropriate services which ultimately improve health outcomes (DH 2009d).

Marmot (2010) suggests that services interventions in adolescent years provide the last opportunity to ensure that health inequalities do not become established.

Lincoln and Earle (2007 cited in Baggott, 2011: 185) explain that 'children and young people's current lifestyles, their environment or economic circumstances may have adverse implications for future adult health'.

Partnership working and involving key stakeholders when planning and implementing such an initiative ensures the right skills are deployed in the training of the school health workforce, development of an assessment tool and care pathway.

(continued)

These may include Child and Adolescent Mental Health Services (CAMHS), education, general practitioners (GPs), medical staff, the National Society for the Prevention of Cruelty to Children (NSPCC), social services and service users. Funding of this type of programme may need to be agreed with commissioners and, as such, be part of an overall strategic approach to improving adolescent health.

Websites

Video link re adolescent health programme and professional skills development, www.rcpch.ac.uk/AHP
Association for Young People's Health (AYPH), http://www.youngpeopleshealth.org.uk/3/resources/17/key-data-on-adolescence/
Self-harm in Children and Young People, handbook, www.chimat.org.uk/resource/item.aspx?RID=105602

Case study written by Gail Lilley, MSc Health Improvement and Well-being student, University of Chester 2013–14

Thinking points

Students should explore the websites and data about adolescent health. Then answer the following questions:

- What are the main mental health issues that adolescents experience?
- What are the societal benefits of implementing this training initiative?
- What health improvement strategies are employed in schools to promote mental health and well-being and why is this important for the future life course?
- What more strategic measures can be undertaken to improve the health of the adolescent population (Viner *et al.* 2012)?

Living and working well

When adulthood is reached, health and well-being will have already been influenced by environmental factors and lifestyle choices and behaviour. Some of the factors that are known to have a positive impact on the life course and positive mental health are employment or being employed or occupied in paid or unpaid work, as opposed to being unemployed or socially isolated. However, disabled people, people with mental health conditions and long-term health conditions are less likely to be in employment. Living near to, or being able to access, green spaces such as parks and leisure areas has a positive impact on physical activity. Changes to lifestyle can still reap benefits, for example, taking more exercise, giving up smoking and eating a healthier diet may improve functional capacity (WHO 2000). Carers with substantial caring roles are also more likely to report health problems. Availing of screening services to detect early stages of disease should be actively promoted to maximize uptake.

The following case study is a proposal to introduce Mental Health First Aid Training in the workplace.

Case study: Health at Work – Proposal to Implement Mental Health First Aid (MHFA) Training for Occupational Health Nurses

Positive mental health is an integral part of an individual's capacity to lead a fulfilled life, including the ability to work. Disturbances to a person's mental well-being can compromise this capacity, diminish functioning at individual level and be a broader loss to society (WHO 2013b).

Certain occupational groups are vulnerable to stress-related mental health problems including nurses, managers, doctors, teachers, farmers and ex-service personnel (NICE 2007). Evidence shows that sickness absence rates are high among NHS employees and those who work the longest hours have the highest sickness and absence rates (DH 2009a).

The MHFA programme was developed in Australia in 2001 – it is the initial help provided to a person developing a mental health problem or crisis. The course aims to give people the skills to recognize signs of mental health distress and to enable them to provide support. It is essentially a train the trainers programme designed to provide early intervention strategies in the workplace.

Part of the success of the programme is due to improved recognition of mental health problems and decreased stigmatization of attendees (Terry 2011). People seeking help early reduce the severity of their condition and subsequent long-term burden to health and mental health systems. Evaluation research is ongoing.

Following consultation with stakeholders and proposal for funding it is recommended that two occupational health nurses are trained to provide the service in the hospital trust (anonymous).

Websites

Mental Health First Aid (Wales), www.mhfa-wales.org.uk/
Mental Health First Aid (England), http://mhfaengland.org/

Case study written by Karen Land, Occupational Health Student, University of Chester 2013–14

Thinking point

Students should explore the websites and data about the effectiveness of MHFA. Then answer the following questions:

- What are the main mental health issues experienced in the workplace?
- What are the societal benefits of implementing this training initiative?
- Why is this programme important for the future life course?
- What strategic measures can be undertaken to improve the health of the workforce in the population?

Ageing well

This is the fastest growing age group in England and the UK. By 2033 it is estimated that approximately 25 per cent of the population will be over 65 years (ONS 2010). Older people are now in the latter stages of the life course and the accumulation of lifestyle factors and choices made in earlier years may be impacting on their current health status. From Figure 3.2 it can be seen that functional capacity will be declining but this can be influenced positively through being active and mentally stimulated. Life expectancy has increased and consequently the length of time spent in post-employment years has resulted in an increased number of people living with mental and physical health challenges. This requires a review of health-care systems and new approaches to delivery of services.

The following case study describes a proposal to improve the health and well-being of the elderly population – dementia care.

Case study: Introduction of a new risk assessment tool to identify early signs and symptoms of dementia

The introduction of a new dementia service was influenced by the local CCGs objective to improve best practice for dementia care. An ageing population will account for increasing prevalence and greater financial expenditure on health and social care costs associated with the disease (DH 2009b). It is estimated that by 2025 1 in 6 people over 65 years will suffer from a form of dementia increasing to 1 in 3 by 2050 (PHE 2013b). The World Health Organization (2012) has declared dementia as a global health priority and recommends that efforts should be made to improve the quality and availability of care with an investment in primary prevention methods.

The proposal aims to increase early diagnosis of dementia by utilizing a risk assessment tool during district nurse (DN) visits. The majority of a district nurse's caseload consists of patients over 65 years of age which reflects the most prevalent age group for dementia (DH 2009b). The assessment tool consist of two parts – the first is case finding and is undertaken based on known risk factors designed to identify patients at high risk of developing dementia in the DN caseload or GP population. The second part of the tool is a series of tick box questions based on common symptoms of dementia to identify early stages of the disease and to facilitate referral to the patient's GP.

There is a distinction between case finding and screening of the whole population, the latter being more expensive and unreliable (NICE 2006). Through early detection outcomes can be improved by timely commencement of medication, treatment of vascular symptoms and other therapeutic interventions such as attending memory clinics, reminiscence therapy, advocating healthier lifestyles and supporting carers.

There are financial implications for training the DN service and other frontline staff as training in dementia care is now mandatory for professionals working with older people. However, early diagnosis, effective support and treatment will reduce the need for residential long-term care and reduce costs (DH 2009b; NICE 2013). NICE (2013) has produced a guide for commissioners of dementia services to improve standards of dementia care, to provide information on integrated approaches to health and social care needs and to enable people to remain in their own homes for as long as possible.

Websites

Alzheimer's Disease website, www.alzheimers.org.uk/

NICE website – Commissioning Dementia Care, www.nice.org.uk/newsroom/news/CommissioningHealthSocialCarePeopleWithDementia.jsp

NICE website – Dementia Care Pathway, http://pathways.nice.org.uk/pathways/dementia

Case study written by Jennifer Clitheroe, District Nurse Student, University of Chester 2013–14

Thinking point

Students should explore the websites about dementia then answer the following questions:

- How and why do dementia services need to change?
- What are the societal benefits of implementing the dementia assessment tool?
- What types of intervention strategies are available?
- Can dementia be linked with earlier stages in the life course (Whalley *et al.* 2006)?
- What approaches can be taken to promote good mental health in the ageing population?

Lifespan and transitions – an international perspective

The World Health Organization focused on promoting health through the life course, with emphasis on women's and children's health, at its World Health Assembly in 2013 (WHO 2013d). It is concerned with a global approach towards achievement of the health millennium development goals (MDGs) in areas of advancing women's and children's health, promoting full vaccination coverage via the Global Vaccine Action Plan 2011–2020, strengthening non-communicable disease policies to promote active ageing and reducing child and maternal mortality. In addition special attention was paid to: violence against women and girls; gender, equity and human rights; and maintaining health and independence in the older population. The health sector has a key role in preventing and addressing these public health concerns worldwide.

Our understanding of life expectancy and life course transitions will be determined by the country or continent in which we live, cultural and religious belief, political factors and health services provision. These factors will be considered from a global perspective with specific examples to highlight the differences.

According to the WHO in its annual report of 2013 (WHO 2013c) the provision of universal health coverage and achievement of the millennium goals by 2015 has the potential to contribute to wider human development based on robust research and strengthening of public health and health services provision. This includes improving health and well-being through health promotion, prevention, treatment and rehabilitation. How this is funded incurs further consideration as all people should have access to the health services they need without financial loss. In turn this will impact on lifespan itself. As life expectancy increases, attitudes and goal posts change.

Transitions in the lifespan are the points at which major change occurs, for example, birth, childhood, adolescence, early and late adulthood, old age and death. These stages in the lifespan and at what point we move from one state to another can vary depending on your perspective. Events are determined physiologically, socially, culturally or as a personal state of mind.

At these points people are also amenable to the impact of health improvement strategies. There is evidence to show that people at these distinct transitional phases in their lives are more receptive to health promotion and improvement strategies. Results from part of the Australian Longitudinal Study on Women's Health (ALSWH) have shown that smoking behaviour among young women is modified by pregnancy and they are motivated to stop as their concern is foremost with the health of the baby rather than their own (McDermott *et al.* 2004). The implications of this are encouraging and support the theory that life events can lead to changes in behaviour.

A similar study about life transitions and changing patterns of physical activity in young women (Brown and Trost 2003) between 18 and 24 years was undertaken as part of the ALSWH. The evidence suggests that life events such as getting married, starting work and having children are linked to changes in lifestyle and decreased levels of physical activity. It is recommended that strategies at these transition points are needed to promote maintenance of activity.

Life expectancy and how it impacts on life course stages and transition

Lifespan itself will influence the length and position of transition. Where lifespan and life expectancy is low then life stages may be shorter, points of transition more distinct or relatively unnoticed.

The age at which childhood begins and ends, whether there is an adolescent phase at all and when adulthood, middle and old age occurs will be influenced by cultural perspectives and life expectancy itself. For example, taking a life expectancy that exceeds 80 years and contrasting with countries which have a life expectancy of under 50 years will greatly influence how people conduct their lives.

An exploration of life expectancy in 2001 and 2011 at birth for both sexes combined has been compared between selected low-, middle- and high-income countries. The objective is to draw the reader's attention to the differences between countries and to contemplate the importance and impact of life course and transitional phases, the length of which may differ significantly.

Sierra Leone is recorded as having the lowest life expectancy in the world today, at 47 years, followed by the Central African Republic, 48 years, and Democratic Republic of Congo (DRC), 49 years. The highest being Japan, at 83 years, Australia, Canada and Sweden, 82 years, the UK, 80 years, and the USA, 79 years. This data can be obtained from the WHO which is usefully contained in an interactive map. See Table 3.2, which is summarized by continent as defined by the WHO.

Table 3.2 Life expectancy at birth – both sexes: some examples

2011	80 years plus	70–79 years	60–69 years	50–59 years	40–49 years
Africa 47–74 (2001 39–72)		Mauritius and Seychelles (74) Algeria (73)	Botswana (66) Ghana (64) Rwanda, Kenya, Ethiopia (60)	Tanzania, Liberia (59) South Africa, Gambia (58) Uganda (56) Zimbabwe (54) Nigeria (53) Angola (51) Lethoso 50	Sierra Leone (47) CAR (48) DRC (49)
Americas 63–82 (2001 58–79)	Canada (82)	USA, Chile (79) Cuba, Barbados (78) Mexico (75) Brazil (74) Dominican Republic (73)	Haiti (63) Bolivia (67) Guatemala (69)		
Eastern Mediterranean 50–82 (2001 49–77)	Qatar (82) Kuwait (80)	UAE, Tunisia (76) Syria (75) Egypt, Iran (73)	Iraq (69) Pakistan (67) Libya (75) Sudan (63) Afghanistan (60)	South Sudan (54) Somalia (50)	
Europe 63–83 (2001 62–2)	Switzerland (83) Spain, Sweden, Italy, France (82) Germany, Ireland, Greece (81) UK, Belgium (80)	Armenia (71) Georgia (72) Albania (72) Hungary (75) Turkey, Poland (76) Denmark (79)	Russian Federation (69) Turkmenistan (63)		

(continued)

Table 3.2 (Continued)

2011	80 years plus	70–79 years	60–69 years	50–59 years	40–49 years
Southeast Asia		Maldives (77)	Timor (64)		
64–77		Sri Lanka (75)	India (65)		
(2001 56–70		Thailand (74)	Indonesia, North Korea (69)		
		Bangladesh (70)			
Western Pacific	Japan (83)	Brunei (77)	Marshall Is. (60)		
60–83	Australia (82)	China (76)	Philippines (69)		
(2001 58–71)	Singapore (82)	Vietnam (75)	Micronesia (69)		
	South Korea (81)	Malaysia (74)	Cambodia (65)		
	New Zealand (81)	Tonga (72)	Papua New Guinea (63)		
		Fiji (70)			

Source: Adapted from WHO (2014).

Changes in life expectancy in the last ten years

What is interesting to note are the changes in life expectancy ranking and rate of change in some countries and reasons for this. In most cases, life expectancy is increasing rapidly at the lower end ranking with a few notable exceptions where improvement has remained static or moved very slightly. For example, the country with the lowest life expectancy in 2001 was Sierra Leone at 39 years following the civil war in the 1990s and, although it still remains the lowest life expectancy in the world, it has increased to 47 in 10 years. Other examples include Zimbabwe which has increased from 43 to 54 years, Rwanda from 44 to 60 years, Uganda from 46 to 56 years and DRC from 47 to 49 years. At this lower end of the world rankings improvement has been delayed due to ongoing conflict resulting in a slow increase such as Sierra Leone, DRC and CAR. Rwanda and Zimbabwe are showing a more rapid recovery following genocide and civil unrest respectively. There are many other factors influencing the ability of a country to develop, such as taking political and financial responsibility, the organization of public health, managing communicable disease and women's and child health reducing infant and maternal mortality. It may be considered that a country's ability to address the millennium goals will play a part in population health and increases in life expectancy.

The country with the highest life expectancy in 2000 was San Marino (82) then Japan (81), Switzerland 80, the UK (78), the USA and Cuba (77), Vietnam (72), India (61). The order at the top in 2011 has changed slightly with small increases in life expectancy resulting in San Marino, Japan and Switzerland now sharing top ranking at 83 years with the UK ranked twenty-third in the world, at 80 years.

Thinking points

Explore the interactive website.

Take examples from countries with life expectancy in the 40s, 50, 60s, 70s and over 80 years and consider where life stages begin and end. They may be selected from the table or the interactive website.

- What factors influence the life course in low-, middle- and high-income countries?
- Take one of the life course stages depending on your professional role or interest and estimate where each stage begins and ends.
- Select a country of your choice and complete Table 3.3.
- Take each of the five life stages.
  - What are the key ages of transition between stages in the selected country?
  - What are the main health and social issues at each stage?
  - How can health and well-being be improved?
  - What specific roles do practitioners have? (For example, health visitor, midwife, school nurse, district nurse, specialist roles, wider care professional roles.)
  - What are the skills that are required?

Table 3.3 Life course stages and transition points

Life stages	Starting well	Developing well	Growing up well	Living and working well	Ageing well
Key ages of transition?					
H&S care issues?					
How can H&WB be Improved?					
Specific roles?					
What are the skills required?					

Conclusion

This chapter has explored the life stages, the impact of the life course and conceptual models. The stages of starting well, developing well, growing up well, living and working well, and ageing well were considered in detail with examples of health problems and health and well-being strategies and initiatives. Case studies in each section allow the reader to explore life stages in more detail with thinking points and questions. Finally discussions on the implications of life expectancy in different countries of the world are suggested for the reader to explore culture and factors influencing the life stages and life course transitions. These emphasize that a one size fits all approach to initiating strategies for improving health and well-being must be tailored to the needs of individuals, communities and populations.

References

Baggott, R. (2011) *Public Health Policy and Politics*, 2nd edn. Basingstoke: Palgrave Macmillan.

Brown W.J. and Trost, S.G. (2003) Life transitions and changing physical activity patterns in young women, *American Journal of Preventive Medicine*, 25(2): 140–3.

Curhan, G.C., Willett, W.C., Rimm, E.B., *et al.* (1996) Birth weight and adult hypertension, diabetes mellitus, and obesity in US men, *Circulation*, 94: 3246–50.

Department of Health (DH) (2009a) *NHS Health and Well-being. Final Report*. London: DH.

Department of Health (DH) (2009b) *Living Well with Dementia: A National Dementia Strategy*. London: DH.

Department of Health (DH) (2009c) *Healthy Child Programme: Pregnancy and the First 5 Years of Life*. London: DH.

Department of Health (DH) (2009d) *Healthy Child Programme: From 5-19 Years Old*. London, DH.

Department of Health (DH) (2010a) *Healthy Lives, Healthy People: Our Strategy for Public Health in England*. London: DH.

Department of Health (DH) (2010b) *Our Health and Well-being Today*. London: DH.

Department of Health (DH) (2011) *Health Visitor Implementation Plan 2011–15. A Call to Action*. London: DH.

Detels, R., Beaglehole, R., Lansang M.A. and Gulliford, M. (2010) *Oxford Textbook of Public Health. Vol.1 The Scope of Public Health*, 5th edn. Oxford: Oxford University Press.

Frankel, S., Elwood, P., Sweetnam, P., Yarnell, J. and Smith G.D. (1996) Birthweight, adult risk factors and incident coronary heart disease: the Caerphilly study, *Public Health*, 110(3): 139–43.

Green, H., McGinnity, A., Meltzer, H. *et al.* (2005) *Mental Health of Children and Young People in Great Britain, 2004*, London: Office for National Statistics. Available at www.esds.ac.uk/doc/5269/mrdoc/pdf/5269technicalreport.pdf (accessed 1 Dec. 2013).

Halfon, N. and Hochstein, M. (2002) Life course health development: an integrated framework for developing health, policy and research, *The Milbank Quarterly*, (80): 3.

Health and Social Care Information Centre and Public Health England (HSCIC and PHE) (2013) *National Child Measurement Programme: England, 2012/13 School Year*. HSCIC. Available at www.hscic.gov.uk/ (accessed 4 Apr. 2014).

Her Majesty's Stationery Office (HMSO) (2008) *The National Child Measurement Programme Regulations 2008*. Available at www.legislation.gov.uk/uksi/2008/3080/pdfs/uksi_20083080_en.pdf (accessed 4 Apr. 2014).

Kiernan, K.E. and Mensah, F.K. (2010) Poverty, family resources and children's early educational attainment: the mediating role of parenting, *British Educational Research Journal*, 37(2): 317–36.

Marmot, M. (2010) *Fair Society, Healthy Lives: Strategic Review of Health Inequalities in England post 2010*, www.marmotreview.org p.126. The Marmot Review

McDermott. L., Dobson, and Russell. A (2004) Changes in smoking behaviour among young women over life stage transitions. *Australian and New Zealand Journal of Public Health*, 28 No. 4

National Health Service (NHS) Choices (2012) Obesity. Available at www.nhs.uk/conditions/Obesity/Pages/Introduction.aspx (accessed 4 Apr 2014).

National Institute for Care and Clinical Excellence (NICE) (2006) *Supporting People with Dementia and their Carers in Health and Social Care*. Available at http://guidance.nice.org.uk/CG42/NICEGuidance/pdf/English (accessed Dec. 2013).

National Institute for Care and Clinical Excellence (NICE) (2007) *Public Health Interventions to Promote Positive Mental Health and Prevent Mental Health Disorders among Adults*. Available at www.nice.org.uk/niceMedia/pdf/mental%20health%20EB%20FINAL%2018.01.07. pdf (accessed 1 Dec. 2013).

National Institute for Care and Clinical Excellence (NICE) (2013) *Quality Standard for Supporting People to Live Well with Dementia*. Available from http://publications.nice.org.uk/quality-standard-for-supporting-people-to-live-well-with-dementia-qs30/introduction-and-overview (accessed Dec. 2013).

Nixon, B. (National CAMHS Workforce Programme) (2011) *Self-harm in Children and Young People Handbook*. UKnix: National CAMHS Support Service.

Office for National Statistics (2010) *Life Expectancy at Birth and at Age 65 by Local Areas in the United Kingdom, 2007–09*. Available at www.statistics.gov.uk/pdfdir/liex1010.pdf (accessed 1 Dec. 2013).

Public Health England (PHE) (2013a) *National Child Measurement Programme. Operational Guidance for the 2013/14 School Year*. London: PHE.

Public Health England (PHE) (2013b) *Improving the Dementia Diagnosis Rate in North East England 2013. An Update on Prevalence Rates; Diagnosis Rates; Crisis Related Hospital Admissions*. Available at www.nepho.org.uk/publications/1218/Improving_the_Dementia_Diagnosis_Rate_in_North_East_England_2013 (accessed 3 May 2014).

Terry, J. (2011) Delivering a basic mental health training programme: views and experiences of mental health first aid instructors in Wales, *Journal of Psychiatric and Mental Health Nursing*, 18(8): 677–86. Available at www.ncbi.nlm.nih.gov/pubmed/21896110 (accessed 3 May 2014).

Viner R.M., Ozer, E.M., Denny, S., *et al.* (2012) Adolescence and the social determinants of health, *Lancet*, 379. Available at www.thelancet.com, (accessed 28 Apr. 2012).

Whalley L.J., Dick F.D. and McNeill, G. (2006) A life-course approach to the aetiology of late-onset dementias, *Lancet*, 5(January). Available at http://neurology.thelancet.com (accessed 4 Apr. 2014).

World Health Organization (WHO) (2012) *Dementia: A Public Health Priority.* Berne: WHO.

World Health Organization (WHO) (2013a) *Review of Social Determinants and the Health Divide in the WHO European Region: Executive Summary.* Copenhagen: UCL Institute of Health Equity.

World Health Organization (WHO) (2013b) *Investing in Mental Health: Evidence for Action.* Available at www.who.int/mental_health/publications/financing/investing_in_mh_2013/en/ (accessed 1 Dec. 2013).

World Health Organization (WHO) (2013c) *World Health Report 2013: Research for Universal Health Coverage.* Available at www.who.int/whr/2013/report/en/ (accessed 4 Apr. 2014).

World Health Organization (WHO) (2013d) Sixty-sixth World Health Assembly – Promoting Health through the Life-Course, Geneva, 20–28 May. Available at www.who.int/maternal_child_adolescent/news_events/events/2013/wha66_report/en/ (accessed 14 May 2014).

World Health Organization (WHO) (2014) *Life Expectancy at Birth. Both Sexes 2012.* Interactive website. Available at http://gamapserver.who.int/gho/interactive_charts/mbd/life_expectancy/atlas.html (accessed 4 Apr. 2014).

World Health Organization (WHO) (n.d.) *Health at Key Stages of Life – the Life-Course Approach to Public Health.* Copenhagen: WHO.

World Health Organization (WHO) and International Longevity Centre-UK (2000) *The Implications for Training of Embracing a Life Course Approach to Health.* HO/NMH/HPS/00.2. Available at www.who.int/ageing/publications/lifecourse/alc_lifecourse_training_en.pdf (accessed 4 Apr. 2014).

4 Lifestyle and health
Alan Massey

Introduction

This chapter aims to promote understanding of lifestyle factors and the choices people make that may improve or impair their health. This includes consideration of specific health issues resulting from affluence and poverty from both UK and global perspectives, and practical approaches to improving health and well-being.

The chapter includes a case study and an exercise based on it. Examples to illustrate UK and global issues, and questions to encourage students to reflect on the key points of the chapter, apply theory to practice, and review the skills required, are integrated throughout.

Definition

According to the *Merriam-Webster On Line Dictionary* (2014) lifestyle is defined as 'the typical way of life of an individual, group, or culture'. This implies that lifestyle is a subjective concept, shaped by our values, attitudes and self-identity, and by socio-environmental influences on how we live our lives and to what purpose. Our values and attitudes towards our health are being debated in the belief that greater understanding of lifestyle factors influencing health, be they biological, behavioural, psychological or socio-environmental, can lead to significant improvements in public health (Jenson 2007). As with all subjective concepts there is little consensus on what a lifestyle is, and therefore on how best to develop theories of how to improve well-being through lifestyle approaches. Moreover, people choose different lifestyles based on their self-identity at different stages of life, and this self-identity is influenced by numerous factors. According to Jenson (2007: 64–5), the term lifestyle can be understood and therefore influenced at three levels:

1 At a structural level, which involves analysis of the variances and similarities of lifestyles between and within countries, societies and cultures as they evolve over time.
2 At the positional level, which involves analysis of the variances and similarities of lifestyles existing in a given society or culture between social groups, layers or classes. The use of power, control and social capital is important here.
3 Finally, at the individual level, which involves analysis of the variances and similarities of the ways in which people lead their lives and express their personality, self-identity and relationships with others.

This chapter explores the lifestyle factors which influence our health, be they self- or socially-constructed, by focusing on the specific impacts of affluence and poverty upon health outcomes. The effects of poverty will be further explored by highlighting influences upon the health of those marginalized in society. Throughout this portrayal, the underpinning theoretical issues will be explored.

Lifestyle factors

The USA's Department of Health and Human Services (2012) defines lifestyles as patterns of individual practices and personal behavioural choices that are related to elevated or reduced health risk. Altering lifestyles and thus reducing the burden of disease on health systems has been a goal of health planners for a number of years. The rationale for addressing lifestyle is best explained by the seminal work of McGinnis and Foege (1993), who pointed out that it is inappropriate to state coronary heart disease (CHD) as the biggest cause of death in the USA; rather, exploration of the patterns of individual practices and personal behavioural choices that had caused people to die from CHD was required. In doing so, they identified that the leading cause of death from CHD in the USA was tobacco use, which accounted for approximately 400,000 deaths per year, followed by diet and exercise patterns, which accounted for approximately 300,000 per year more. These authors similarly identified alcohol use, infections, sexual behaviour, accidents and drug use as major causes of mortality and morbidity. Using this approach, they highlighted that half of the annual mortality in the USA in 1993 was premature, and that with modification to lifestyles these premature deaths could be prevented or deferred. Four key lifestyle choices emerged as significantly affecting health – smoking, diet, regular exercise and excessive alcohol consumption – and addressing these has become a public health imperative. It was also evident that those utilizing negative health behaviours tended to lie in socially disadvantaged groups, and that cultural and social patterns of behaviour are evident in lifestyle choices.

Traditionally, governments across the globe have been slow to address lifestyle issues owing to criticism that interfering with an individual's ability to make autonomous decisions regarding their health is paternalistic. Compounding this inaction is that much of the evidence surrounding the influence of lifestyle choices is contested due to the multi-causational pathways of disease. Typically, governments will only intervene in lifestyle choices if the behaviour in question has health consequences for secondary parties and if the evidence of a causal pathway is clear (Tones and Green 2010).

Thinking point

Improvements in lifestyle choices have come to be dominated by four elements: a healthy diet, regular exercise, smoking and alcohol consumption. In your opinion is it appropriate to utilize lifestyle choices as a measure of a healthy lifestyle via mortality and morbidity rates, given the contested nature of evidence in this field?

Health behaviours

The aforementioned definition of lifestyle and the surrounding discussion is reflected in behavioural explanations of lifestyle choices. Within this field of research one explanation for the differences in lifestyle choices is the concept of adaptive and maladaptive health behaviours. When faced with the daily stressors of life, individuals react with habitual patterns of behaviour, through thought and emotion. Adaptive behaviours reflect an individual's ability to manage and make sense of potential threats, and to respond in a way that addresses or minimizes perceived threats. On the other hand, maladaptive behaviours are those that inhibit a person's ability to adjust to particular situations; rather, people elect behaviours which reduce anxiety, but do not affect the root causes of perceived threats (Connor and Norman 2005). In terms of health, maladaptive behaviours include factors such as smoking, drinking and illicit drug use (Gilmour and Williams 2012). The following clinical case study presents an accurate demonstration of how maladaptive behaviours present within public health practice and society.

Case study

A female client 60 years of age attended an employer-funded lifestyle screening session. The client was employed full-time within an administrative/clerical role. During the screening process the client became emotional when questioned regarding work–life balance and disclosed that in addition to working full-time, she was also the sole carer for her elderly mother, who was suffering from dementia, since the death of her husband. The client confided that she found the management of work–life balance significantly stressful, and that she was beginning to utilize alcohol as a coping mechanism. A dependency was clearly starting to develop from alcohol consumption in excess of 28 units per week. The client was also overweight despite consuming a healthy diet: excess alcohol, compounded by an inability to initiate a regular exercise regime owing to a lack of personal time and undertaking an occupational role that required the client to sit for most of her working day, made weight management difficult. The client was exhibiting signs of stress and anxiety owing to the evident lack of control she possessed within both her employment role and her personal life.

Case study by Jacqueline Cinnamond.

Lifestyle choices: culturally or socially constructed?

In exploring current perspectives on lifestyle choices and health outcomes we need to revisit Jenson's (2007) criteria and ask which if any of his levels has the biggest influence on our lifestyle. Is it influenced predominantly at the structural level, where the actions of the state become significant, as there is a requirement for the creation of structures and systems conducive to well-being? Is health influenced predominantly by our situation within society, and by the culture, accepted beliefs, attitudes and actions of distinct sections or layers of society, or does responsibility for our health predominantly lie with each of us through our ability to make choices as free agents in society? Finally, is lifestyle a mixture of each element and therefore best addressed by a partnership approach?

Throughout history, the question of whether society should have primacy over the individual has perplexed scholars from all branches of the sciences (Giddens 2009), and throughout the world, health systems have been developed which reflect this fundamental issue: should personal responsibility for health be paramount, or should the state intervene in health issues to protect the national interest? In finding a balance between personal and state responsibility, health services tend to be based on concepts embodied in Beveridgean, Bismarckian and consumer sovereignty models of health care. The choice of model is based on the ability of nation states to develop health infrastructures and to generate societal values of acceptability. The WHO (2013) argues that in developing countries the state has a large part to play in introducing the infrastructure needed to assure environmental controls for good sanitation, protection from and prevention of infectious diseases, and access to clean air, water and food. Emphasizing the need for different approaches between developed and developing countries, the WHO (2013) points out that within developed countries such as Japan, inhabitants can expect to live for 83 years and their health will be challenged predominantly by non-communicable diseases or diseases associated with ageing, while in countries with low life expectancy, such as Sierra Leone where the average individual will live for 47 years, their health will be challenged predominantly by communicable diseases in addition to issues of resources for health such as adequate food and water.

Within the developed world, through the need to address the root causes of chronic disease rather than the environmental causes of disease, the role of the state in restricting free choice becomes blurred (Baggott 2010). In recent years the advent of the salutogenic model of well-being, and the growth of the neoliberal agenda, has led to a partnership approach to addressing lifestyle issues. This challenges the dualist ideological perspectives, such as the liberal–individualist perspective or the paternalism–utilitarianism approach, by the merging of individualism and state intervention in partnership approaches to health. One example of this within the developed world is put forward by Giddens (2009), who argues that we need to combine the influences of structure and agency, and move away from ideologically opposed approaches to addressing health (Haralambos and Holborn 2000). Central to these factors is the idea of access to resources, which is heavily constrained by an individual's power status, and by the use of power by or on each person. Within the developed and developing world, then, each nation state faces different challenges in supporting people to achieve a good lifestyle balance.

Within the field of psychology a wealth of research exists demonstrating the health outcomes of a perceived lack of power. This body of research commenced with Walter Cannon's theory of homeostasis, which indicates that because environments are continuously changing then humans must adapt if they wish to grow and survive (Christiansen and Matuska 2006). It is our ability to adapt to the stressors of everyday life which has a significant influence on our health. Christiansen and Matuska outline four factors that are important in achieving a good lifestyle balance:

- Achieving a positive time balance spent between such factors as the search for safety and security and the amount of time (and energy) spent on factors such as belonging, love and societal acceptance.
- The fulfilment of social roles allowing us to portray our lifestyle in a positive manner, both to society and ourselves. Social roles are felt to be important as they bring responsibilities and demands as well as choices and resources.
- Role strain and role burden are important in two distinct ways. First, role strain is reduced by our ability to fulfil the obligations placed on us by societal expectations and our values of our own roles, and by our ability to meet, delegate or modify those responsibilities and values. Secondly, having a greater number of roles in life generally means that we are able to balance our achievements by an increased number of social support mechanisms.
- Finally, achieving a good role balance is important, as if an individual is able to fully engage with various roles in life with care and attention, then this is reflected positively in factors such as problem solving and creativity.

Research in these areas has identified some of the factors which create negative stress in individuals and therefore have negative consequences for health. North *et al.* (1993) advocate that employee stress similar to that observed within the case study can be best measured using the demand–control–support model. This three-dimensional methodology demonstrates that if the psychological demands of employment are correlated with inadequate control and social support, then employees are predisposed to work-related stress, anxiety and, potentially, to depression. Although in the case study the client's stress was contributed to by the work–life interface, and was not solely a direct result of her employment role, having low control over work and family life can have the same outcome.

Lifestyle choices and social disadvantage

Whether or not the health habits of the socially disadvantaged are free and rational choices is the focus of much research. For example, oppositional cultural theorists suggest that the cultural and environmental conditions experienced by people within the lower social classes means that many individuals will oppose mainstream health beliefs; instead they view mainstream behaviours as lacking resonance with their lived experience, and reject behaviour patterns of authority figures and cultures in favour of replication of the unhealthy habits of significant others (Hinshelwood and Skogstad 2000). Gostin and Hodge (2007) expand this argument and suggest that all health choices are so entrenched in social structures that the idea of personal choice is an illusion. According to Deaton (2011: 14), 'poor people lead heavily constrained lives, in terms of money, time and choices', and must rely on their physical and mental resources within an environment that quickly erodes these factors, inevitably leading to poorer health outcomes. Tones and Green (2010) argue that improving health and well-being is a political and ethical imperative, and that we should avoid blaming individuals for their lifestyle choices. They argue that individuals are aware of the negative health outcomes of their behaviour, but utilize maladaptive behaviours to help them cope with a challenging existence. They are the victims of their circumstances and not of their behaviours.

Thinking point

In your opinion do you agree with the position put forward by the oppositional cultural theorists that life is full of choices; however, people rarely get to make them! Or do you feel that most of our choices regarding our own lifestyle are made on an individual level?

Stewardship as a new way of governing for health

According to Baggott (2010), most recent approaches to dealing with lifestyle choices within democratic states seek to avoid paternalism via state intervention wherever possible; instead they use more subtle tools aimed at stewardship. Developed in the early part of the new century and championed by the WHO, stewardship is a more ethically acceptable approach to influencing health and well-being. The concept of stewardship was born out of a growing awareness of the need to balance individualistic and collective responsibility for health within the neoliberal agenda, and the need for governments to promote and shape environments that respect personal responsibility while creating environments conducive to good health. Policy makers and governments should adopt an approach which coordinates multi- and inter-sectoral action for health, aimed at achieving socially acceptable and desired goals which lead to a good life.

The subtle tools available to governments include such incentivizing and de-incentivizing elements as changes to taxation or risk reduction strategies. This form of stewardship is evident in the approach of the Nuffield Council on Bioethics to public health initiatives. This takes the form of a ladder (Figure 4.1) of interventions based on the right of choice/autonomy. At the bottom of the ladder is the option to do nothing, and the proposed interventions take incremental steps involving increasing state activity. At the top of the ladder is the step of eliminating choice. With each higher step taken, the right of autonomy is reduced, and careful consideration must be given to ensure the intervention is proportionate to the size of the problem in terms of health outcomes and cost (Nuffield Council on Bioethics 2007).

If governments are to act as stewards, then an understanding of responsibility for health is paramount. Getting people to alter their lifestyle is one option; addressing the socially constructed factors that influence or determine people's health is another. Much of the previously discussed work on creating environments conducive to health is influenced by reports such as the Whitehall Studies 1 (Marmot *et al.* 1978) and 2 (Whitehall II Study 2004), the Black Report (Department of Health and Social Security [DHSS] 1980), and the work of Dahlgren and Whitehead (1992) with their determinants of health model.

The Whitehall Studies 1 and 2 have been influential as they identified a socioeconomic gradient of health outcomes and behaviours. These studies commenced in the late 1960s and found that individuals in the lower socio-economic groups could

| Eliminate choice |
| Restrict choice |
| Guide choice by disincentives |
| Guide choice by incentives |
| Guide choice by changing the default policy |
| Enable choice |
| Provide information |
| Do nothing |

Figure 4.1 Ladder of interventions
Source: Nuffield Council (2007).

expect to experience poorer health than their more affluent counterparts. Socio-economic status is felt to influence health in three distinct ways: first, access to health care; secondly, via environmental exposure to health enhancing or detracting elements; and, finally, through health behaviours. Marmot (2010) indicates that within a developed country such as England, the difference in life expectancy between higher and lower socio-economic groups could be as much as seven years. Status, and hence the control individuals had over their working environment, was found to be significant. The second Whitehall Study (commencing in 1985) continued to explore the reasons for differences in health outcomes between diverse socio-economic groups, and identified in particular the relationship between work, stress and health. The findings of this report are significant, as it identified that the impact lifestyle choices have on health outcomes (particularly cardiovascular disease) is not as great as might be expected. These studies indicate that perhaps the most important factors to address are social gradients and the variations in health experienced as a consequence of occupational stratification. In general terms the WHO (2013) define a social gradient as a person's position in any given society based on their socio-economic position: the lower a person's socio-economic position, the worse their health. This is evidenced on a global scale, and as such the social gradient in health means health inequalities affect everyone (WHO 2013).

Thinking point

In your opinion do you feel that your position in society is as important to your health as your health behaviours?

Social stratification and its influence on lifestyle

Rowlingson (2011) indicates that the most likely explanation for the effects of social gradients on health inequality lies in two areas. Firstly, on an internal level social gradients lead to status anxiety, in which anxiety and therefore stress is created by income inequality which places people in a hierarchical competition for resources; this social stratification affects an individual's status in society, challenging their self-esteem and self-efficacy. Secondly, on an external level those who lack the power to make autonomous decisions in their work suffer from relations of domination.

There is widespread acknowledgement that the social gradient of health inequality can begin as early as *in utero*, with the socio-economic status of the expectant mother and the environmental factors that surround her – for instance, poor nutritional intake, consumption of excessive alcohol and cigarette smoking throughout pregnancy – having a significant effect on the cognitive development of the foetus. Furthermore, inadequate housing and maternal stress also have negative effects on foetal development (WHO 2007; Marmot 2010). The causal relationship continues after the child is born: the residential environment within which infants are raised can have a profound detrimental effect upon their mental well-being. In particular, children living in inadequate housing have been found to possess elevated levels of stress hormones. Furthermore, deprivation in terms of substandard heating, lack of physical exercise and insufficient cognitive stimuli has been shown to impede children's development. As the children progress along their life trajectory they tend to become socially marginalized as teenagers, and the inequalities experienced in terms of financial, educational and social provision can become emotionally manifest through feelings of low self-esteem and stress brought about by an absence of control over their lives, where they live and their employment opportunities. As employees, the relationship between lower social position and lower ranking employment status results in an absence of control over their employment role. When lack of control over the individual's life is coupled with a low ranking occupation role and inadequate social support within the employment setting, psychological ill health can ensue as a result of work-related stress (Whitehall II Study 2004).

Thinking point

In both the developed and developing worlds the need for a well-educated and healthy population is becoming increasingly important to ensure economic stability and growth. What do you feel governments should do to respond to this fact?

How do poverty and affluence affect health?

As we have seen, a wealth of research indicates that the more affluent you are, the better health outcomes you can expect. Across the globe an individual's socio-economic standing can be utilized to understand their likely health outcomes. A great deal of research has also been undertaken to identify the factors which influence or determine our health, and in this the work of Dahlgren and Whitehead for the WHO European Office in the early 1990s is seminal. These authors sought to produce tools which could be used by policy makers across the globe to consider and address the factors that determine health, and developed the Rainbow Model of Health which has been utilized in structuring attempts to address health and particularly health inequalities.

Dahlgren and Whitehead highlight that there are inherent variations in health outcomes for human beings. Each of us is more or less susceptible to disease, depending on our genetic strengths and weaknesses, our gender, and our luck in acquiring and fighting disease. As biological entities, we are open to health threats from a variety of sources. What lies at the heart of this model is awareness that these variations in health should be random. Therefore, if systematic variations in health outcomes appear, then the differences must be socially constructed and as such are a health inequality. Health or social inequalities have three essential features: they are systematic, socially produced (and therefore modifiable) and unfair (Dahlgren and Whitehead 1992). However, as the case study demonstrates, the ability of individuals to exert control over such factors depends on far-reaching aspects of their socio-economic environment. For example, low socio-economic position and the health inequalities that individuals are exposed to as a result can be predetermined from conception, and have the potential to continue throughout their life trajectory (North *et al*. 1993; Acheson 1998; WHO 2007; Black 2008; Kirkwood *et al* 2008; Boorman 2009; Marmot 2010; Department of Health 2011). Consequently, the success of any future policy proposal to address the social gradient of health and health inequalities depends largely on its ability to empower individuals to make positive changes to improve their physiological and psychological well-being.

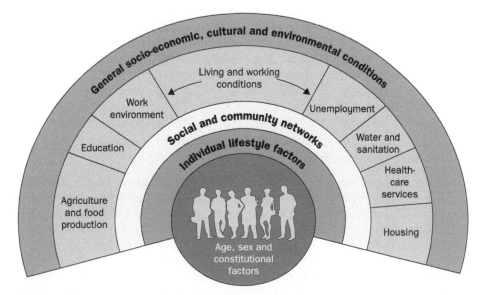

Figure 4.2 Rainbow model of health

Source: Dahlgren and Whitehead (1991).

In devising proactive approaches to health, policy makers and researchers have turned their attention away from simply extending life through the biomedical model, to identifying factors which extend and enhance a healthy life. There are several alternative health models of interest to researchers. However, only the genetic model, the socio-economic model, and the lifestyle model are considered at this point.

Models of health and lifestyle

The genetic model

The genetic model is one which seeks to identify the genetic causes of health and well-being, and as such is biological in nature. Genetic screening and counselling, for example, have proved useful in identifying and to some extent controlling genetic risk through changes in lifestyle and health behaviours. However, its proactive potential is still emerging (Thirlaway and Upton 2009). In utilizing this model as an example of how poverty affects health, I use access to agriculture and food production as an example. According to the UK's Department of International Development (2014), almost 1 billion people worldwide go hungry every day. This is matched by a further 1 billion people who are undernourished, that is, who are not receiving enough vitamins and minerals to sustain a healthy body. These figures are expected to double in the next twenty to thirty years. For expectant mothers, malnutrition or being undernourished means that the development of a healthy child is compromised, leading to changes in epigenomes (Kaati *et al.* 2007). Similarly, for those children born without regular access to the nutrients required for the development and maintenance of a healthy immune system, their health is compromised both in the short and long terms. To put this into context, in the developing world 165 million children under the age of 5 are malnourished or undernourished, which translates into increased death rates from communicable diseases (Department of International Development 2014). The genetic model of health offers insight into how people can understand their genetic history and therefore take steps to mitigate their own risk factors for health. Similarly, pharmacogenomics offers the potential to improve medicines management by tailoring it to individual needs. Finally, this model offers the potential to fight disease at the genetic level (National Human Genome Research Institute 2014).

The socio-economic model

The basic premise of this model is that health is influenced to a greater degree by sociological, environmental and economic factors than by the biological mechanisms of disease. According to this model, the greatest influences on our life and health maps are our psychosocial environment (social relationships, social capital, and so on), physical environment (heat, cold, radiation, and so on), chemical environment (pollutants in the air, water, soil, food, and so on.), biological environment (plants, animals, and so on) and our economic environment (access to work, disposable wealth, and so on). There is now an abundance of evidence to support the relationship between health and the socio-economic environment. For example, in 2008 the WHO published its final report on the social determinants of health, which sought to abolish avoidable health inequalities within a generation by addressing the circumstances in which people grow, live, work and age (WHO 2008: 3). This report clearly highlights the dominant socio-economic factors that influence health when present in an individual's environment, and it includes such emerging themes as early childhood development, globalization, health systems, urbanization, employment conditions, social exclusion, women and gender equity, public health conditions which should have priority, and means of measurement and of gathering evidence. Similarly, Sir Michael Marmot, the chair of the Commission on Social Determinants of Health for the WHO, undertook a review which explored differences in health and well-being among social groups in England, and set out how policy makers could best address the evident health inequalities in our lives which are due to socio-economic factors (Marmot, 2010). The report concluded that reducing health inequalities requires action in six distinct policy arenas:

1   Give every child the best start in life.
2   Enable all children, young people and adults to maximize their capabilities and have control over their lives.
3   Create fair employment and good work for all.
4   Ensure a healthy standard of living for all.
5   Create and develop healthy and sustainable places and communities.
6   Strengthen the role and impact of preventive measures against ill health.

Link and Phelan (1995), in their theory of fundamental causes, seek to explain differences in health outcomes by highlighting that the ability to access resources, such as social cohesion, social influence, money, knowledge, prestige and power, depends on socio-economic status; those in the lower socio-economic bandings have less access to and influence over those factors which improve health. Access to appropriate resources is fundamental in the development of a healthy lifestyle, and since the mid-nineteenth century the access of those in the higher socio-economic groups to innovation and knowledge is evidenced by the development of disparities in health.

How do poverty and affluence affect health – specific health issues

Deaton (2011) explains innovation and its effects succinctly by citing the use of anti-retroviral drugs. Affluent countries have access to these drugs and inhabitants of affluent countries can expect a longer lifespan owing to their ability to fight disease. Those in poorer countries are less likely to have access to these medical innovations. This example is evidence of the inverse equity hypothesis, which indicates that within nation states those in the higher socio-economic groups benefit first from health innovations. This simple fact widens health inequalities across time; as innovations become more widely available, the poorer socio-economic groups begin to have improved health, but never actually catch up in terms of health gain (Victora *et al.* 2000).

    Health inequalities exist within affluent countries, as those with knowledge of the latest innovations and treatments will attend consultations armed with an understanding of effective and efficient treatments. Practitioners of a higher quality will attend to them and can draw on a greater range of resources. Poorer members of society will have less knowledge, will be attended to by less able practitioners and will have limited resources.

As Deaton (2011) indicates, education is a useful way of exploring health inequalities and why disparities influence health. Good education is a resource which pervades the other determinants of health. The lower socio-economic groups tend to have lower levels of parental education, while this is reversed in higher socio-economic groups; high-quality state or private education tends to mean increased earning power as an adult through choice of occupation. Earning power reinforces the cycle of choice by allowing those with disposable income to choose healthy or unhealthy behaviours. Occupation also determines health owing to the inherent risks faced in the work performed. For example, society rewards those with a good education by offering them work which requires predominantly cognitive skills. Those who have not attained educational success may be offered work which requires predominantly manual skills. Therefore, a construction worker is exposed to greater health risks, such as physical harm, chemical harm, biological agents of disease and psychological distress, while apart from psychological risk a bank manager has much lower levels of exposure to these mechanisms of disease. Cutler *et al.* (2010) point out that education can also be used to directly improve health, as a good education gives you the knowledge and resources required to navigate factors affecting health during adulthood.

Deaton (2011) also outlines that the impact of socio-economic factors on health and well-being is only part of a much wider phenomenon. He indicates that rather than differences in income and status causing health variances between social groups, it is inequality itself which is harmful to all.

The lifestyle model

The lifestyle model of health has emerged as one mechanism to address the dichotomy inherent in the other models, which deal predominantly with the structural or biological determinants of health or the role that human agents play in determining their own health map. The lifestyle model, which is now emerging as a central research theme for policy makers, requires greater understanding not only of factors which prevent ill health, but of those factors which enhance health and well-being. Discussing the work of Antonovsky and his model of salutogenesis, Cattan and Tilford (2006) highlight that research has turned its attention to the resources people need and the capacities people have or need in order to create health and well-being. Antonovsky clarified thinking by highlighting that:

> Contemporary Western medicine is likened to a well-organized heroic, technologically sophisticated effort to pull drowning people out of a raging river. Devotedly engaged in this task, often quite well rewarded, the establishment members never raise their eyes or minds to inquire upstream, around the bend in the river, about who or what is pushing all these people in. (Antonovsky 1987: 90, in Cattan and Tilford 2006: 18)

His salutogenic model rejected both the biomedical foundations underpinning definitions relating to health and well-being and the dichotomy between health and disease. Antonovsky indicated that health is a continuum and is constantly challenged by our everyday existence. The difference in health outcomes lies in a person's ability to have a sense of coherence when coping with the challenges of existence. In his formulation, the sense of coherence has three components:

- Comprehensibility – a belief that things happen in an orderly and predictable fashion, and a sense that you can understand events in your life and reasonably predict what will happen in the future.
- Manageability – a belief that you have the skills or ability, the support, the help or the resources necessary to take care of things, and that things are manageable and within your control.
- Meaningfulness – a belief that things in life are interesting and a source of satisfaction, that things are really worthwhile, and that there is good reason or purpose to care about what happens.

By applying this sort of model we can see that people structure their philosophy of health around a risk analysis of various healthy (and not so healthy) habits, identifying those habits which provide them with a quality of life they find acceptable.

One such model is Ronald Labonte's model of health (Labonte 1998a), which incorporates a desire for social transformation based on the core public principles of advocacy, enablement and mediation (Figure 4.3). He indicates that three things

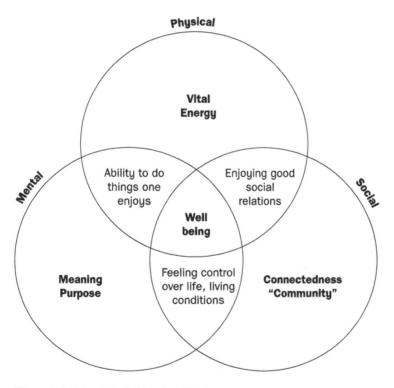

Figure 4.3 Labonte's fields of well-being

Source: Labonte (1998b).

need to be in place to experience health and well-being: physical capability (including vitality and energy); mental health (essentially described as having meaning and purpose in life); and a social context of connection to family and others in the community (National Health Service Scotland 2003). This model seeks to highlight that the quality of a person's life is as important as a person's biological state of health. In seeking to address health and lifestyle, therefore, health planners wishing to transform individuals or communities need to develop systems which address both the prevalence of cases and the causes of health inequalities.

Social exclusion

As we have seen, an individual's health is influenced by structural, material and psychosocial factors. Inherent within these is consideration of the amount of control we can exercise or the amount of control exercised upon us, which shapes our constructs of self-identity, self-efficacy and positional role in society. These can create feelings of engagement or exclusion, depending on the existence of elements such as local or national civic structures, social networks, and family and friends. Considering that the stated aim of public health in the twenty-first century is to address health inequalities (WHO 2014), dealing with those on the margins of society has become a practice imperative. However, some social groups remain at the margins despite societal, economic, political and structural changes designed to create social equity.

Social exclusion is defined by Silver (2007: 15) as 'a multidimensional process of progressive social rupture, detaching groups and individuals from social relations and institutions and preventing them from full participation in the normal, normatively prescribed activities of the society in which they live'. This removal of people from mainstream support mechanisms can occur at individual, social class, group, community or country level. Victims of social exclusion can be characterized in two ways: those who 'voluntarily' exclude themselves, such as certain religious groups, and those who are coercively marginalized, such as drug users, the unemployed or the homeless (Sagric *et al.* 2007). At the individual level, social exclusion usually occurs via the mechanism described in the Black Report (DHSS 1980) as social drift. Here an individual's social position is eroded owing to ill health, leading to reduced opportunities to access resources conducive to good health and consequently reduced social position. Similarly, as the social status of individuals changes through factors such as unemployment or homelessness, their altered position leaves them at the margins of mainstream society. These individuals tend to have poor control over their lives and little access to supportive resources. This leads to poor health outcomes owing to reducing self-efficacy, increasing social isolation, material deprivation and the potential to adopt maladaptive health behaviours. Individuals can then become engrained in these cultures owing to restricted access to those factors which define social class – power, income and prestige – resulting in reduced social mobility and decreased lifestyle choices.

Case study exercise

Please reacquaint yourself with the case study on page 65.

According to National Health Service Scotland (2003), a useful tool in understanding the value of Labonte's model in seeking improvements in lifestyle is a tree exercise. This provides a framework to discuss how health outcomes are a product of social determinants. It is best undertaken in small groups belonging to the same community, and should have a community focus.

Directions:

1 Draw a bare tree with roots, a trunk, and branches.
2 List what you consider to be the dominant disease outcomes likely within this case study (depression, cancer, etc.). List these diseases as the leaves on the tree.
3 Next, list the lifestyle behaviours (lack of exercise, poor diet, etc.) you feel contribute to the disease outcomes. List these on the trunk of the tree.
4 Now list the social, economic, and political determinants that influence the behaviours described (carers' rights, alcohol policies, etc.). List these determinants at the roots of the tree.
5 These determinants represent the 'root causes of disease'. Describe how some of the root causes impact on health outcomes through behaviours (lack of a healthy canteen in the workplace impacts on diet and therefore diabetes), while others impact on health outcomes directly (air pollution leads to respiratory disease).

This exercise can be repeated at the community level and is helpful in understanding the social, environmental and lifestyle choices that influence well-being.

Summary

Within this chapter we have identified that addressing lifestyle choices is a public health imperative, given the burden of disease attributed to them. In exploring the impact of unhealthy lifestyle behaviours it is important to consider that people cope with the daily struggle for resources in differing ways, based on their personal beliefs of what quality of life means to them. The daily struggle to obtain resources, be it physical, psychological or sociological, means that people approach health behaviours in different ways based on their life circumstances. These decisions on accessing resources can be influenced by a range of factors inherent in the society in which they reside. Special attention needs to be provided to those on the margins of society who have little or no control over the resources for health.

References

Acheson, D. (1998) *Independent Inquiry into Inequalities in Health*. London: Department of Health. Available at www.archive.official-documents.co.uk/document/doh/ih/part1a.html (accessed Dec. 2013).

Baggott, R. (2010) *Public Health: Policy & Politics*, 2nd edn. London: Palgrave Macmillan.

Black, C. (2008) *Review of the Health of Britain's Working Age Population: Working for a Healthier Tomorrow*. Available at www.dh.gov.uk/publications (accessed Dec. 2013).

Boorman, S. (2009) *NHS Health and Well-being Final Report*. Available at www.dh.gov.uk/publications (accessed Dec. 2013).

Cattan, M. and Tilford, S. (2006) *Mental Health Promotion: A Lifespan Approach*. Maidenhead: McGraw-Hill.

Christiansen, C.H. and Matuska, K.M. (2006) Lifestyle balance: a review of concepts and research, *Journal of Occupational Science*, 13(1): 49–61.

Connor, M. and Norman, P. (2005) *Predicting Health Behaviour*. Maidenhead: McGraw-Hill Education.

Cutler, D.M., Lleras-Muney, A. and Vogl, T.S. (2010) Socioeconomic status and health: dimensions and mechanisms, NBER Working Paper No. w14333. Available at http://ssrn.com/abstract=1267564 (accessed Jan. 2014).

Dahlgren, G. and Whitehead, M. (1991) *Policies and Strategies to Promote Social Equity in Health*. Stockholm: Institute for Future Studies.

Dahlgren, G. and Whitehead, M. (1992) *Policies and Strategies to Promote Social Equity in Health*. Background document to WHO strategy paper for Europe. Copenhagen: World Health Organization.

Deaton, A. (2011) What does the empirical evidence tell us about the injustice of health inequalities? Available at http://papers.ssrn.com/sol3/papers.cfm?abstract_id=1746951 (accessed Dec. 2013).

Department of Health (2011) *No Health without Mental Health: A Cross-government Mental Health Outcomes Strategy for People of All Ages*. Available at www.dh.gov.uk/mentalhealthstrategy (accessed Dec. 2013).

Department of Health and Human Services (2012) *What is a Healthy Lifestyle*. Available at www.healthfinder.gov (accessed Oct. 2013).

Department of Health and Social Security (DHSS) (1980) *Inequalities in Health: Report of a Research Working Group*. The Black Report. London: Department of Health and Social Security.

Department of International Development (2014) *Reducing Hunger and Malnutrition in Developing Countries*. Available at www.gov.uk/government/policies/reducing-hunger-and-malnutrition-in-developing-countries (accessed Feb. 2014).

Giddens, A. (2009) The life-course, in M. Haralambos and M. Holborn (eds) *Sociology; Themes and Perspectives*, 7th edn. London: HarperCollins.

Gilmour, J. and Williams, L. (2012) Type D personality is associated with maladaptive health-related behaviours, *Journal of Health Psychology*, 17(4): 471–8.

Gostin L.O. and Hodge, J.G. (2007) Global health law, ethics and policy, *The Journal of Law, Medicine and Ethics*, 35(4): 519–25.

Haralambos, M. and Holborn, M. (2000) *Sociology: Themes and Perspectives*, 7th edn. London: HarperCollins.

Hinshelwood, R.D. and Skogstad, W. (2000) *Observing Organizations: Anxiety, Defence and Culture in Health Care*. London: Routledge.

Jenson, M. (2007) Defining lifestyle, *Environmental Sciences*, 4(2): 63–73.

Kaati, G., Bygren, L.O., Pembrey, M. and Sjostrom, M. (2007) Transgenerational response to nutrition, early life circumstances and longevity, *European Journal of Human Genetics*, 15(7), 784–90.

Kirkwood, T., Bond, J., May, C., McKeith, L. and Teh, M. (2008) *Foresight Mental Capital and Well-being Project. Mental Capital through Life: Future Challenges*. London: Government Office for Science. Accessed at www.foresight.gov.uk (accessed Jan. 2014).

Labonte, R. (1998a) *A Community Development Approach to Health Promotion*. Edinburgh: Health Education Board for Scotland.

Labonte, R. (1998b) A model of health and well-being, in Scottish Community Development Centre (2003) *LEAP for Health; Learning, Evaluation and Planning*. Glasgow: NHS Scotland.

Link, B.G. and Phelan, J. (1995) Social conditions as fundamental causes of disease, *Journal of Health and Social Behaviour*, 35(special issue): 80–4.

Marmot, M. (2010) *Fair Society, Healthy Lives: Strategic Review of Health Inequalities in England post 2010*. Available at www.marmotreview.org (accessed Jan. 2014).

Marmot, M.G., Rose, G., Shipley, M. and Hamilton, P.J. (1978) Employment grade and coronary heart disease in British civil servants (Whitehall Study 1). *Journal of Epidemiology and Community Health*, 32(4): 244–9. Doi:10.1136/jech.32.4.244.PMC 1060958.PMID 744814.

McGinnis, J.M. and Foege, W.H. (1993) Actual causes of death in the United States, *Journal of the American Medical Association*, 270(18): 2207–12.

Merriam-Webster On Line Dictionary (2014) Available at www.merriam-webster.com/dictionary/lifestyle (accessed Feb. 2014).

National Health Service Scotland (2003) *Insight – Case Studies in Community Development and Health in Scotland*. Available at www.healthscotland.com/documents/133.aspx (accessed Jan. 2014).

National Human Genome Research Institute (2014) *Health Issues in Genetics*. Available at www.genome.gov/10001872 (accessed Jan. 2014).

North, F., Syme, S., Feeney, A., Head, J., Shipley, M. and Marmot, M. (1993) Explaining socio-economic differences in sickness absence: the Whitehall II study, *British Medical Journal*, 306(6874): 361–6.

Nuffield Council on Bioethics (2007) *Public Health: Ethical Issues*. Available at www.nuffield-bioethics.org/public-health/public-health-policy-process-and-practice (accessed Jan. 2014).

Rowlingson, K. (2011) Does income inequality cause health and social problems? Available at www.jrf.org.uk/sites/files/jrf/Rowlingson-Income-eBook.pdf (accessed Jan. 2014).

Sagric, C., Radulovic, O., Bogdanovic, M. and Markovic, R. (2007) Social marginalisation and health. *Acta Medica Medianae*, 46(2), 49–52.

Silver, H. (2007) *The Process of Social Exclusion: The Dynamics of an Evolving Concept*. Manchester: Chronic Poverty Research Centre. Available at www.chronicpoverty.org/ (accessed Jan. 2014).

Thirlaway, K. and Upton, D. (2009) *The Psychology of Lifestyle: Promoting Healthy Behaviour*. London: Routledge.

Tones, K. and Green, J. (2010) *Health Promotion: Planning and Strategies*, 2nd edn. London: Sage.

Victora, C.G., Vaughan, P.J., Barros, F.C., Silva, A.C. and Tomasi, E. (2000) Explaining trends in inequities: evidence from Brazilian child health studies, *Lancet*, 356(9235), 1093–8.

Whitehall II Study (2004) *Work Stress and Health: The Whitehall II Study*. Available at www.ucl.ac.uk/whitehallII (accessed Oct. 2013).

World Health Organization (WHO) (2007) *Early Child Development: A Powerful Equalizer*. Geneva: WHO. Available at www.who.int/social_determinants/resources/ecd_kn_report_07_2007.pdf?ua=1 (accessed Dec. 2013).

World Health Organization (WHO) (2008) *Closing the Gap in a Generation: Health Equity through Action on the Social Determinants of Health. Final Report of the Commission on Social Determinants of Health*. Geneva: WHO.

World Health Organization (WHO) (2013) *Research for Universal Health Coverage*. Geneva: WHO.

World Health Organization (WHO) (2014) *Millennium Development Goals*. Available at www.who.int/topics/millennium_development_goals/en/ (accessed Oct. 2013).

5 Behavioural approaches to health and well-being

Donna Hart

Introduction

The question of how to effectively enable individuals and populations to make sustainable behaviour changes that have positive effects on their health and well-being is not easily answered, given the current political and economic climate. Demographic changes including increases in life expectancy, chronic long-term conditions and population size clearly indicate the need for effective long-term behaviour change. It is vital for those involved in public health and well-being to take cognizance of the current culture within healthcare that may threaten the philosophical and ideological underpinnings of public health. The Francis Report (2013) identifies the negative impact of economically driven targets being given greater emphasis than quality patient care. Gillam (2013), discussing the Francis inquiry, asserts that the commodification of health care has intensified the factors placing pressure on the health-care system, and that this commodification has resulted from the market-oriented policies introduced by the UK Coalition government formed in 2010. He goes on to note that these continued and unnecessary 'reforms' are likely to perpetuate some of the pervasive conditions identified by Francis. Gillam believes that the government will continue with its programme, which expects the NHS to make savings of £20 billion by 2015. Public health and well-being practitioners can be expected to become dispirited; even with the most creative accounting measures, it will be extremely challenging to support the move from a prescriptive, reactive public health approach to an individual/population proactive approach, given the current financial constraints.

It is therefore vital for all who have a role in engaging individuals and populations in public health and well-being to be enthusiastic, passionate, knowledgeable, realistic and critically discerning as regards approaches and models to facilitate healthy behaviour change.

Theoretical perspectives

The use of theories to underpin behaviour change interventions can clarify the intentions of the intervention or programme. Webb *et al.* (2010) suggest that theory can identify the construct to be addressed (for example, values or motivation), the mechanisms influencing behaviour change techniques (for example, vicarious learning in modelling), and the populations most likely to benefit (for example, those who are socially excluded). There is a wide body of knowledge relating to behaviour change which attempts to explain the predicates of human behaviour. There are two predominant areas of theory. First is theory relating to psychological models that attempt to describe why and how people change their behaviour: for example, the health belief model (Rosenstock 1966; Becker 1984); the theory of planned behaviour (Fishbein and Ajzen 1975; Ajzen 1991); the social cognitive theory (Bandura 1986); and the transtheoretical 'Stages of Change Model' (Prochaska and DiClemente 1983). There are many excellent texts that present in-depth overviews of these theoretical models (Rutter and Quine 2002; Berry 2004; Corcoran 2007). The second dominant area of theory relates to communication and persuasion theory which attempts to inform how information is most effectively imparted (Robertson 2008).

A widely utilized model is the transtheoretical 'Stages of Change Model' of Prochaska and DiClemente (1983), due to its perceived applicability to a range of behaviours and its recognition that it is likely that people may relapse in their attempts at changing behaviour before achieving sustained maintenance of change. The model conceptualizes behaviour change as a process rather than an isolated event, and identifies five main stages of behaviour change: precontemplation, contemplation, preparation, action and maintenance. The model also offers ten further psychological and social processes of change which facilitate the individual's transition through the five stages. Tables 5.1 and 5.2 show how the model can be applied to eating a healthier diet and are based on the work of Prochaska and DiClemente (1983).

Thinking point

Consider the extent to which the aspects of the 'Stages of Change Model' are evident in the case study written by Bree Tomlinson, a recently qualified Specialist Community Practitioner in District Nursing.

Table 5.1 Stages of change

Stage of change	Related description
Precontemplation	The consumption of an unhealthy diet with no intention to change current dietary behaviour
Contemplation	The consumption of an unhealthy diet but with some intention to adopt a healthier diet in the near future
Preparation	The introduction of some healthy foods with the intention to increase healthy eating in the near future
Action	The consumption of a healthy diet adopted and maintained for several months
Maintenance	The consumption of a healthy diet fully adopted and maintained for more than six months

Table 5.2 Social and psychological processes of change

Process of changing dietary behaviour	Example of process
Consciousness raising	Awareness of messages and information received relating to a healthy diet
Dramatic relief	An emotional reaction to information relating to the dangers of eating an unhealthy diet
Environmental re-evaluation	A consideration of arguments that suggest an unhealthy diet may be detrimental to the environment, for example the increased packaging related to processed food
Helping relationships	Having others who listen to experiences of individuals attempting to make dietary changes
Self re-evaluation	Feelings of guilt and disappointment related to the consumption of an unhealthy diet
Stimulus control	Not having unhealthy foods readily available
Social liberation	Experiencing changes in society which make it easier to adopt a healthier diet
Reinforcement management	The individual rewards themselves when a healthy diet is consumed
Self-liberation	Being committed to consuming a healthy diet
Counter-conditioning	Preferring a healthy diet to an unhealthy diet

Case study: Hoarding and the district nurse

Hoarding is a complex issue that requires understanding from professionals to provide effective services (Bratiotis *et al.* 2011). This understanding must go beyond the identification of hoarding from other related conditions to insight into associated co-morbid mental and physical health problems. It is often these problems that lead to the district nurse's input; in this case the patient had a chronic leg ulcer. Compulsive hoarding is often a hidden problem. By the nature of what the district nurse does, we can often be the first to uncover a problem that is chronic and progressive (Fleury *et al.* 2012) and in this case very well established.

An elderly gentleman, Mr W, was referred to the district nurses via the local pharmacist. He had been frequently attending to purchase dressings over several months. When the pharmacist engaged Mr W in conversation, it became apparent that Mr W was attempting to treat a leg wound without any specialist input. With his consent the pharmacist made contact with us.

On arrival at Mr W's property the garden was cluttered with various objects and it was difficult to reach the front door, presenting a health and safety risk to professionals coming to the property as well as to Mr W himself, which is common in these cases (Frost *et al.* 2000). As this was a privately owned home, Mr W has great

(continued)

control over the circumstances under which professionals are permitted to enter (Bratiotis *et al.* 2011), and although previously consenting to the referral he did not agree to any member of our team entering.

Using the Transtheoretical Model (Prochaska *et al.* 1992) a successful behaviour change in Mr W followed. Although Mr W had refused the district nurses access he did agree to attend our treatment clinic for timed appointments. This was seen as essential to success as we were able to build up trusting relationships with Mr W over a period of time. As the Nursing and Midwifery Council (2004) highlights, sustained relationships with those in need are essential in improving health and well-being. Mr W's perceptions and beliefs about the care he could benefit from gradually changed as he successfully moved through the distinct stages of the model towards a behaviour change (Rutter and Quine 2002).

In stage one, precontemplation, Mr W displayed behaviour typical of a person without any intention to change (Rutter and Quine 2002). Although this can often be because the person has no awareness of the issue, it was not the case with Mr W. He displayed behaviour typical of that of a hoarder hiding a problem. He had a well-established mechanism for dealing with the outside world (Thomas 1998) and avoiding people entering his home. This could be seen as Mr W preferring not to interact with people, as hoarders often do (Pertusa *et al.* 2008), but Mr W actually enjoyed company, just not in his home, therefore the treatment room was the perfect solution.

Gradually as Mr W became more familiar with the team and the environment he progressed to stage two of the model, contemplation (Rutter and Quine 2002). He began to talk about his home and his concerns with those he knew. He would listen to options that would be available to him in the future and ask questions about what this help would entail.

This led to a quick progression to stage 3 of the model, preparation. He began to recognize the lack of good nutrition due to lack of cooking facilities, and the poor sleeping arrangements due to no bedroom access, as contributory factors to his deteriorating health and skin integrity. These are common problems within the hoarding population (Marchand and McEnany 2012). Although recognition of these issues was progress, Mr W would not allow any action to be taken and refused referrals to other services, requesting very long periods to think over suggestions. It eventually became apparent his reluctance came out of fear of being labelled and losing control. Negative labels and stereotyping can prevent people from seeking help (Making Every Adult Matter, 2008).

Over time this did change, as the team persevered with Mr W's care and he began to discuss the realities of accepting help. Contributory factors were his deteriorating health and a fast-approaching winter. Mr W began to wish to use his home and his belongings for their intended purpose, for example, to sleep in a bed in a bedroom and be safe and warm during the colder months.

At this stage Mr W had progressed to stage four, action. He was keen to engage with other services, while often asking the district nurses for advice; he came to this decision himself. A breakthrough came when he accepted help in clearing some of his home while he went to respite care for two weeks. He was clear that this was a

(continued)

short-term arrangement and could see the benefit for his health, but was adamant he would return home. He reported to the house daily to monitor progress and to maintain some control, but did not hinder the process. The district nurse team visited regularly and, with some good nutrition, sleep and general rest, Mr W's legs improved.

Finally, Mr W's progression to the final stage of the model, maintenance, was quickly and completely instigated by himself. At the end of his respite stay he returned home. Although his home was now a much safer environment, considerable work still needed to be done and Mr W decided he did not want to stay. He took a large amount of his possessions to his small residential home room and arranged a permanent stay. He enjoyed the company, food and general care so much he did not feel any great attachment to his lifelong home. The residential staff got to know him well, and were accommodating to his vast amount of belongings as long as it did not become unsafe. The district nurses continued to visit and his legs healed, weight increased and general well-being improved. Several months later Mr W sold his home to a local builder, deciding he never needed to return.

Case study by Bree Tomlinson.

Persuasion and communication theory underpins all psychological models of behaviour change and the transtheoretical model (Prochaska and DiClemente 1983). It can be applied throughout the five stages and tailored to the stage of change process that the individual or population is at; for example, guidance on how to eat more healthily when eating in restaurants would be useful for someone who has adopted a healthy diet, but not for someone in the precontemplation stage.

Robertson (2008) suggests that there are two main theories of persuasion and communication of relevance to behaviour change: the elaboration likelihood model and the communication-behaviour change model. When considering the latter Robertson explains how McGuire's (1989, cited in Robinson 2008) inputs and outputs demonstrate the complexity of the communication and persuasion process, and act as a useful guide for those designing interventions to maximize the effectiveness of the message journey.

Inputs in the persuasion process are:

- Source: who is going to deliver the message and are they credible, personable and can act as a role model?
- Message: what particular information will be included and how will it be structured?
- Channel: how will the message be conveyed, via literature or radio, for example, and nationally or locally?
- Receiver: who is the message aimed at and what is their culture, lifestyle and socio-economic position?

- Destination: what is the aim of the message in terms of outcomes, for example a raising of awareness or a behaviour change?

Responses to each of the above inputs need to occur before the individual can move through the stages. Outputs in the persuasion process include:

- exposure to the message
- taking notice of the message
- liking and becoming interested in the message
- understanding the message
- developing the skills to respond to the message
- attitude change in response to the message
- memory storage of the content of the message
- be able to recollect the message
- decide on the basis of retrieval
- behave in accordance with decision
- reinforcement of desired behaviour (adapted from McGuire 1989, cited in Robertson 2008).

Robertson (2008) describes the elaboration likelihood model devised by Petty and Cacioppo (1986) as a way of determining the likely degree of persuasion by considering the level of scrutiny an individual gives to a message. The model suggests that the degree of scrutiny is dependent on motivation; those who are less motivated consider a message peripherally (peripheral processing), leading to a lesser likelihood of a change in behaviour. Conversely, more motivated people will apply much closer scrutiny to a message (central processing), leading to a greater likelihood of behaviour change.

The assumption that utilizing theory leads to more effective behaviour change interventions continues to be debated (Webb *et al.* 2010). When reviewing evidence for the effectiveness of stage-based interventions at increasing activity levels for more than six months, Adams and White (2004) assert that despite these being widely adopted there is little evidence of longer-term success in achieving behaviour change. Given the range and complexity of theoretical perspectives presented as models relevant for behaviour change, those engaging in public health and well-being may find it difficult to decide on the most appropriate approach to behaviour change. Ryan (2009) suggests that health professionals may find mid-range theory more useful in this context, as it explains particular phenomena or situations and is therefore more usable when informing practice.

It can be argued that motivation is a phenomenon common to both behaviour change theory and persuasion and communication theory. There are many similarities seen when comparing and contrasting models of behaviour change, some apparent differences being merely the use of different language with the same meaning. Dixon (2008) identifies that concepts relating to a person's self-belief in their ability to undertake the behaviour change (confidence) and a person's wish to engage in a particular behaviour (motivation) feature in all the main behaviour change theories. Furthermore Orji *et al.* (2012) assert that self-efficacy is the strongest determinant that influences healthy behaviour change within all key models.

Recently updated National Institute for Care and Clinical Excellence guidance (NICE 2014a) recommends behaviour change interventions should be underpinned by a range of evidence and theory, and interestingly identifies motivation and context as significant factors in achieving behaviour change. This recognition adds further value to the consideration of mid-range theory. Those attempting to influence behaviour change clearly need to be cognizant of established evidence and theory such as that provided by NICE. However, this needs to be coupled with an ability to critically discern the most appropriate theories to be utilized, along with consideration of particular phenomena (for example, motivation and context).

Person-centred approaches

Person-centred approaches are based on the central premise of collaboration between the individual and the practitioner. Along with deciding the most appropriate approach to be taken, there is consideration of the individual's personal context including health inequalities. The NICE guidance (2014a: 5) outline principles for those working with individuals, emphasizing that interventions should be selected that both support and motivate individuals to:

- understand the short-, medium- and longer-term consequences of their health related behaviours, for themselves and others
- feel positive about the benefits of health-enhancing behaviours and changing their behaviours
- plan their changes in terms of easy steps over time
- recognize how their social contexts and relationships may affect their behaviour, and identify and plan for situations that might undermine the changes they are trying to make
- plan explicit 'if-then' coping strategies to prevent relapse
- make a personal commitment to adopt health-enhancing behaviours by setting and recording goals to undertake clearly defined behaviours in particular contexts, over a specified time
- share their behaviour change goals with others.

Key aspects of the above principles are particularly reflected in two approaches to individual behaviour change: motivational interviewing and cognitive behavioural therapy (CBT).

Motivational interviewing is a person-centred dialogue in which the individual is encouraged to explore their current motivations to change and their reasons for resistance to change. During motivational interviewing the practitioner will facilitate the individual to minimize any resistance to behaviour change. MacDowall *et al.* (2006) assert that motivational interviewing offers an alternative to a traditional disease-focused approach to behaviour change. Motivational interviewing emphasizes the individual's perspective of the advantages and disadvantages of changing their behaviour, and only incorporates strategies such as goal setting with the individual's agreement (MacDowall *et al.* 2006).

CBT originated as an approach to treat those with psychological distress and is a structured, time-limited and active form of therapy (Whitfield and Davidson 2007). A cognitive behavioural approach recognizes the influence of emotions (such as feelings and mood), cognitions (such as thoughts and beliefs), physiology (such as health status) and behaviour (such as events and actions) on an individual's experiences and behaviour. MacDowall *et al.* (2006) suggest remembering the following key concepts when applying a cognitive behavioural approach to understanding health behaviour:

- Health-related behaviour is learned from childhood onwards and if unchallenged can become increasingly habitual.
- Individuals respond to their behaviour being rewarded (positive reinforcement) by increasing that behaviour, and decrease a behaviour if it causes a negative consequence. Individuals also increase a behaviour if it causes the removal of an unpleasant situation (negative reinforcement), which is often achieved through avoiding the unpleasant situation.
- A CBT approach can achieve harm reduction which aims to minimize the risk of adverse health effects from a behaviour, and is sometimes a more realistic aim than complete cessation of a particular behaviour.
- The overall aim of an intervention based on a CBT approach is to both identify and stop habitual unhealthy behaviour and cognitions, and replace them with more healthy and adaptive behaviours.

Both motivational interviewing and a CBT approach may involve goal setting, cognitive reframing and relapse prevention.

Thinking point

When considering the above and undertaking further reading relating to individual approaches, which concepts feature across individual approaches and can be cross-referenced to the NICE principles?

Politically there has been an increasing emphasis on individual responsibility for health, sometimes disguised behind an exhortation for choice and autonomy. Individual approaches to behaviour change clearly 'fit' within a context of individuals taking responsibility for their own health. However, there are two significant barriers to the effectiveness of individual approaches: the wider determinants of health and economic factors.

The evidence linking lower socio-economic status with poorer health is incontrovertible. Acheson (1998), Marmot (2010) and Buck and Frosini (2012) highlight the consistent socio-demographic gradient in relation to the prevalence of multiple risky behaviours, with those in lower social classes and with lower levels of education being more likely to engage in multiple lifestyle risks. Maryon Davies and Jolley (2010) argue that appealing to an individual's sense of personal responsibility is fruitless if the individual lacks opportunities to make healthier choices, due to social or economic circumstances.

Aside from opportunistic brief interventions, individual approaches to behaviour change can be time intensive and therefore relatively expensive. The Royal College of Nursing (RCN 2012) has recognized that there is much criticism of the NHS offering a 'sickness service' rather than a 'wellness service'. Research undertaken by the Faculty of Public Health (Maryon Davies and Jolley 2010) asking the public how much of the health budget was spent on keeping people well and promoting healthier lifestyles – that is, wellness rather than illness – resulted in an average figure of 29 per cent. This is in marked contrast with the actual figure of 4 per cent of the overall health budget going to public health. Considering the likelihood of NHS funding effectively being frozen for several years to come, it will be a major challenge for practitioners to secure resources to initiate evidence-based individual behaviour change approaches.

Population approaches

It is widely recognized that the behaviour of individuals, communities and populations is a key determinant of their health status (NICE and WHO Europe 2010). The World Health Organization recognizes the growing incidence of long-term conditions across the world's populations, identifying that the current burden of disease faced by older people is a combination of both living with poor health and dying prematurely (WHO 2012). This report highlights that while disease patterns are different across high-income and low- to middle-income countries, all the leading conditions in all countries are non-communicable and therefore potentially avoidable. Public Health England (2013) have asserted that it is at least equally important to address health inequalities along with the smoking, excessive alcohol consumption, high levels of inactivity, obesity and poor diets that we know are significant factors in ill health. Given the increase in health inequalities it will be interesting to monitor the progress of Public Health England in tackling them. It may be that the new structure of the NHS outlined in the Health and Social Care Bill 2012, which places public health services working locally alongside local authorities and clinical care commissioning groups, may be more effective at meeting local health needs and addressing health inequalities. Public Health England have asserted that for too long the focus has been on treatment and illness as opposed to prevention and resilience, and that they will work both locally and nationally to improve the public's health. In their recent document outlining their priorities for 2013–14 they identify the following five key priorities:

1   Helping people to live longer and more healthy lives by reducing preventable deaths and the burden of ill health associated with smoking, high blood pressure, obesity, poor diet, poor mental health, alcohol and insufficient exercise.
2   Reducing the burden of disease and disability in life by focusing on preventing and recovering from the conditions with the greatest impact, including dementia, anxiety, depression and drug dependency.
3   Protecting the country from infectious diseases and environmental hazards, including the growing problem of infections that resist treatment with antibiotics.
4   Supporting families to give children and young people the best start in life, through working with health visitors and school nurses, family nurse partnerships and the Troubled Families programme.

5   Improving health in the workplace by encouraging employers to support their staff, and those moving into and out of the workforce, to lead healthier lives (Public Health England 2013: 6).

Public Health England, along with other national policy makers, professionals or agencies who have a remit to influence behaviour change within populations, have a range of evidence to support their work. The updated NICE pathway overview of behaviour change (2014b) offers the following principles for selecting interventions aimed at populations.

Recommended action: deliver population-level policies, interventions and programmes tailored to change specific, health related behaviours. These should be based on information gathered about the context, needs and behaviours of the target population(s). They could include:

- Fiscal and legislative interventions.
- National and local advertising and mass media campaigns (for example, promotion of positive role models and general promotion of health enhancing behaviours).
- Point of sale promotions and interventions (for example working in partnership with private sector organizations to offer information, price reductions or other promotions) (NICE 2014a: 3).

When focusing on programmes and interventions aimed at communities NICE (2014a) emphasize the importance of building on and fostering the strengths of a community and the relationships within a community. Their principles include:

- Improve self-efficacy.
- Promote resilience and build skills, by promoting positive social networks and helping to develop relationships.
- Promote access to the financial and material resources needed to facilitate behaviour change (NICE 2014a: 6).

It is evident that the concepts of levels of intervention including legislation and community empowerment are firmly embedded within current theories, approaches and guidance relating to behaviour change.

Community empowerment

There is an increasing focus on defining and meeting health and well-being needs at a local level, communities' views on their health needs and communities' participation in meeting these needs (Health and Social Care Act 2012), and on the need to address health and societal inequalities – the Marmot Review, *Fair Society, Healthy Lives* (Marmot 2010) and the public health policy paper *Healthy Lives, Healthy People* (DH 2010a).

Community empowerment involves considering several related concepts, including community development, community participation, community inclusion, social capital and capacity building (Sines *et al.* 2013). A useful principle of empowerment is offered by MacDowall *et al.* (2006: 153) who assert that:

While using people's local knowledge in programme planning does not in itself promote empowerment, involving all members of a community in decision making does. Participation without power is not the goal of development, but participation as an outcome of empowerment is. Community development programmes seek to equip people with the knowledge, skills and support necessary to allow them to participate in decisions at the level of their choice.

This principle highlights that the redistribution of power within communities is vital to the process of empowerment. Laverack (2007) describes empowerment as a process whereby communities gain more influence and control over the resources and decisions that affect their lives, including wider health determinants. It is important for those attempting to influence the health and well-being of communities through empowerment to be cognizant of all relevant concepts and be critically discerning as to the true level of community decision making being allowed. Public Health England assert that 'improvement in the public's health has to be led from within communities, rather than directed centrally' (2013: 2).

Low physical activity rates across the lifespan are a major concern, and it is interesting to consider the facilitation of community empowerment in relation to health and well-being initiatives originating from sporting events watched nationwide (Sines *et al.* 2013). The benefits of the legacy from major sporting events such as the London Olympics may positively impact on health and well-being. A core principle and philosophical premise of the London 2012 Olympic bid was the promise of legacy (Weed 2010). The material benefits of such legacy, for example improvements within the economy and local infrastructure, will have a direct impact on the determinants of health relating to the local population. The less measurable effects of legacy, including interest in physical activity and the motivation to change behaviour, are worthy of consideration particularly when considering the success of the Change 4 Life initiative (DH 2010b). Change 4 Life encourages individuals to make sustainable behaviour changes to their everyday lives. Similarly local public health and well-being initiatives can capitalize on the inspiration and motivation generated by legacy, by encouraging individuals and populations to make small changes to increase their activity levels, by trying new activities and setting challenges.

Prest and Partridge (2010) advocate the value of developing public health and well-being initiatives that harness the interest created by world stage sporting events, and translate this interest into motivation to change behaviour. They describe one such collaborative project designed by NHS Dorset, Active Dorset and Dorset County Council, which reflects Olympic and Paralympic values including inspiration and determination, and has a free interactive website at its core. This Team Dorset Challenge supports the local population to take part in activities and challenges in groups, as local focus groups identified that the population in Dorset were more likely to participate with others than on their own (Prest and Partridge 2010).

When attempting to effect behaviour change within populations, the importance of involving the identified population with the social marketing strategy cannot be overestimated. It is vital that the public health and well-being concern or issue is matched with the motivations, needs and barriers relating to the population group or audience at which any initiative is aimed. Jackson (2009) proposes that good social marketing goes beneath the surface and utilizes a range of methods including qualitative research (face-to-face interviews and focus groups) and geodemographic profiling, in order to convey messages that truly influence positive shifts in behaviours in population groups across the lifespan. Consideration also needs to be given to ethical concerns regarding the advertising of unhealthy food and drink by sponsoring companies.

Local areas away from where a sporting event took place have challenges relating to resources, in that their area will not receive all the structural benefits afforded to the area which hosts a major event. It can be argued that the geographical location of the London Olympics added to health inequalities between regions.

The intervention ladder

The ladder of intervention was devised by the Nuffield Council on Bioethics and described in their 2007 report, *Public Health: Ethical Issues*. This intervention ladder is a useful tool for the public, policy makers, professionals and anyone engaged in public health, to facilitate consideration of the rationale, justification, effectiveness and acceptability of any public health initiative that aims to influence behaviour change. The level of intrusiveness and restriction of freedom increases with each rung of the ladder.

- Eliminate choice. Legislate to completely eliminate choice; for example, the compulsory wearing of seatbelts, a ban on smoking in public places and the proposal that smoking in cars while a child is a passenger should be banned.
- Restrict choice. Legislate to restrict the choices available to people; for example, banning the use of a potentially harmful chemical or a harmful ingredient from foods. Alternatively, a healthy ingredient can be added to food. A more controversial intervention is the adding of fluoride to the water in some areas.
- Guide choices through disincentives. Economic disincentives can be put in place to influence people not to engage in unhealthy activities; for example, increasing taxation on alcohol, tobacco and environmentally harmful cars.
- Guide choices through incentives. Economic incentives; for example, reduced taxation on environmentally efficient cars.
- Guide choices through changing the default policy. Making the regular choice the healthy choice and the less healthy choice the default option; for example, providing healthy options for school dinners as standard with less healthy foods available on request.
- Enable choice. Facilitating behaviour change by making the healthy choice accessible; for example, offering a free exercise programme or providing toothbrushes in all schools.
- Provide information. Provide education and information to the public; for example, as part of a range of interventions to increase exercise levels.
- Do nothing or simply monitor the current situation (adapted from Nuffield Council of Bioethics 2007).

The Nuffield Council of Bioethics (2007) describe the ladder of intervention as a progression of steps that move from individual autonomy, freedom and responsibility up to full state intervention and responsibility. They assert that a key function of the ladder is to facilitate the consideration of alternative interventions and their level of intrusiveness, and not to allow absolute judgements. Within the context of the wider determinants of health, however, the degree to which individuals or populations are able to enact their responsibility varies. Nonetheless the ladder can be a useful framework for those engaged in attempting to influence behaviour, allowing them to deliberate the balance of the benefits of an intervention between individuals and populations.

In terms of democracy, popularity and appealing to voters, governments face an inherent challenge in balancing their responsibility and duty to foster the health of the population, and maintaining people's personal liberty. Legislation versus personal freedom and responsibility is a perennial debate which, along with levels of intervention, can be considered within the context of 'nudging' and 'shoving'. Branson *et al.* (2012) explain that by introducing subtle alterations within the environment, it is possible to influence the behaviour of populations without coercion. Thaler and Sunstein (2008) who conceptualized nudging define its aim as modifying any feature of the choice architecture without restricting any options that lead to an alteration in behaviour. Shoving can be described as usually including legislative or fiscal measures in order to change behaviour. Branson *et al.* (2012) assert that the shoving approach is clearly more paternalistic and interventionist than a nudging approach.

An example of nudging is the provision of recycling containers and regular collection in order to make positive environmental behaviour the easy choice. A shoving-approach example is the legislated ban on smoking in public places. There is clear evidence that legislation has worked and saved lives: Sims *et al.* (2010) identified a reduction in heart attacks since the smoking ban. While generally supported by the public, the ban was a courageous public health shove and demonstrates how significant population behaviour change can be influenced while retaining public support. The Faculty of Public Health (Maryon Davies and Jolley 2010) highlight that the evidence of behaviour change related to individual responsibility is less clear and assert that health inequalities are a major barrier which government policy needs to address.

Interestingly, evidence gained by the Faculty of Public Health (Maryon Davies and Jolley 2010) demonstrated that the general public are in favour of more radical action by government, including legislation that improves the public's health and well-being, than government assumes. Nudging can occur two ways, and the public voice and momentum can nudge public health planners and governments into taking action.

The world's governments increasingly focus on the need for behaviour change, owing to many factors, including the current and projected demographic picture, increasing health inequalities, an increase in people living with long-term conditions, medical advances, behaviour-related risks to the environment, escalating health and social care costs, global economic uncertainty, instability and debt. Two recent significant events have emphasized the urgency of the need for behaviour change in populations across the world.

The first, in February 2014, was the publication of the World Cancer Report by the International Agency for Research (IAR 2014a), the specialist cancer agency of the World Health Organization. The report identifies the significant rise in cancer across the world, with 14 million new cases in 2012, predicted to rise to 22 million cases a year within the next two decades. The report asserts that while even the richest countries will face significant challenges in sustaining increased cancer care and treatment costs, developing countries will certainly be unable to do so. As the report identifies, this health inequality is compounded due to developing countries being disproportionately affected with higher numbers of new cancer cases and fewer health resources. The strongest message that the report conveys, and leaves no doubt that urgent action is required, is that around half of these new cancer cases could be prevented if current evidence was appropriately implemented.

The second significant event was the Richard Dimbleby Lecture 'A New Multilateralism for the 21st Century' delivered by Christine Lagarde, the managing director of the International Monetary Fund (IMF), on 3 February 2014. Whilst the essence of the lecture (IMF 2014) is the identification of tensions in global economic sustainability, Lagarde identifies three key issues – demographics, environmental degradation and income inequality – which have resonance with those responsible for influencing behaviour change.

Demographics

The world population is growing and ageing. In 30 years it will have increased by 2 billion, and by 2020 there will be more people over 65 than under 5 for the first time ever. The geographical distribution of old and young people is changing, with regions such as South Asia and Africa experiencing a sharp increase in their young population, while Japan, China and Europe's populations are shrinking and ageing. Ageing countries will need to look after their older generation, and countries with young populations will need to focus on education and the provision of enough jobs.

Environmental degradation

The world will experience growing food, water and energy scarcity as the twenty-first century progresses, with nearly half the population living in areas of water shortage. The results of climate change will adversely affect the world's vulnerable populations most. One example is that a significant proportion of the land that grows maize in sub-Saharan Africa will not be able to support the crop by 2030. One part of the solution relates to energy utilization and the fact that we are subsidizing the behaviour that is destroying our planet. Energy needs to be priced correctly and energy subsidies phased out.

Income inequality

Disparity in incomes has been rising in most countries, with 70 per cent of the world's population living in countries where income inequality has risen. An example is India where the worth of the billionaire community has increased 12 times in recent years, which is enough funds to eliminate absolute poverty in India twice over. The IMF knows that courageously designed spending and tax policies can reduce inequality in income.

In a policy briefing relating current public health reforms, the Royal College of Nursing (RCN 2012) strongly assert the need for government to recognize and take action on the links between poverty, poor housing and social isolation and poorer mental and physical health. They argue that preventative aspects of public health must be prioritized in order for health inequalities to be reduced (RCN 2012).

Thinking point

When considering the above assertions from the World Cancer Report and Christine Lagarde's speech, what do you think should be the balance between individual choice and legislation, and the balance between the concepts of nudge and shove?

Summary

National and global predictions relating to both increasing health inequalities and the increasing incidence of long-term conditions are indicative of how high the stakes are; addressing health and well-being is an urgent priority. Practitioners need to demonstrate a critical consciousness in relation to both the evidence supporting behaviour change interventions and the financial climate in which they are practising. The greater emphasis on local health and well-being needs within the new public health funding system is positive. However, practitioners need to champion public health and well-being initiatives that ensure populations are not disadvantaged by the inappropriate allocation of resources through poor commissioning. It is also vital that all those engaged in attempting to change behaviour are always cognizant of the complexity and impact of health inequalities and health determinants. Practitioners need to be brave in ensuring that they are represented within the commissioning process.

References

Acheson, D. (1998) *Independent Inquiry into Inequalities in Health: Recommendations*. London: Department of Health.

Adams, J. and White, M. (2004) Why don't stage-based activity promotion interventions work? *Health Education Research*, 20(2), 237–43.

Ajzen, I. (1991) The theory of planned behaviour, *Organizational Behaviour and Human Decision Processes*, 50(2): 179–211.

Bandura, A. (1986) *Social Foundations of Thought and Action: A Social Cognitive Theory*. Englewood Cliffs, NJ: Prentice-Hall.

Becker, M.H. (ed.) (1984) *The Health Belief Model and Personal Health Behaviour*. Thorofare, NJ: Slack.

Berry, J.W. (2004) Fundamental psychological processes in intercultural relations, in D. Landis, M. Bennett and J. Bennett (eds) (2004) *Handbook of Intercultural Training*, 3rd edn. Thousand Oaks, CA: Sage.

Branson, C., Duffy, B., Perry, C. and Wellings, D. (2012) *Acceptable Behavior? Public Opinion on Behaviour Change Policy*. London: Ipsos MORI.

Bratiotis, C., Sorrentino Schmalisch, C. and Stekette, G. (2011) *The Hoarding Handbook*. Oxford and London: Oxford University Press.

Buck, D. and Frosini, F. (2012) *Clustering of Unhealthy Behaviours over Time*. London: Kings Fund.

Corcoran, N. (2007) *Communicating Health: Strategies for Health Promotion*. London: Sage Publications.

Department of Health (DH) (2010a) *Healthy Lives, Healthy People: Our Strategy for Public Health in England*. London: DH.

Department of Health (DH) (2010b) *Change 4 Life. One Year On: In Support of Healthy Weight, Healthy Lives*. London: Department of Health.

Department of Health (2012) *Health and Social Care Act*. Available at www.legislation.gov.uk/ukpga/2012/7/contents/enacted (accessed Jan. 2014).

Dixon, A. (2008) *Motivation and Confidence: What Does it Take to Change Behaviour?* London: Kings Fund.

Fishbein, M. and Ajzen, I. (1975) *Belief, Attitude, Intention and Behaviour: An Introduction to Theory and Research*. Reading, MA: Addison-Wesley.

Fleury, G., Gaudette, L. and Moran, P. (2012) Compulsive hoarding: overview and implications for community health nurses, *Journal of Community Health Nursing*, 29(3): 154–62.

Francis, R. (chair) (2013) *Report of the Mid Staffordshire NHS Foundation Trust Public Enquiry* (Francis Report) London: The Stationery Office.

Frost, R., Steketee, G. and Williams, L. (2000) Hoarding: a community health problem, *Health and Social Care in the Community*, 8(4): 229–34.

Gillam, S. (2013) The Francis Inquiry: a lost opportunity? *Quality in Primary Care*, 21(4): 205–6.

International Agency for Research (IAR) (2014) *World Cancer Report*. Geneva: World Health Organization.

International Monetary Fund (IMF) (2014) *A New Multilateralism for the 21st Century: The Richard Dimbleby Lecture*. Available at ww.imf.org/external/np/speeches/2014/020314.htm (accessed Feb. 2014).

Jackson, A. (2009) Can social marketing bring about long-term behaviour change? *Perspectives in Public Health*, 129(6): 260–1.

Laverack, G. (2007) *Health Promotion Practice: Building Empowered Communities*. Maidenhead: Open University Press.

Macdowall, W., Bonell, C. and Davies, M. (2006) *Understanding Public Health: Health Promotion Practice*. Maidenhead, Open University Press.

Making Every Adult Matter (2008) *A Four-point Manifesto for Tackling Multiple Needs and Exclusions*. London: Making Every Adult Matter.

Marchand, S. and McEnany, G. (2012) Hoarding's place in the DSM-5: another symptom, or a newly listed disorder? *Issues in Mental Health Nursing*, 33(9), 591–7.

Marmot, M. (2010) *Fair Society, Healthy Lives: Strategic Review of Health Inequalities in England post 2010*. Available at www.marmotreview.org (accessed Jan. 2014).

Maryon Davies, A. and Jolley, R. (2010) *Healthy Nudges: When the Public Wants Change But the Politicians Don't Know It*. London: Faculty of Public Health.

National Institute for Care and Clinical Excellence (NICE) (2014a) *Behaviour Change Overview. NICE Pathway*. London: NICE.

National Institute for Care and Clinical Excellence (NICE) (2014b) *Behaviour Change: Individual Approaches. NICE Public Health Guidance 49*. London: NICE.

National Institute for Care and Clinical Excellence (NICE) and World Health Organization Europe (2010) *Health Systems and Health-related Behaviour Change: A Review of Primary and Secondary Evidence*. Copenhagen: WHO Regional Office for Europe.

Nuffield Council on Bioethics (2007) *Public Health: Ethical Issues*. Available at www.nuffield-bioethics.org/public-health/public-health-policy-process-and-practice (accessed Jan. 2014).

Nursing and Midwifery Council (2004) *Standards of Proficiency for Specialist Community Health Nurses*. London: Nursing and Midwifery Council.

Orji, R., Vassileva, J. and Mandryk, R.L. (2012) Lunch time: a slow-casual game for long-term dietary behavior change, *Personal and Ubiquitous Computing*. doi: 10.1007/s00779-012-0590-6.

Pertusa, A., Fullana, M., Singh, S., Alonso, P., Menchon, J. and Mataix-Cols, D. (2008) Compulsive hoarding: OCD symptom, distinct clinical syndrome, or both? *American Journal of Psychiatry*, 165(10): 1289–97.

Petty, R. and Cacioppo, J. (1986) *Communication and Persuasion: Central and Peripheral Routes to Attitude Change*. New York: Springer Verlag.

Prest, S. and Partridge, R. (2010) 2012 Olympics: A catalyst for behaviour change? *Perspectives in Public Health*, 130(6): 257–8.

Prochaska, J.O. and DiClemente, C.C. (1983) Stages and processes of self-change of smoking: toward an integrative model of change, *Journal of Consulting and Clinical Psychology*, 51(3): 390–5.

Prochaska, J. O., DiClemente, C. C. and Norcross, J. C. (1992). In search of how people change: applications to addictive behaviours, *American Psychologist*, 47(9): 1102–14.

Public Health England (2013) *Our Priorities for 2013/14*. London: Public Health England.

Robertson, R. (2008) *Using Information to Promote Healthy Behaviours*. London: Kings Fund.

Rosenstock, J.M. (1966) Why people use health services, *Millbank Memorial Fund Quarterly*, 44(3): 94–124.

Royal College of Nursing (RCN) (2012) *Going Upstream: Nursing's Contribution to Public Health*. Available at www.rcn.org.uk/__data/assets/pdf_file/0007/433699/004203.pdf (accessed Jan. 2014).

Rutter, D. and Quine, L. (2002). *Changing Health Behaviour*. Buckingham: Open University Press.

Ryan, P. (2009) Integrated theory of behaviour change, *Clinical Nurse Specialist*, 23(3): 161–72.

Sims, M., Maxwell, R., Bauld, L. and Gilmore, A. (2010) Short term impact of smoke-free legislation in England: retrospective analysis of hospital admissions for myocardial infarction, *British Medical Journal*, 340: c2161. doi: 10.1136/bmj.c2161

Sines, D., Aldridge-Bent, S., Fanning, A., Farrelly, P., Potter, K. and Wright, J. (eds) (2013) *Community and Public Health Nursing*, 5th edn. Chichester: Wiley.

Thaler, R.H. and Sunstein, C.R. (2008) *Nudge: Improving Decisions About Health, Wealth and Happiness*. London: Caravan Books.

Thomas, N. (1998) Hoarding, *Journal of Gerontological Social Work*, 29(1): 45–55.

Webb, T., Joseph, J., Yardley, L. and Michie, S. (2010) Using the internet to promote health behaviour change: a systematic review and meta-analysis of the impact of theoretical basis, use of behaviour change techniques and mode of delivery on efficacy, *Journal of Medical Internet Research*, 16(1): e19.

Weed, M. (2010) How will we know if the London 2012 Olympics and Paralympics benefit health? *British Medical Journal*, 340(c2202): 1205–6.

Whitfield, G. and Davidson, A. (2007) *Cognitive Behavioural Therapy Explained*. Abingdon: Radcliffe.

World Health Organization (WHO) (2012) *Good Health Adds Years to Life*. Geneva: WHO.

6 Social justice and global perspectives on health improvement and well-being

Dr Mzwandile (Andi) Mabhala

Introduction

This chapter critically defines social justice. It openly declares that its analysis of social justice is situated within a particular political position, and explains why that position is taken in relation to public health and inequalities in health. It proposes that, in a just society, the primary function of the state should be to produce policies that enable all members of society to have fair and genuine access to opportunities to obtain the social goods that determine health and well-being.

It goes on to critically review the literature on three differing theories of social justice – the libertarian, utilitarian and egalitarian philosophies – particularly their fundamental claims regarding equality and fairness in the distribution of privilege and deprivation. It notes that egalitarian theories are consistent with the social justice principles of equality and fairness, on the understanding that egalitarian philosophy proposes an equal distribution of social goods; and as the evidence suggests that health inequalities are rooted on an uneven distribution of social goods, egalitarian theories are proposed as a suitable approach for addressing inequalities in health. Furthermore, evidence shows that egalitarian approaches which place more emphasis on health – as opposed to health care or access to health services – provide a better solution to the social injustice of health inequalities.

This chapter uses examples from the UK, South Africa and elsewhere to explain why egalitarian social justice principles provide a perfect fit with the practice of public health policy. It also justifies why health, as opposed to health care, has special moral importance for social justice in health inequalities, and argues that, if health and social policies are to have any chance of reducing health inequalities they will have to pay more attention to health rather than health services.

This chapter claims that for public health practitioners to make real differences to health inequalities, they need to place their arguments within broader social policies. It recognizes that some of the measures to reduce health inequalities may interfere with the liberty of free market capitalism, and appreciates the reluctance by liberal governments to do this, but identifies four areas where governments could make inroads without interference: poverty, education, housing and unemployment.

Defining social justice

Politicians of all colours increasingly use the concept of social justice as a political slogan to promise that they will produce fair distributive policies. However, judgements about what constitute fairness are subject to different political organizations' underpinning principles, values and ideologies. The lack of a stable, ideologically bounded interpretation of fair distribution of social goods makes the concepts of social justice malleable by proponents of contrasting political ideologies.

Unlike politicians who use the concept of social justice without being explicit about their philosophical stance, in this chapter, fairness and equality are understood to be two main pillars of social justice. It takes a similar view to Powers and Faden (2006) in that social justice is seen as the moral foundation of public health and health policy. Powell *et al.* (2012) subscribe to the viewpoint which positions social justice as the idea of creating a society or institution based on the principles of equality and solidarity, that understands and values human rights and that recognizes the dignity of every human being. This view is shared by several other writers; for example, Krieger and Birn (1998) define social justice as deliberate actions based upon recognition that all social groups are not treated equally in a society. Similarly, Gostin and Powers's (2006) account of social justice stresses the fair distribution of common advantages and common burdens. Hofrichter (2003) proposes that social justice demands an equitable distribution of collective goods, institutional resources and life opportunities. These views of social justice in relation to public health are based on strong evidence that inequalities in the distribution of social goods are fundamental causes of the uneven distribution of health and disease in our society (Marmot 2007, 2010, 2011). It is therefore proposed that social justice goals in relation to public health should promote health equality as a basic social right (Hofrichter 2006).

Philosophical perspectives

In a just society, the primary function of the state should be to produce policies that provide fair and genuine access to the opportunities for those social goods that determine health and well-being. Analysis of this position is framed around three very different but highly influential philosophical approaches to social justice: libertarianism, utilitarianism and egalitarianism (Ruger 2004). The primary bases of comparison between them are their claims pertaining to equality and fairness in the distribution of privileges and deprivation, and their position on the role of the state in distribution of social goods.

Core to the libertarian philosophy is the premise that individuals have 'full ownership', meaning that individuals have full immunity or protection against the 'non-consensual' loss of their rights to self-ownership except where an individual violates the rights of others (Almgren 2007). In the dominant libertarian vision of civil society, collective well-being is best achieved through the exercise of individual free will and self-responsibility in the context of a laissez-faire market economy (Almgren 2007).

Libertarians are concerned mainly with limiting the adverse effect of government interference with the ability of individuals to exercise control over their own life (Powers and Faden 2006; Almgren 2007). The libertarian view is that because illness, unemployment and even old age are risks intrinsic to human existence, it is the role and responsibility of individuals to protect themselves through mechanisms such as pension schemes, insurance and savings (Almgren 2007). While this perspective can be seen as fair, it is only fair if one assumes that everybody has the same start in life; it ignores the fact that in some societies there are people who have limited ability to self-protect. In societies where the libertarian view is dominant, the state tends to place more trust in the power of free markets to address the determinants of social inequalities, such as poverty, income, employment, unemployment, and security mechanisms for old age, maternity or childcare.

This view is unsuitable as a model for tackling health inequalities, as social justice is a moral and ethical issue rather than a legal issue; there are no legal arguments for some people to enjoy all social goods supportive of their health and well-being, while others have none, but there is a moral and ethical argument. This view of social justice does nothing to promote social mobility. Taken to the extreme, libertarians would be relatively unconcerned with problems of extreme deprivation or extreme abundance as long as the extreme of abundance is acquired through legal means. This view is inconsistent with the international declaration of social protection in United Nations General Assembly Resolution 65/1 of 2010, which affirms there is a duty upon member states to ensure they produce policies that entrench social protection as a human right that all citizens can expect (United Nations General Assembly 2010).

The origin of the utilitarian perspective on social justice begins with Aristotle's notion of distributive justice, which in essence views the just distribution of goods and benefits of society as a legitimate function of the state. In simple form the utilitarian principle states that utility should be distributed in accordance with whichever scheme yields the maximum good to the maximum number of people (Powers and Faden 2006; Almgren 2007). Taken at face value, this suggests that society should be organized on highly rational terms to achieve the maximum social goods for the most number of persons (Powers and Faden 2006). Taken to the extreme, utilitarians would be relatively unconcerned with problems of extreme deprivation or extreme abundance as long as the maximum good to the maximum number of outcomes is served (Daniels *et al.* 2004, 2007).

The perspective proposed in this chapter stands in stark contrast to both utilitarian and libertarian viewpoints. This chapter argues that the egalitarian perspective closely matches the ideals of social justice – fairness and equality. Egalitarians are neither maximizers nor proponents of a single measure of utility (Powers and Faden 2006). In general, egalitarian theories propose that persons are provided with an equal distribution of certain goods, such as health care, but most proposals of egalitarian theories are cautiously formulated to avoid making equal sharing of all possible social benefits a requirement of social justice (Ruger 2004).

However, the position adopted in this chapter contrasts with that of egalitarian theorists who focus on health care; it favours the version that qualifies the 'right to equal health' rather than health care – the egalitarian approach that focuses on the connection between health and the socio-economic and environmental conditions in which people live. It shares the view that social justice requires that all persons be given opportunities to attain the conditions necessary to be healthy (Sudhir *et al.* 2004). This proposal is based on long-established evidence that social class, as determined by educational attainment, social position and level of control in occupation, is a major determinant of the patterns and distribution of disease and mortality (Kawachi *et al.* 1997; Daniels *et al.* 2004). Furthermore it has long been known that an individual's chances of life and death are patterned according to social class; the more affluent and educated people are, the longer and healthier their lives (Kawachi *et al.* 1997; Bayer *et al.* 2007).

Public health researchers such as Marmot (2010) and Mackenbach and Bakker (2003) have repeatedly demonstrated that the greater the degree of socio-economic inequality within a society, the steeper the gradient of health inequality. As a result, a middle income group in a less equal society will have worse health than a comparable or even poorer group in a society with greater equality (Kawachi *et al.* 1997; Daniels *et al.* 2004, 2007; Bayer *et al.* 2007). The emphasis should not be placed on the pattern of distribution of health outcomes or solely on access to health care, but on the broader social systems and processes underlying health inequalities (Rose 1992; Gwatkin 2000; Sudhir *et al.* 2004). This chapter shares Rawls's view that the social conditions into which somebody is born have a profound impact on what they can achieve and aspire to achieve (Rawls 1971). Therefore, the principles of social justice should aim at regulating the terms of basic structures of society, that is, society's main political, social and economic institutions, in a way that enables an equal opportunity for all, not just the few. This argument is based on the premise that society's achievements and failures in health may contain important information about the injustice of particular social arrangements (Gwatkin 2000; UK Health Watch 2005).

The deductive standpoint here is that these structures contain various social positions, and that people born into different positions have different expectations of life determined in part by the political system as well as by economic and social circumstances (Kawachi *et al.* 1997; Daniels *et al.* 2004, 2007; Bayer *et al.* 2007). It has been argued that some institutions of society favour certain starting places over others (Beauchamp 1975, 2003; Hofrichter 2003; Peter 2004). This view was best articulated by Rose (1992) who stated that socio-economic deprivation includes a whole constellation of closely interrelated factors – such as lack of money, overcrowded and substandard housing, living in a poor locality, poor education, unsatisfying work or actual unemployment – which reduce social approval and self-esteem. In turn this constellation of deprivations leads to a wide range of unhealthy behaviours, including smoking, alcohol excess, poor diet, lack of exercise and a generally lower regard for future health (Rose 1992). He goes on to argue that political effort should be focused on three broad components of deprivation, each of which profoundly influences health and where some progress would be possible even in the face of economic inequalities: these are education, housing, and unemployment (Rose 1992). Arguably, these are areas where the government could make a real difference without necessarily interfering with free economic enterprise. However, while these factors have detrimental effects on health, they sit outside the health sector; therefore the policy to address them is likely to be developed with little or no consideration of health effects. That means for public health practitioners to make a real difference in tackling inequalities in health, they need to place their argument within broader social policy, not just within health.

Collectivism versus individualism

Gostin and Powers (2006) explain that one of the roles of social justice in relation to public health is identifying and ameliorating patterns of systematic disadvantage that undermine the well-being of people – for instance, those whose prospects of good health are limited because their life choices are not even remotely like those of others. The recognition that there are people who have limited prospects of choice raises questions about the neoliberal, libertarian policy which promotes choice. For example, *Equity and Excellence: Liberating the NHS* (DH 2010a) made reference to choice 83 times in a 57-page document. As Krieger (2011) asked, is it their choice that some people live in the worst part of the town? Is it their choice that some people live near sources of radiation that put their children at risk? Is it their choice that some live near the worst forms of pollution, that they have no clean water, or are there systems that allow these people to live in such conditions? Is it their choice that 3.5 million children live in poverty in the UK today (Child Poverty Action Group 2013)?

Other writers have also challenged the perception that health is a personal choice, for instance, the classic article by Krieger and Birn (1998) in which they describe social justice as the foundation for public health. This followed an earlier article which challenged the popular ideological message that individual short-comings are at the root of ill health (Krieger and Bassett 1993). They advocate a perspective of public health which puts emphasis on the collective and structural aspects of individual shortcomings or voluntary risks, challenging attempts to narrowly and persuasively limit public attention to the behaviour of the individ-uals, and exposing myths that 'blame the victim' (Beauchamp 1975, 2003; Krieger and Bassett 1993; Krieger and Birn 1998).

The implications of this shift of public health focus from individual risk factors to collective and structural aspects means that public health practice and public health institutions must pay more attention to identifying and addressing the socio-economic determinants of health. This view is supported by several social justice theorists who recognize that, while there are multiple causal pathways to numerous dimensions of disadvantage, of particular concern for social justice are poverty, substandard housing, poor education, unhygienic and polluted environ-ments, and disintegration (Kawachi *et al.* 1997; Kass 2001; Bayer *et al.* 2007). There is a plethora of evidence that these factors are also fundamental socio-economic and environmental determinants of health (Marmot 2004, 2005, 2007, 2009, 2010,

2011). Concurring, Powers and Faden (2006) assert that social justice concerns securing and maintaining the social conditions necessary for a sufficient level of health and well-being for everyone.

Beauchamp (1975, 2003) highlights the ethical implications for public health practitioners. They conceive of public health as an ultimately and essentially ethical enterprise committed to the notion that all persons are entitled to protection against the hazards of this world, and to the minimization of death and disability in society (Beauchamp 2003; Hofrichter 2003; Powers and Faden 2006). Consequently, Beauchamp (1975, 2003) maintains that social justice involves changing society so that claims for freedom, equality and democracy receive adequate expression, and so that the politics by which people pursue these goals gain acceptance as being normal rather than exceptional and suspect. Beauchamp (1975, 2003) further argues that under social justice all persons are equally entitled to such key ends as health protection or minimum standards of income. Gostin and Powers (2006) assert that the social justice view of public health is logically and ethically justified if one accepts the vision of public health being the protection of all human life.

This perspective adds an ethics dimension to the widely accepted view of public health. Furthermore it defines public health as an institution charged with promoting human welfare by bringing about a certain kind of human good, the good of health (Powers and Faden 2006). Seeing public health as ultimately rooted in an egalitarian tradition is the vision of social justice.

UK policy perspective

In recent years the notions of fairness and equality have been promoted as driving principles behind the ambitious policies of all major UK political parties (Cutler and Waine 2013). The most recent evidence of this could be seen when the UK Coalition government outlined their policy objectives, which included a promise to 'ensure that fairness is at the heart of [their] decisions so that all those most in need are protected' (HM Government 2010: 7). This reflected resonance with their predecessor Labour governments, who in their 1997 manifesto and earlier policy documents promised to create a fairer society (Labour Party 1997). Both governments expressed commitment to develop a public health strategy to tackle inequalities in health, even though there were clear differences on how that might be achieved (DH 1997, 2010a, 2010b; Labour Party 1997; HM Government 2010). In *The Coalition: Our Programme for Government* the Coalition government pledged to 'investigate ways of improving access to preventative healthcare for those in disadvantaged areas to help tackle health inequalities' (HM Government 2010: 28).

A cursory view at the Conservative-led Coalition government's public health White Paper, *Healthy Lives, Healthy People* (DH 2010b) gives an impression of commitment to fairness and equality. This White Paper was replete with references to tackling inequalities in health. If one considers the expressed commitment to fairness and equality without considering the underpinning ideology, one might erroneously expect the expressed moral imperative in public health policies to be tempered with concerns for those who experience health benefits as well as who are exposed to hazards that harm health (Rose 1992; Kass 2001; Beauchamp 2003; Gostin and Powers 2006; Powers and Faden 2006; Almgren 2007).

However, the Coalition government identified their key priority as reducing budget deficits and paying down the public debt. The methods they proposed to achieve these goals reflected their ideological belief in the superiority of the free market (Scott-Samuel *et al.* 2014). This ideological belief creates an unequal society and, as this chapter demonstrates, it is the poorest who bear the greatest burden (Cutler and Waine 2013; Scott-Samuel *et al.* 2014). The opposition Labour Party's criticism has been mainly of the speed with which this is being done, when in fact the method is more problematic than speed. The methods chosen by the Coalition government to reduce budget deficits focused mainly on cuts – cutting tax, public spending and social welfare benefits. As Jacobs (2014) argues this method makes it inevitable that the poor will bear the greatest burden, because spending goes to those on low incomes, while most taxes are paid on higher incomes.

The UK government has produced policies that are said to put money back directly to the revenues and help to pay debt: these include the increase in value added tax (VAT); the cap on individual benefits; the housing benefit penalty being applied to those with a spare room (bedroom tax); the localization of council tax benefit; the abolition of the social fund; the conversion of disability living allowance into personal independence payments with more restrictive eligibility criteria; the removal of legal aid for welfare benefits advice; cuts in higher education funding and increased tuition fees; and the paring back by most councils of basic social care services. All of these affect the poor and most vulnerable groups. On the other hand, the redistributive policies introduced by the government have included cuts in corporation tax, introducing the 'help to buy' scheme and raising the personal income tax threshold to £10,000. All these are designed to benefit those earning higher incomes because those on low incomes do not earn enough to benefit from the tax-free allowance, nor do they have the financial credit to benefit from the 'help to buy' scheme (Jacobs 2014). Regrettably these policies attract very little challenge from the official opposition party, even though they adversely affect the creation of a society of greater social justice and public good.

Inevitably, these changes will also have an impact on other determinants of health, including inequalities in access to higher education which, in itself, has an impact on social mobility and potential income. Scott-Samuel *et al.* (2014) argue that these policies, particularly 'help to buy' and cuts in corporation tax, simply reflect the political right's ideological belief in the superiority of the market; nonetheless, these policies are inconsistent with both evidence of the value of upstream interventions when tackling health inequalities and the expressed commitment to 'improving public health, tackling health inequalities' (DH 2010b: 9). The evidence has shown that tackling health inequalities requires greater attention to fair distribution of social goods (Mackenbach and Bakker 2003; Mackenbach *et al.* 2003). As Marmot states, 'health inequalities are unfair and putting them right is a matter of social justice' (Marmot 2010: 29).

Case study

The Trussell Trust, one of the charity organizations that runs food banks in the UK, has reported the biggest increase in UK food bank use. In 2013 they reported a 170 per cent rise in numbers turning to food banks. According to the trust, almost 350,000 people have received at least three days' emergency food from Trussell Trust food banks during the last 12 months, nearly 100,000 more than anticipated and close to triple the number helped in 2011–12. The trust reported that the rising cost of living, static incomes, changes to benefits, underemployment and unemployment have meant increasing numbers of people in the UK have hit a crisis that forces them to go hungry. Figure 6.1 was developed by the Trussell Trust to illustrate the rise in food bank use over recent years:

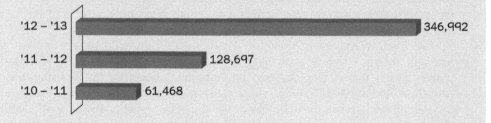
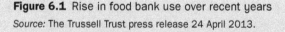

Figure 6.1 Rise in food bank use over recent years
Source: The Trussell Trust press release 24 April 2013.

The Trussell Trust's Executive Chairman, Chris Mould, says: 'Politicians across the political spectrum urgently need to recognize the real extent of UK food poverty and create fresh policies that better address its underlying causes. This is more important than ever as the impact of the biggest reforms to the welfare state since it began start to take effect.'

The trust presented evidence that shows the reasons for the use of food banks (see Figure 6.2).

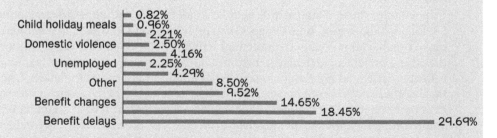

Figure 6.2 Voucher distribution by type of crisis
Source: The Trussell Trust, press release 24 April 2013.

Thinking point

The increase in use of food banks has triggered contrasting views about redistributive policies and poverty, and food poverty in particular. To some the increase in use of food banks is driven by publicity. For example, one politician commented: '[F]ood banks do a good service, but they have been much in the news. People know they are free. They know about them and they will ask social workers to refer them. It would be wrong to pretend that the mass of publicity has not also been a driver in their increased use.'

Others such as Policy Exchange (a leading UK think tank) claim that draconian sanctions on benefit claimants are forcing people to use food banks (Miscampbell 2014). In a letter to the *Sunday Telegraph*, 43 of the most senior Roman Catholic clerics in England and Wales explained to the government how benefit reforms have torn away the safety net for the poor and hungry, creating a crisis (Royston 2013; The Children's Society 2013). In response to this criticism the government argue that they are giving unemployed Britons 'new hope and responsibility' by cutting their benefit payments, and claim that welfare reforms are part of a 'moral mission' for the country (Bingham and Dominiczak 2014).

What are your views? How well do you think the current government is doing on fairness and equality?

Global perspective

At the Millennium Summit of the United Nations (UN) in 2000, 189 UN member states committed to help achieve eight millennium development goals. Persistent extreme poverty was identified as one of the world's most pressing and deep-seated problems, and members pledged to halve the rates of poverty by 2015 (UN 2000). At this summit fundamental values including freedom, equality, tolerance and solidarity, which together spelt a firm commitment to social justice, were accepted by all member states as the guiding spirit for all MDG efforts (Kabeer 2011). Thirteen years later the UN (2013a) reported on the progress that has been made towards eradication of extreme poverty; however, it noted that the economic and financial crisis, which in many ways provided a pretext for a narrative which promoted austerity policies, has had a negative effect on this goal. It reported that one in eight people in the world still go to bed hungry, despite major progress. It pointed out that progress has not been evenly experienced across the world, with some parts including China, Indonesia and Malaysia making significant progress, while for other regions progress has been slow (UN 2013a).

It has been argued that the countries that pursued policies underpinned by the fundamental principles of social justice – fairness and equality – have taken bigger strides towards achieving the MDGs than those where there are a lot of injustices and inequalities. In particular, the countries that made improvements to socio-economic determinants including income inequalities, educational attainment, employment and power have seen greater achievements. Malaysia is being held up as a country in which far-reaching affirmative action policies with respect to education, land ownership, public service employment, and ownership of companies seemed to have worked (Kabeer 2011). Kabeer argues that its success stemmed from the simultaneous pursuit of both affirmative action and structural economic change (Kabeer 2011).

The evidence suggests that the countries that have been slow to promote egalitarian policy have poor outcomes compared to those that have fewer inequalities. South America (historically one of the most unequal regions in the world) provides a good example where inequalities in access to opportunities for human development have had an impact on progress towards poverty reduction. As Kabeer (2011) observed in Mexico, the poorest southern states (Chiapas, Oaxaca and Guerrero), which are home to around 75 per cent of the country's indigenous peoples, report far lower levels of education than the national average and far higher maternal mortality ratios.

Similarly, sub-Saharan Africa (SSA) has the highest rates of poverty in the world and is home to some of the most unequal countries in the world (Kabeer 2011; UN 2013a, 2013b). South Africa is reported to be one of the few countries in the region that is on track to meet most of the MDGs, but its average improvements mask deeply entrenched inequalities (Kabeer 2011). While poverty has fallen in the post-apartheid period, the decision by the ruling African National Congress (ANC) to adopt neoliberal policies created uneven distribution of social goods (Kabeer 2011). According to the World Health Organization (2014) the neoliberal framework adopted by South Africa in 1994 included:

- fiscal discipline – strict criteria for limiting budget deficits
- financial liberalization – interest rates should ideally be market determined
- increasing foreign direct investment (FDI) – by reducing barriers
- privatization – state enterprises should be privatized
- deregulation – abolition of regulations that impede the entry of new firms or restrict competition (except in the areas of safety, environment and finance)
- a reduced role for the state.

The post-apartheid neoliberal policies provided a narrative that explained the current crisis of South African capitalism, characterized by high unemployment (particularly youth unemployment), high wages, declining standards in state primary and secondary education, increased demand for private primary and secondary education, a decline in standards in government health facilities, increased demand for private health care, and low productivity (Mbeki 2009). The root cause of this crisis can be traced to a compromise deal reached between Black upper ruling classes and capitalist forces in the Congress for Democratic South Africa II (CODESA II), whereby the black elite caved in to the capitalist forces' promise of payment for protection of multinational corporations (Mbeki 2009). This deal led to the aggressive preservation and promotion of the free market, alongside the stripping out of states' ability to provide social protection to the large poor black underclass (Mbeki 2009).

The impact the CODESA II transformation continues to have on other key social determinants of health inequalities is in many cases dramatic. For example, according to Hodgson (2012) the Euromonitor international analyst, South Africa has the most unequal income distribution in the world with a Gini Index of 63.6 per cent in 2011. Privatization and tendering of the main utilities (water, gas, roads construction, telecommunications and electricity) and state enterprises (such as South African Rail) are believed to have reduced the state's power to provide social protection and tackle growing unemployment. According to Statistics South Africa (2013), the unemployment rate in the country was 24.1 per cent in the fourth quarter of 2013.

In this aggressive pursuit of free market competition, it is the poorest (predominantly black) classes who bear the greatest burden. Regrettably, this ideology attracts no challenge from the Democratic Alliances (DA), the South African official opposition party, whose criticism is mainly of corruption. Admittedly, corruption has had a great impact on the distribution of privileges in South Africa. However, it largely explains the ideology described by Mbeki as 'reparation ideology – whereby the black elites who see themselves as previously disadvantaged individuals (PDI) see their mission as extracting reparations from those who put them in a disadvantaged position' (Mbeki 2009: 69). It also explains the relationship between the state and black elites, who use their previous disadvantaged status to justify using the state to advance their material interests rather than to serve the needs of the people. All this is done under the disguise of Black Economic Empowerment (BEE), a scheme whereby leaders of the black resistance movement were bought off with what looked like a transfer to them of massive assets at no cost. This legitimized multinational corporations' payments to black politicians; dangling BEE before the black underclasses keeps them hoping that one day they too will receive a fairer share of South African wealth.

Thinking point

Thandiwe is 58 years old and has lived in one of the squatter camps in Johannesburg for the past 30 years. She is talking to her local council, expressing her disappointment that after 19 years in power the ANC government has not been able to improve people's living environment. She cites jobs, education, housing and sanitation among many things that the ANC has not been able to deliver. She explains that education and job opportunities have in fact got worse since the ANC came into power. The local council member glibly replies: 'This is new South Africa: choices have never been wider, you are free to do whatever you want, you can do the job you choose, you can choose which school you want to send your children to. What is stopping you?'

This reflects the different views of those who believe it is the role of the state to influence the distribution of social goods and those who believe in free choice. What are your views?

Conclusion

The chapter has critically reviewed the literature, unearthing several dimensions of social justice including philosophical, political, ethical and socio-economic dimensions. The political dimension is that public health policy, in order to fulfil its mission to protect and improve the public's health, must attend more forcefully to issues of health inequalities and their root causes in social and economic inequalities. Social justice involves changing society so that claims for freedom, equality and democracy receive adequate expression, and so that the politics by which people pursue these goals gain acceptance as being normal rather than exceptional and suspect.

The socio-economic dimension of social justice is based on recognition that while there are multiple causal pathways to numerous types of disadvantage, of particular concern for social justice are poverty, substandard housing, poor education, unhygienic and polluted environments, and disintegration.

The ethical dimension is rooted in fairness and equality, two key attributes of social justice. It is based upon recognition that not all social groups are treated equally in a society. It stresses the fair disbursement of common advantages and the sharing of common burdens, and demands an equitable distribution of collective goods, institutional resources and life opportunities.

References

Almgren, G. (2007) *Health Care Politics, Policy and Services: A Social Justice Analysis*. New York: Springer.

Bayer, R., Beauchamp, D.E., Gostin, L.O. and Jennings, B. (2007) *Public Health Ethics*. Oxford: Oxford University Press.

Beauchamp, D.E. (1975) Public health: Alien ethics in a strange land? *American Journal of Public Health*, 65(12): 1338–9.

Beauchamp, D.E. (2003) Public health as social justice, in R. Hofrichter (ed.) *Health and Social Justice: Politics, Ideology and Inequality in the Distribution of Disease*. San Francisco, CA: Jossey-Bass.

Bingham, J. and Dominiczak, P. (2014) *Cutting Benefits Part of a 'Moral Mission', Cameron Tells New Cardinal*. Available at www.telegraph.co.uk/news/politics/david-cameron/10647538/Cutting-benefits-part-of-a-moral-mission-Cameron-tells-new-Cardinal.html (accessed 21 Mar. 2014).

Child Poverty Action Group (2013) *Child Poverty Facts and Figures*. Available at www.cpag.org.uk/child-poverty-facts-and-figures (accessed 4 Mar 2014).

Cutler, T. and Waine, B. (2013) But is it 'fair'? The UK Coalition government, 'fairness' and the 'reform' of public sector pensions, *Social Policy & Administration*, 47(3): 327–45.

Daniels, N., Kennedy, B. and Kawachi, I. (2004) Justice and health inequalities, in A. Sudhir, F. Peter, A.K. Sen and A. Sen (eds) *Public Health, Ethics and Equity*. Oxford: Oxford University Press.

Daniels, N., Kennedy, B. and Kawachi, I. (2007) Why justice is good for our health: determinants of health inequalities, in R. Bayer, D. Beaucamp, L.O. Gostin and B. Jennings (eds) *Public Health Ethics*. Oxford: Oxford University Press.

Department of Health (DH) (1997) *The New NHS: Modern, Dependable*. London: DH.

Department of Health (DH) (2010a) *Equity and Excellence: Liberating the NHS*. Available at www.dh.gov.uk/prod_consum_dh/groups/dh_digitalassets/@dh/@en/@ps/documents/digitalasset/dh_117794.pdf (accessed 15 Apr. 2011).

Department of Health (DH) (2010b) *Healthy Lives, Healthy People: Our Strategy for Public Health in England*. Available at www.dh.gov.uk/prod_consum_dh/groups/dh_digitalassets/documents/digitalasset/dh_124040.pdf (accessed 31 Nov. 2010).

Gostin, L.O. and Powers, M. (2006) What does social justice require for public's health? Public health ethics and policy imperatives, *Health Affairs*, 25(4): 1053–60.

Gwatkin, D.R. (2000) Health inqualities and the health of the poor: what do we know? What can we do? *Bulletin of the World Health Organization*, 78(1): 3–7.

Hodgson, A. (2012) *Income Inequality Rising across the Globe*. Available at http://blog.euromonitor.com/2012/03/special-report-income-inequality-rising-across-the-globe.html (accessed 21 Mar. 2014).

HM Government. (2010) *The Coalition: Our Programme for Government*. London: HM Government.

Hofrichter, R. (2003) *Health and Social Justice: Politics, Ideology, and Inequity in the Distribution of Disease*. San Francisco, CA: Jossey-Bass.

Hofrichter, R. (ed.) (2006) *Tackling Health Inequities Through Public Health Practice: A Handbook for Action*. Battle Creek, MI: W.K. Kellogg Foundation.

Jacobs, M. (2014) *The Coalition Government is Proving as Ideologically Radical as Those of Thatcher and Attlee*. Available at http://blogs.lse.ac.uk/politicsandpolicy/archives/33399 (accessed 21 Mar. 2014).

Kabeer, N. (2011) *MDGs, Social Justice and the Challenge of Intersecting Inequalities. Policy Brief*. Available to www.soas.ac.uk/cdpr/publications/pb/file66938.pdf (accessed 11 Mar. 2014).

Kass, N.E. (2001) An ethics framework for public health, *American Journal of Public Health*, 91(11): 1776–82.

Kawachi, I., Kennedy, B.P., Lochner, K. and Prothrow-Stith, D. (1997) Social capital, income inequality, and mortality, *American Journal of Public Health*, 87(9): 1491–8.

Krieger, N. (2011) *Epidemiology and the People's Health: Theory and Context*. New York: Oxford University Press.

Krieger, N. and Bassett, M. (1993) *The Health of Black Folk: Disease, Class and Ideology in Science*. Bloomington, IN: Indiana University Press.

Krieger, N. and Birn, A.E. (1998) A vision of social justice as the foundation of public health: commemorating 150 years of the Spirit of 1848, *American Journal Public Health*, 88(11), 1603–6.

Labour Party (1997) *Ambitions for Britain – 2001 Manifesto*. London: Labour Party.

Mackenbach, J.P. and Bakker, M. (2003) *Reducing Inequalities in Health: A European Perspective*. London: Routledge.

Mackenbach, J.P., Bos, V., Andererson, O., *et al.* (2003) Widening socioeconomic inequalities in mortality in six Western European countries, *International Journal of Epidemiology*, 32(5): 830–7. Available at http://ije.oxfordjournals.org/content/32/5/830.full.pdf+html (accessed Oct. 2009).

Marmot, M. (2004) Tackling health inequalities since the Acheson Inquiry, *Journal of Epidemiology Community Health*, 58(4): 262–3.

Marmot, M. (2005) Social determinants of health inequalities, *Lancet*, 365(9464): 1099–104.

Marmot, M. (2007) Achieving health equity: from root causes to fair outcomes, *Lancet*, 6736(370): 1153–63.

Marmot, M. (2009) Closing the health gap in a generation: the work of the Commission on Social Determinants of Health and its recommendations, *Global Health Promotion*, 16(23): 23–7.

Marmot, M. (2010) *Fair Society, Healthy Lives: Strategic Review of Health Inequalities in England post-2010*. Available at at www.instituteofhealthequity.org/Content/FileManager/pdf/fairsocietyhealthylives.pdf (accessed 12 Dec. 2010).

Marmot, M. (2011) *Social Determinants of Health – What Doctors Can Do*. Available at http://www.google.co.uk/url?sa=t&rct=j&q=people%20do%20not%20want%20health%20because%20it%20gives%20them%20jobs%20they%20want%20health%2C%20marmot%20&source=web&cd=5&ved=0CEAQFjAE&url=http%3A%2F%2Fbma.org.uk%2F-%2Fmedia%2FFiles%2FPDFs%2FWorking%2520for%2520change%2FImproving%2520health%2Fsocialdeterminantshealth.pdf&ei=bn4LUoDhFsnKhAfwy4DADg&usg=AFQjCNFcEGJEywCN7nMo1OxrX9c0_maamA (accessed 14 Aug. 2013).

Mbeki, M. (2009) *Architects of Poverty: Why Africa Capitalism need Changing*. Johannesburg: Picador Africa.

Miscampbell, G. (2014) *Smarter Sanctions: Sorting Out the System*. London: Policy Exchange.

Peter, F. (2004) Health equity and social justice, in A. Sudhir, F. Peter, A.K. Sen and A. Sen (eds) *Public Health, Ethics and Equity*. Oxford: Oxford University Press.

Powell, M., Johns, N. and Green, A. (2012) *Social Justice in Social Policy*. Available at www.social-policy.org.uk/lincoln2011/PowellJohnsGreen%20P7.pdf (accessed 25 Apr. 2014).

Powers, M. and Faden, R. (2006) *Social Justice: The Foundations of Public Health and Health Policy*. Oxford: Oxford University Press.

Rawls, J. (1971) *A Theory of Justice*. Cambridge: Harvard University Press.

Rose, G. (1992) *The Strategy of Preventive Medicine*. Oxford: Oxford University Press.

Royston, S. (2013) *Bishops' Letter Highlights Severe Cuts in Benefit Up-Rating Bill*. Available at www.childrenssociety.org.uk/news-views/our-blog/bishops-letter-highlights-severe-cuts-benefit-rating-bill (accessed 4 Mar. 2014).

Ruger, P.J. (2004) Health and social justice, *The Lancet Public Health*, 364(18): 1075–80.

Scott-Samuel, A., Bambra, C., Collins, C., Hunter, D.J., McCartney, G. and Smith, K. (2014) The impact of Thatcherism on health and well-being in Britain, *International Journal of Health Services*, 44(1): 53–71.

Statistics South Africa (2013) *Quarterly Labour Force Survey: Quarter 4, 2013*. Pretoria: Statistics South Africa.

Sudhir, A., Peter, F., Sen, A.K. and Sen, A. (2004) *Public Health, Ethics, and Equity*. Oxford: Oxford University Press.

The Children's Society (2013) Letter from 43 bishops, in The Children's Society (ed.) *Letter*. London: The Children's Society.

UK Health Watch (2005) *The Experience of Health in an Unequal Society*. Available at www.pohg.org.uk/support/publications.html (accessed 23 Mar. 2006).

United Nations (UN) (2000) *The Millennium Development Goals Eight Goals for 2015*. Available at www.undp.org/content/undp/en/home/mdgoverview.html (accessed 1 Mar. 2014).

United Nations (UN) (2013a) *The Millennium Development Goals Report 2013*. New York: United Nations.

United Nations (UN) (2013b) *World Day for Social Justice: UN Urges Action to End Poverty, Overcome Inequality*. Available at www.un.org/apps/news/story.asp?NewsID=47180&Cr= Inequality&Cr1 (accessed 11 Mar. 2014).

United Nations General Assembly (2010) *United Nations General Assembly Resolution 65/1: Keeping the Promise: United to Achieve the Millennium Development Goals*, Vol. 65/1, p. 51. New York: United Nations General Assembly.

World Health Organization (WHO) (2014) *Trade, Foreign Policy, Diplomacy and Health*. Available at www.who.int/trade/glossary/story094/en/ (accessed 13 Mar. 2014).

7 | Environmental and external influences on health and well-being

Alan Massey

Introduction

The chapter considers the wider determinants of health, including the natural and built environments and other external factors influencing the health and well-being of individuals, communities and populations.

Pruss-Ustan and Corvalan (2006) define the environment in relation to health and well-being as all physical, chemical and biological factors external to a person and all the related behaviours which arise in response to those factors. It is prudent to think of environments as ecosystems. An ecosystem is a community of living organisms (for example plants and animals), as well as non-living components (such as air, soil and buildings), which interact to form a system. All organisms depend on their environment for the basic resources for life (for example clean water and nutritious food). Increased access to these resources, coupled with awareness of factors which cause or promote disease and their removal from or reduction within environments in which humans exist, has led to significant improvements in health. Similar improvements have followed changes in sociological factors such as the provision of suitable housing, the introduction of less hazardous processes in the workplace, and the reduction of poverty. However, the process of accessing resources conducive to health and well-being can have negative effects on the ecosystems on which we depend. For example, food production causes damage to arable land owing to the use of pesticides and other chemicals, and air quality is reduced owing to pollution. The relationship between human development and the use of environmental resources generates great debate of ethical, legal and social issues, due to the need to ensure sustainability of those resources. According to the World Health Organization (2014a) the major environmental factors requiring action are:

- air quality (indoor and outdoor)
- surface and ground water quality
- toxic substances and hazardous wastes (indoor and outdoor)
- homes and communities
- infrastructure and surveillance
- global environmental health.

In terms of global health, we can see two distinct lines of enquiry. In the developing world, the necessity to address the traditional environmental threats to health remains paramount. Within the developed world, where many of the traditional environmental threats have been mitigated through management, evidence is emerging of the need to consider other threats, including psychosocial environmental influences. When considering the management of environments, we also must consider the impact of human activity on the manageable use of the planet's resources. This last point is evidenced by the continuing increase in the human population: by 2050 the world's population will reach 9 billion people. This will inevitably lead to increased demand for resources. Increases in land and water use, pollution due to industrialization in the developing world, and greenhouse gases coupled with changing weather patterns, together mean that global environmental sustainability becomes of paramount importance (WHO 2014a).

Environmental sustainability offers opportunities to research conditions which influence our well-being. It can offer insight into the yet poorly understood interaction between humans and their environment, and how humans are influenced at biological, physiological and psychological levels. Similarly, the impact of environmental cultures on human health requires greater understanding (Hall and Lamont 2009). Within this chapter we shall explore the built, rural and natural environments and their impact on health, the impact that specific settings have on human health and well-being, and the WHO's attempts at health promotion via the settings agenda. We shall also examine the role of specific institutions in the creation of cultures conducive to health, and finally explore the impact of environmental factors on sustainable health improvement.

Access to environmental resources and adverse health effects

Natural, rural and built ecosystems are important to health as they provide the basic resources we need in order to exist. All ecosystems not only affect our physical health; they are also important as they structure our experience of daily life and consequently how we feel about ourselves. It is for this reason that well-being must be considered when exploring the effects of the environment on health. The balance we achieve in the daily search for resources is set within a context which can erode or nourish us physically and mentally.

The balance of ecosystems is changing, leading to the depletion of some basic resources. We shall focus on two ecosystems: rural and urban. These have been chosen to illustrate trends in human habitation and their effect on health and well-being.

During the past century, there has been a shift from people predominantly inhabiting rural ecosystems to predominantly inhabiting urban ecosystems; by 2050 it is estimated that seven out of ten people will live in urban ecosystems, as opposed to the two out of ten who lived there 100 years ago. The United Nations indicates that at present the move to urbanization is dominated by city living. Currently, 468 cities around the globe (known as megacities) have 10 million inhabitants or more. This migration towards urban living is set to continue, particularly in developing countries, and has had a significant impact on health with a

50 per cent reduction in the number of people living in extreme poverty in the last decade alone (UNEP 2012). However, large-scale migration will create difficulties for the developing world, such as access to health care and appropriate housing, disease caused by communal living and unsanitary conditions, and access to resources for healthy living such as clean water and nutritious food. For example, at present 1 billion people in the developing world live in urban slums, and this will rise to 2 billion by 2030 (United Nations Population Fund 2007a).

Both urban and rural ecosystems influence our health in several ways. The following three examples illustrate the effect of living in differing ecosystems but are by no means a comprehensive list.

The physical environment

In urban areas, outdoor facilities for exercise and recreation can be scarce or difficult to access for many residents. Air quality is poorer leading to a rise in chronic diseases associated with pollution, for example, asthma and coronary heart disease. Housing can be substandard, leading to increases in infectious diseases.

In rural areas residents, particularly women, fare worse in the major lifestyle indicators than their urban counterparts. They consume tobacco and alcohol in greater quantities, exercise less and have less nutritious diets (Winters 2013). Rural residents lack access to built facilities such as gyms, street lighting and pavements, making exercise difficult. However, they enjoy fresher food, cleaner air and less crime.

The social environment

In urban areas there may be large disparities in socio-economic position, higher rates of physical violence and crime, and psychological stressors associated with increased density. Population density is also responsible for increased accident rates and an increase in mental health issues.

By contrast, in rural areas residents can expect long-lasting and more meaningful social networks, community affiliation and shared life experiences with community self-help and reciprocity (United Nations Population Fund 2007b).

Access to health care

In urban systems people have increased access to health-care facilities. However, the socially disadvantaged are likely to face barriers to accessing state or privately funded health services. Many will be without health insurance due to insufficient contributions made to taxation systems. This means that they access emergency services when necessary and do not engage in preventative health-care services.

Rural residents may have restricted access to health care, particularly in the developing world where people are geographically remote from health-care provision. They, like their socio-economic counterparts in the cities, are likely to be uninsured and attended to by less able practitioners (Winters 2013).

For the developing world, the trend for migration towards urban living will create difficulties in providing the resources needed for health and well-being, inevitably leading to negative health consequences. For example, 1.8 billion people lack access to safe drinking water, leading to approximately 2 million deaths per year from diarrhoea alone. The greatest burden is currently felt by the newborn, young children and the elderly. In addition, 2.6 billion people do not have access to effective sanitation (United Nations Population Fund 2007b). Similarly, human existence exposes us to considerable levels of background radiation, most markedly from the sun. Background radiation exposure is also contributed to by 'Naturally Occurring Radioactive Material (NORM)' originating from soil, air and water (Tillman 2007: 367), and therefore found within the food and drink that the population consumes. Furthermore, the global population is exposed daily to background radiation resulting from nuclear catastrophes and war (Tillman 2007).

Consequently, the incessant search for resources for living is leading to an increase in environmental risk factors for disease, particularly:

* pollution
* microbes in air, water and soil
* contaminants in food
* weather conditions (droughts, heatwaves)
* natural disasters (earthquakes, floods)
* pesticides
* pests and parasites
* radiation
* poverty
* lack of access to health care.

As we can see, environmental health not only creates opportunities to improve health, but also to reduce or increase social injustice as poor environmental quality affects the most vulnerable in society, such as the young and those whose health status is already compromised.

Thinking point

Ecosystem management is important within the health and well-being agenda as there is a requirement to ensure the equitable and sustainable use of resources to create health. In your opinion, how do you feel the need for economic sustainability can be merged with the need for environmental sustainability?

Evidence of influence

One challenge facing planners is our restricted knowledge of environmental effects on health. The following environmental factors are examples where we have sound evidence of effect (Healthy People 2020 2013):

* exposure to hazardous substances in the air, water, soil, and food
* physical, biological and psychosocial hazards
* nutritional deficiencies
* the built environment.

For example, the case for the harmful effects of air, water and soil pollution has been clearly made. Similarly, evidence outlining the effect of socio-economic factors on health is strong. Our scientific understanding of how the drain on environmental resources is influencing the balance within ecosystems is far more contentious, as is our understanding of how ecosystems affect well-being. In examining these latter elements in detail, factors such as societal structures, the role of state institutions and human flourishing (eudemonic factors), as well as factors which make life pleasant (hedonic factors), need to be considered.

Exploration of these elements has occurred throughout history and at present is a thriving area of social research. Concepts such as social capital, addressing health inequalities and the effect of material factors on well-being have increased our understanding of the impact of some of the determinants of health, such as economic influences and the socio-economic gradient of health (Hall and Lamont 2009). In terms of biological responses to environmental determinants, Hall and Lamont indicate that there are three productive areas of research. First, how the stress response system affects biological health, where the over-release of hormones such as cortisol has a negative long-term health effect. Secondly, the serotonergic system, which plays a role in generating positive emotions associated with social interactions or negative emotions linked with the lack of social relations; this area of research is dominated by pharmacological treatments for conditions such as depression. Finally, development of the brain, particularly in early childhood and adolescence, is known to play a role in our reflective consciousness, which structures thoughts around our sense of perceived purpose, meaning and identity (Hall and Lamont 2009).

However, the same cannot be said about our understanding of sociological explanations of health and how relational factors influence health and well-being, which rely on a poorly understood mechanism (Hall and Lamont 2009). Research into relational factors is required as there is growing awareness that the socio-economic explanation of the evident health gradient between social classes is only part of a wider picture. The idea that wealth equals health is now being challenged because addressing health inequalities, access to health services and differences in health behaviours deals only with a minority of the issues (Hall and Lamont 2009). Wealth does affect health, though paradoxically for many individuals wealth does not equal improved quality of life. For example, if socio-economic factors were the dominant element in the health gradient, then the more affluent countries would experience the best health. However, in certain wealthy societies health outcomes mirror those of less affluent countries. The USA is a classic example of this anomaly. Citizens of the USA, one of the most affluent countries in the world, do not enjoy the best health in the world as one might expect. Male citizens of the USA on average spend $8608 per year on healthcare. In Cuba an average male will spend $430 on theirs, and yet these two countries evidence the same life expectancy (WHO 2014a).

Evidence is emerging that the relational environment is just as important as economic factors. One example of research in this area has been encapsulated within *The Spirit Level* (Wilkinson and Pickett 2009). Exploring the effect of income inequality, *The Spirit Level* argues that a wide range of health and social-care problems are attributable to national equity, that is, the gap between rich and poor. Where there is a significant gap there is an erosion of societal trust, which leads to increased anxiety and encourages unhealthy consumption amongst the disadvantaged, in turn leading to illness and disease. The work concludes that those countries which do the best for their citizens are those with narrow income differences. In terms of affluence the book raises interesting questions, revealing that above a certain threshold increased material wealth does not significantly improve health. These findings are contentious and the study's methodological rigour has been questioned in some quarters. However, there is a growing body of evidence to suggest income inequality affects health negatively, and little evidence to suggest the opposite effect (Rowlingson 2011).

We have identified in earlier chapters that an individual's health and well-being can be eroded by the daily struggle to attain the basic resources for health. Research is beginning to indicate that this is also true of a person's social resources. The daily struggle to find psychological resources for health, including our symbolic representation, also influences our well-being (Hall and Lamont 2009); research into symbolic representation highlights the important role of social relations within communities, environments and settings in which people reside and work. This includes the strength of social relations, the trust individuals have in others, and social position. All these factors are important in creating social resources to manage challenges to our well-being, and to combat the erosion of health. In the past few decades, the neoliberal agenda has changed the role of social relations and, in particular, the role of state institutions in the development of symbolic representation. The move from paternal liberalism (where choice is offered and the state intervenes when it feels inappropriate choices are being made) to liberal paternalism (individuals have more choice with the state only intervening as a last resort), has seen a rise in personal responsibility for health (Department of Health 2010). Symbolic representation has been engulfed in the risk agenda, leading to cultures where human identity is viewed as secondary to the creation of wealth, goods and production (MacEachen 2000). However, liberal paternalism does offer the prospect of proactive environmental architecture; governments can create social resources for health or they can remove them. The traditional mechanism of providing greater access to health care and of changing health behaviours has addressed some key health inequalities. However, more needs to be done to address physical and mental well-being by primary prevention methods, focusing environments and communities towards health enhancement in order to ameliorate the erosion of health and well-being (Hall and Lamont 2009).

Newton (2007), as part of her work for the Well-being in Developing Countries research group, reviewed the evidence surrounding the influence of the natural environment and its effects on both objective and subjective measures of well-being. Newton notes that research – much of it linked to issues of mental health and well-being – has been undertaken on the effects of providing green spaces in urban environments. There is a link between green environments and spatial variables, which are known to affect subjective measures of happiness (Brereton et al. 2008). Kellert et al. (2011), in their outline of the biophilia theory, indicate that humans evolved in a sensory-rich environment that was, and is, critically important to human health and well-being. Building on the work of Wilson (1984), this notion indicates that humans have an innate emotional affiliation with nature for its cognitive, aesthetic, intellectual and spiritual meanings, besides its role as a source of physical sustenance. The theory suggests that our identity and fulfilment as rational beings depends on our relationship with nature and the environment; for example, provision of communal spaces in urban environments is linked to improvements in social cohesion and mental well-being (Pretty *et al.* 2005). Interestingly, depletion of the natural environment is known to decrease happiness through factors such as decreased security, reduction of certainty and feelings of loss. Table 7.1 outlines how the natural environment influences health and well-being using the typology of biophilia values of Kellert *et al.*

Thinking point

The ideas discussed above raise some interesting questions. For example, why are some societies more effective than others in creating positive health outcomes via consideration of environmental and social factors? What is it about the cohesiveness of your own particular society that adds to or detracts from the health and well-being of your community?

Table 7.1 Kellert's typology of biophilia values

Term	Definition	Function
Utilitarian	Practical and material exploitation of nature	Physical sustenance/security
Naturalistic	Satisfaction from direct experience/contact with nature	Curiosity, outdoor skills, mental/physical development
Ecologistic-Scientific	Systematic study of structure, function and relationship in nature	Knowledge, understanding, observational skills
Aesthetic	Physical appeal and beauty of nature	Inspiration, harmony, peace, security
Symbolic	Use of nature for metaphorical expression, language, expressive thought	Communication, mental development
Humanistic	Strong affection, emotional attachment, 'love' for nature	Group bonding, sharing, cooperation, companionship
Moralistic	Strong affinity, spiritual reverence, ethical concern for nature	Order and meaning in life, kinship and affiliational ties
Dominionistic	Mastery, physical control, dominance of nature	Mechanical skills, physical prowess, ability to subdue
Negativistic	Fear, aversion, alienation from nature	Security, protection, safety

The development of the settings approach

In line with the concept offered by general systems theory – that the whole is greater than the sum of its parts – the settings approach has developed to deal with health and well-being via the interrelated systems that make up a setting in which people live, work and play (Scriven and Hodgins 2011). Systems-level thinking offers the promise that a coherent and integrated model can be developed to improve research, policy and knowledge in the complex field of health planning. The Ottawa Charter formalized the ideas to diminish reductionist health planning set out by the WHO in its Health for All strategy (1984), replacing it with a strategy based on the premise that 'health is created and lived by people within the settings of their everyday life; where they learn, work, play and love' (WHO 1986). The settings agenda is predominantly associated with the health promotion movement and incorporates principles such as community participation, partnership working, empowerment and social equity (WHO 2014a). For example, the Sundsvall Statement of 1992, the Jakarta Declaration 1997, the Bangkok Charter 2005 and the Nairobi Call for Action 2009 collectively endorse the need for the development of supportive environments for health (Scriven and Hodgins 2011). Settings such as cities, workplaces, hospitals, care institutions and schools currently utilize this approach to facilitate the improvement of public health throughout the world (WHO 2014b). The following example indicates how a setting such as the workplace can influence the environment and consequently health and well-being.

The WHO (2011) affirms that internationally almost 20 per cent of fatalities from cancer can be ascribed to radiation exposure within the living and working environment, which amounts to over a million deaths annually. Cancer Research United Kingdom (2012) has published global figures revealing that almost 13 million cancer diagnoses are registered each year, of which approximately 8 million result in fatalities. Moreover, occupational cancer remains the principal cause of work-related death among employees, both within the UK and globally (Global Occupational Health Network 2006; International Metalworkers Federation 2007). International estimates suggest that approximately 20 per cent of all atmospheric cancers are directly linked to the working environment, giving rise to almost 1.5 million employee fatalities annually (Hamalainen *et al.* 2007; WHO 2011). This equates to occupational cancer contributing to between 4 and 20 per cent of all cancer diagnoses within the global population (Boffetta and Kogevinas 1999; Nurminen and Karjalainen 2001; Barone-Adesi *et al.* 2005; Global Occupational Health Network 2006; Health and Safety Executive 2012; Trades Union Congress 2012). However, there is significant recognition that employment is beneficial to health; it is an intricate and essential aspect of human existence that enables individuals to extract not only income, but also a sense of social inclusion that increases self-esteem (Yuill and McMillian 1998; Brown and Trevino 2006; Waddell and Burton 2006).

The underpinning philosophy of the settings approach is that the culture of a setting is built around environmental systems which are inclusive, synergistic and targeted towards the health and well-being of people in these settings (Green and

Tones 2010). Consequently, to create positive well-being outcomes, planners need to shape not only the physical environment, but also social and cultural environments. This should be done by careful analysis and utilization of systems within a setting or organization, to ensure that either the setting or organization adopts a holistic approach to promoting health. This philosophy is based on an ecological, not a reductionist, perspective. The ecological model moves us away from the dominance of personal risk and health behaviourism, to a focus on the interaction between man and the subsystems of the ecosystem (Green and Tones 2010). The ecological model lends itself to issues of well-being as it moves beyond the simplistic notion of disease and health risk factors, instead accepting that people are not victims of their own behaviours and that people's behaviours are shaped via complex environmental influences (Scriven and Hodgins 2011).

The work of Bronfenbrenner (Bronfenbrenner and Ceci 1994) is important in the development of this view. He postulates that analysis of social and cultural environments should take place together with understanding of people's personal attributes and the complexity of their situations over time. This analysis can be achieved via exploration of the multiple layers – Bronfenbrenner called them the micro, meso, exo and macro systems – within which people exist. His work focused on human development, but can be utilized in a number of ways and has interesting areas of synthesis when applied to exploring health and well-being.

A micro system is the one closest to an individual and contains the elements that an individual has direct contact with; these elements have the greatest influence on us and are bidirectional. This system is fundamental in shaping our views around structure and agency, and contains, for example, our family and peers. The meso level moves us beyond bidirectional influences by connecting the systems which form the structure of our environment, and is based on communication channels and relationships within our environment – for example, the connection between home and workplace. The exo level defines the larger social system in which people live. This influences our socialization, but not via direct contact; for instance, by community laws and regulations. Finally, the macro system contains the cultures, values and customs of a system. According to Hall and Lamont (2009), culture and ethics exercised within settings provide useful explanations of why some communities have better health outcomes than others, irrespective of affluence.

Thinking point

Dahlgren and Whitehead's (1991) rainbow model of health (see Figure 7.1) is an example of a Bronfenbrenner-style analysis. Can you reflect on the influences on your well-being within your own environment using a layered model?

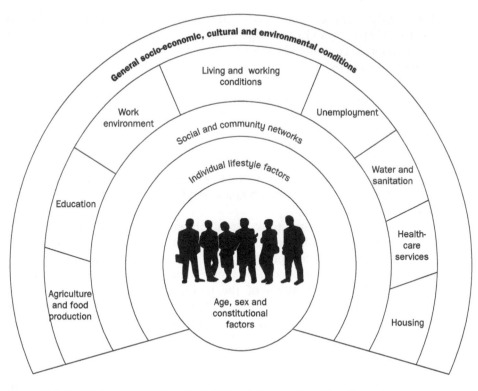

Figure 7.1 Dahlgren and Whitehead's (1991) rainbow model of health

Source: www.healthknowledge.org.uk

Why address settings for health?

The settings approach can be applied in a variety of environments ranging from cities, towns and villages to single institutions such as care homes, schools and workplaces. Its fundamental advantage is that it offers points of access to communities requiring primary prevention, and to individuals who may not regularly engage with health education or health services (Dooris 2011). The settings approach is an excellent mechanism to enable practitioners to achieve the five domains for action set out by the WHO within the Ottawa Charter. According to the WHO (2014b) it:

- focuses attention on where health is promoted and sustained
- sets easily recognized boundaries for action
- easily identifies potential partners
- provides opportunities to observe and measure the impact of interventions for health gain
- offers excellent potential, both for pilot testing and as a vehicle for sustainable change in society.

Green and Tones (2010) indicate that the settings model has to address some key issues if it is to become widely accepted. For example, no two settings are the same, and transfer of successful elements from one setting to another is difficult. The realization of shared goals and visions within settings can be problematic; the scale of some settings means that the ideals set out in the Ottawa Charter are difficult to realize, leading to disillusionment. Settings for health can actually increase health inequalities rather than reduce them. Partnership working and the exercise of collective power can be difficult due to vested interests. Owing to misunderstanding of conceptual drivers, the settings approach has led to a rebranding of personalized health education. Finally, many practitioners do not have the practical skills to implement the models and principles of the settings approach.

To address these issues various implementations of the settings approach have emerged (Dooris 2011: 21):

- The 'passive' model, where the problems and solutions rest within the voluntary control of the individual. The setting itself is secondary. An example is health education within schools, where the school provides the opportunity to reach groups of young people to teach them about keeping healthy.
- The 'active' model, where part of the problem lies with the individual and part with the setting, and the behaviour of individuals can be influenced by the setting. For example, infection control in hospitals requires regular hand washing by staff. This is supplemented by education and via environmental action through provision of improved washing facilities, and introduction of policies and staff training.
- The 'vehicle' model, based on an understanding that the problem and the solution lie within the setting, but that the path to change involves taking incremental steps on specific topics. The vehicle for change is the topic-focused initiative, but the setting rather than the individual needs to be the focus for change. An example is weight reduction programmes for sedentary workers: here education is offered while the organization restructures its welfare facilities (food, exercise and job rotation systems).
- The 'organic' model, which places emphasis on the role of individuals within the organization in changing the system in the longer term. The problem is within the system and the solution lies in changing processes and structures; for example, facilitating and strengthening community action. This method resembles the community development model and has at its heart quality improvement methods.
- The 'comprehensive' model, which aims to make changes to structure and processes within the organization, but considers that these are not largely within the control of individual staff as in the organic model. Examples include the development of healthy policies and enacting changes to systems.

This typology of healthy settings practices demonstrates that the settings approach moves beyond the premise that a workplace, school or care setting is where health promotion work can take place, to the premise that understanding the social, economic, environmental, organizational and cultural contexts is necessary to influence health and well-being (Dooris 2011).

The role of institutions in well-being

The word 'institution' can be defined in several ways, though for our purposes we use a sociological perspective. An institution is any structure or instrument of social order which shapes the behaviour of a community. Institutions have a social purpose, structuring individual activity by organizing the rules that govern behaviour (Giddens 2013). Before considering how institutions can affect health, it is prudent to briefly review the development of sociological theories describing how social institutions affect health. Here the influential work of Durkheim, Marx and Weber will be briefly outlined.

Emile Durkheim is considered the founding father of sociology, owing to his belief that sociology was a distinct form of research and should study phenomena attributable to society at large rather than via specific actions of individuals (Calhoun *et al.* 2012). Durkheim analysed how societies were being restructured in the modern age to address the loss of traditional and religious constructions of society. He viewed societies as comprising interrelated institutions, joined by personal relations and collective consciousness, and utilized the phrase 'institutions' to highlight that collective beliefs and modes of behaviour are evidenced by collective action. The concept of collective action is important for health as it provides our sense of self, and with community support as well as the capacity for emotional support (Hall and Lamont 2009).

Karl Marx and Max Weber approached sociology from a different perspective, as both were primarily political and economic commentators whose research assigned more weight to the role of individuals in society, social class structures and the oppressive elements of social structures (Calhoun *et al.* 2012). Weber highlighted how economics sought solutions to social problems and that social authority could be exercised over people through state institutions. This perpetuates the dominance of social class structures as well as material advantage. These concepts affect our health via how socially connected we feel and by our status in societal hierarchies (Calhoun *et al.* 2012). Marx highlighted how individuals' health is influenced by their social position; in particular by social class, status and the exercise of power. These theories highlight how social resources such as status and collective consciousness are influential in terms of individuals' sense of well-being.

As an example of how institutions can shape the behaviours of individuals, I shall focus on workplaces as a setting for health. Adults in employment spend approximately one-third of their lives in the workplace (Rogers 2002), so it has the potential to shape our health significantly. Work is seen as a central activity for humans in constructing feelings of self-worth, self-identity and self-efficacy. People can have instrumental or affective attitudes to work. People with an affective attitude view it as a means to an end: it is important in accessing the resources required for a healthy lifestyle (such as food and recreation), but in itself work carries little or no intrinsic value. People with an instrumental outlook see work as rewarding for its own sake, and would continue to work irrespective of other considerations such as financial gain. As well as meeting our psychological needs, however, the workplace as an environment can be detrimental to health. The workplace has four distinct environmental threats to health – physical, chemical, biological and psychological (Rogers 2002). According to Johada and Rush (1980), on a psychological level people have an inherent need for collective ventures, in order to feel useful and have a sense of belonging. These, together with a need for time structure, and social contact, identity and status, are essential elements for us to feel a sense of well-being.

Case study

A female, 45 years old, attended a sickness absence clinic for a review appointment after being off work for almost six months. The client, who has a partner and two adolescent daughters in secondary education, worked full-time as a health-care assistant on a busy surgical ward within a large National Health Service Trust, and has been in her employment role for ten years. She intentionally worked day shifts, so that she would be available for her daughters when they returned home from school. She stated that she enjoyed her employment role, and had previously demonstrated a good attendance record. The client's sickness absence emerged in the form of stress, anxiety and depression when she developed problems within her personal life, and found the subsequent stress of finding a work–life balance was too much to bear. The client had a long history of depression and self-harm, which she has experienced since adolescence, and during the course of her absence she had also been diagnosed with chronic fatigue syndrome. The client stated that she has no friends, and although she expressed that she had a good professional relationship with her work colleagues she did not socialize with them outside work. This sense of isolation was compounded by the fact that during the course of her six-month sickness absence, neither her manager nor work colleagues had contacted her to see how she was doing. Utilizing the healthy settings typology, can you judge which approach would be best suited to dealing with this case study? How might you go about improving the physical and psychosocial environments for this client?

Healthy workplaces

Hancock (2011), in her review of healthy workplace initiatives, identifies a compelling need for the developed world to take proactive steps to improve the health of an ageing workforce at risk from chronic disease. Evidence is emerging that workplaces as institutions for health and well-being need to take the following steps, for economic, social and ethical reasons:

- Monitor the health status of the workforce and identify the environmental, biological, social and cultural risks to health.
- Create healthy workplaces, which drive healthy behaviours, based on shared ownership of health and well-being outcomes.
- Design comprehensive health-care systems, based on the public health model, which drive healthy behaviours.
- Implement strategic health and well-being programmes.

Hancock also indicates that in the developing world, workplaces not only need to address the primary environmental threats to health (physical, chemical, biological and psychological), but also the trend away from communicable diseases and towards non-communicable diseases. For example, the WHO (2014b) indicates that currently 13 million people a year are diagnosed with cancer, and predicts this will rise to 24 million by 2035, as the global population increases and people in the developing world start to be afflicted in greater numbers by non-communicable diseases. As we have seen, 50 per cent of all deaths in the developed world are attributed to lifestyle choices and are therefore modifiable. Workplaces in the developing world therefore need to ensure that they create cultures, environments and systems which deal with the four dominant lifestyle issues.

Emerging environmental threats to health and well-being

According to the United Nations Environment Programme (UNEP 2012), the need for global environmental stewardship has arrived simply because humans are fundamentally altering the planet and environmentally constructed changes to fragile ecosystems can no longer be ignored. Human activity has modified all the planet's ecosystems, such as the oceans, the land systems, freshwater systems and the atmosphere. Much of this has taken place at a chemical level, warming our atmosphere, harming our oceans, changing increasing areas of land to deserts and reducing access to freshwater supplies, which mean that maintaining access to basic resources for health will become increasingly difficult.

There is a pressing global need to improve our knowledge and understanding of these threats and how they interact, and to adopt proven solutions where possible. Evidence in these key areas is often contested and there is a clear need to reach consensus for action. Degradation of ecosystems threatens our health as it erodes the building blocks on which our health is built. As mentioned earlier, access to nutritious food and clean water is an obvious example of the problems faced. However, limited access means that in future people will have to relocate to areas where these resources exist, and this migration will increase civil instability between and within nation states (Myers 2009). Myers continues that global climate change means people will experience more frequent extremes of weather, such as heatwaves and excessive rains, increasing natural disasters and altered exposure to infectious diseases, owing to changes in the make-up and living habits of vectors, hosts and pathogens. For example, since 1980 the number of devastating natural disasters has doubled and this trend is forecast to continue (Myers 2009). As we have seen the earth's atmosphere is degrading, leading to increasing deaths from cancers, and heart and respiratory diseases, due to air pollution. Higher temperatures will further increase the amount of heart and respiratory diseases due to the formation of low level ozone clouds. Similarly, respiratory diseases such as asthma are increasing due to rising levels of carbon dioxide in our atmosphere (Myers 2009). As the developing nations eradicate many basic environmental threats to health, then rates of non-communicable diseases will increase. This will inevitably lead to a strain on access to health care.

The long-term implications of the changing chemistry of ecosystems means that efforts at ecosystem management must occur in several key areas to ensure sustainable consumption of the planet's resources. According to UNEP (2012) these key areas include:

- climate change
- exposure to infectious diseases
- water and food scarcity
- natural disasters and human conflicts
- population movement
- harmful substances and hazardous waste.

The simple fact that these issues are highly complex, have multi-causality and often have long latency periods has traditionally translated into inaction. One issue facing the world is that as ecosystems degrade, the developed world at present has the capacity to replace resources from geographically dispersed ecosystems. This leads to its insulation from the effects of environmental degradation in the developing world. The need for economic and social expansion in the developing world leads to issues of social injustice and eco-parochialism. However, the United Nations is seeking via its millennium goals and its post-2015 development framework to reach a consensus among all nations for action against what it describes as the biggest public health threat (UNEP 2012).

Myers (2009) concludes his report for the United Nations Foundation with a note of optimism. He indicates that the need to address the health impacts of global environmental change is upon us. However, as climate change is a threat magnifier it focuses increasing attention on environmental threats to health which have proven solutions and are mainly preventable. What is required is a change of attitudes on a global level, and greater cooperation across countries and sectors to work in partnership to address these issues. As such, it offers an opportunity to have one world and not a developing and a developed world.

Summary

Within this chapter we have identified that the environment has significant effects on health and well-being. The search for resources for health is leading to changes in ecosystems essential for our physical and psychological health and well-being. How our environment affects health is relatively well understood in terms of physically and sociologically constructed causes of disease. What is less clear is how our well-being is influenced by our relationship with the environments and settings in which we live, work and play. We have seen that all these factors require further research and careful management if we are to maintain the advances in human health achieved via management of the environments in which we exist. However, with this management comes the need for resource sustainability. If we are to continue to expand as a species, then we must understand in detail the effects of the environment on humans and the effect of humans on the environment.

References

Barone-Adesi, F., Richard, L. and Merletti, F. (2005) Population attributable risks for occupational cancer in Italy, *International Journal of Occupational and Environmental Health*, 11(1): 23–31.

Boffetta, P. and Kogevinas, M. (1999) Introduction: epidemiologic research and prevention of occupational cancer in Europe, *Environmental Health Perspectives*, 107(2): 229–31.

Brereton, F., Clinch, J.P. and Ferreira, S. (2008) Happiness, geography and the environment, *Ecological Economics*, 65(2): 386–96.

Bronfenbrenner, U. and Ceci, S.J. (1994) Nature-nurture reconceptualized in developmental perspective: a biological model, *Psychological Review*, 101(4): 568–86.

Brown, M. and Trevino, L. (2006) Ethical leadership: a review and future directions, *Leadership Quarterly*, 17: 595–616.

Calhoun, C., Gerteis J. and Moody, J. (2012) *Contemporary Sociological Theory*. London: Wiley.

Cancer Research United Kingdom (2012) *Cancer Incidence Statistics*. Available at www.cancer-researchuk.org/cancerinfo/cancerstats/incidence (accessed Dec. 2013)).

Dahlgren, G. and Whitehead, M. (1991) *Policies and Strategies to Promote Social Equity in Health*. Stockholm: Institute for Future Studies.

Dahlgren, G. and Whitehead, M. (1992) *Policies and Strategies to Promote Equity in Health*. Copenhagen: WHO Regional Office for Europe. Available at http://whqlibdoc.who.int/euro/-1993/EUR_ICP_RPD414(2).pdf (accessed May 2014).

Department of Health (2010) *Healthy Lives, Healthy People: Our Strategy for Public Health in England*. Available at http://www.dh.gov.uk (accessed Feb. 2013).

Dooris, M. (2011) Part one: health promotion principles and the settings approach, in A. Scriven and M. Hodgins (eds) (2011) *Health Promotion Settings: Principles and Practice*. London: Sage.

Giddens, A. (2013) *The Constitution of Society: Outline of the Theory of Structuration*. Cambridge: Blackwell.

Global Occupational Health Network (2006) *Prevention of Occupational Cancer*. Available at www.who.int/occupational_health/publications/newsletter/gohnet11e (accessed Feb. 2014).

Green, J. and Tones, K. (2010) *Health Promotion: Planning and Strategies*, 2nd edn. London: Sage.

Hall, P.A. and Lamont, M. (eds) (2009) *Successful Societies: How Institutions and Culture Affect Health*. Cambridge: Cambridge University Press.

Hamalainen, P., Takala, J. and Saarela, K. (2007) Global estimates of fatal work-related diseases, *American Journal of Industrial Medicine*, 50: 28–41. Available at www.onlinelibrary.wiley.com/doi/10.1002/ajim.20411/abstract (accessed Feb. 2014).

Hancock, C. (2011) *Workplace Health Initiatives: Evidence of Effectiveness*. Available at www.c3health.org/wp-content/uploads/2009/09/Workplace-health-initiatives-review-of-the-evidence-v-1-20111205.pdf (accessed Feb. 2014).

Health and Safety Executive (2012) *Cancer*. Available at www.hse.gov.uk/statistics/causdis/cancer/index.htm (accessed Feb. 2014).

Healthy People 2020 (2013) *Environmental Health*. Available at www.healthypeople.gov/2020/topicsobjectives2020/overview.aspx?topicid=12 (accessed Feb. 2014).

International Metalworkers Federation (2007) *Occupational Cancer: Zero Cancer*. Available at http://www.imfmetal.org/index.cfm?c=15620&1=2 (accessed Sept. 2012).

Johada, M. and Rush, H.J. (1980) *Work, Employment and Unemployment: An Overview of Ideas and Research Results in the Social Science Literature*. Hove: Science Policy Research Unit, University of Sussex.

Kellert, S. R., Heerwagen, J. and Mador, M. (2011) *Biophilic Design: The Theory, Science and Practice of Bringing Buildings to Life*. Hoboken, NJ: John Wiley.

MacEachen, E. (2000). The mundane administration of worker bodies: from Welfarism to Neoliberalism, *Health, Risk & Society*, 2(3): 315–27.

Myers, S.S. (2009) *Global Environmental Change: The Threat to Human Health.* Geneva: United Nations Foundation.

Newton, J. (2007) *Well-being and the Natural Environment: A Brief Overview of the Evidence.* Available at www.apho.org.uk/resource/item.aspx?RID=91094 (accessed Oct. 2013).

Nurminen, M. and Karjalainen, A. (2001) Epidemiologic estimate of the proportion of fatalities related to occupational factors in Finland, *Scandinavian Journal of Work, Environment and Health,* 27(3): 116–213.

Pretty, J., Peacock, J., Sellens, M. and Griffin, M. (2005) The mental and physical health outcomes of green exercise, *International Journal of Environmental Health Research,* 15(5): 319–37.

Pruss-Ustan, A. and Corvalan, C. (2006) *Preventing Disease Through Healthy Environments.* Geneva: WHO.

Rogers, B. (2002) *Occupational and Environmental Health Nursing: Concepts and Practice.* London: Wiley.

Rowlingson, K. (2011) *Does Income Inequality Cause Health and Social Problems?* Available at www.jrf.org.uk/sites/files/jrf/Rowlingson-Income-eBook.pdf (accessed Sept. 2012).

Scriven, A. and Hodgins, M. (2011) *Health Promotion Settings: Principles and Practice.* London: Sage.

Tillman, C. (2007) *Principles of Occupational Health and Hygiene: An Introduction.* Sydney: Allen & Unwin.

Trades Union Congress (2012) *Occupational Cancers: The Figures.* Available at www.tuc.org.uk/workplace/tuc-20569-f0.cfm (accessed Feb. 2014).

United Nations Environment Programme (UNEP) (2012) *Current Changes in Approaches to Environmental Policy.* Available at www.unep.org/ (accessed Feb. 2014).

United Nations Population Fund (2007a) *State of the World's Health: Unleashing the Potential for Urban Growth.* Available at www.unfpa.org/pds/ (accessed Feb. 2014).

United Nations Population Fund (2007b) *State of the World Population.* Available at web.unfpa.org/swp/2007/english/chapter_1/urbanization.html (accessed Feb. 2014).

Waddell, G. and Burton, K. (2006) *Is Working Good for your Health and Well-being?* Cardiff and Huddersfield: Cardiff University and University of Huddersfield Press.

Wilkinson, R. and Pickett, K. (2009) *The Spirit Level: Why More Equal Societies Almost Always Do Better.* London: Allen Lane.

Wilson, O. (1984) *Biophillia, the Human Bond with Other Species.* Cambridge, MA: Harvard University Press.

Winters, C.A. (2013) *Rural Nursing: Concepts, Theory and Practice,* 4th edn. London: Springer Noble.

World Health Organization (WHO) (1984) *Health for All Targets.* Copenhagen: WHO.

World Health Organization (WHO) (1986) *Ottawa Charter for Health Promotion.* Geneva: WHO.

World Health Organization (WHO) (2011) *Environmental and Occupational Cancers: Fact Sheet no. 350.* Available at www.who.int/mediacentre/factsheets/fs350/en/ (accessed Sept. 2012).

World Health Organization (WHO) (2014a) *Environmental Health.* Available at www.who.int/topics/environmental_health/en/m (accessed Mar. 2014).

World Health Organization (WHO) (2014b) *Introduction to Healthy Settings.* Available at www.who.int/healthy_settings/about/en/ (accessed Mar. 2014).

Yuill, C. and McMillian, I. (1998) *Sociology and Occupational Therapy: An Integrated Approach.* London: Churchill Livingstone.

8 Commissioning for health improvement and well-being

Frances Wilson and Moyra Baldwin

Introduction

How the government and local health and social care organizations commission for health improvement and well-being in England is fundamental to the services provided, the type of interventions and local initiatives undertaken. Changes to the National Health Service (NHS) and commissioning strategy in the UK will affect future service provision. As established under the Health and Social Care Act 2012 the Department of Health and local government will be new partners in commissioning integrated services. This partnership will influence how health needs are assessed, interagency and partnership working, and the growth of social enterprises which will have a direct impact on service delivery and health outcomes in the short, medium and long terms. Commissioning is a process by which the most up-to-date, cost-effective and evidence-based health and social care services can be provided for the public. It has gained momentum in recent years to the point where commissioning is the kernel of health services provision in England.

In this chapter students are introduced to the principles and policies underpinning commissioning and how the NHS landscape is changing in England. Roles of commissioners and stakeholders are analysed and the commissioning stages explored. Alternative systems of health and social care commissioning are analysed from within and outside the UK.

Defining commissioning

The many definitions of commissioning and the different terminology adopted by various commissioning agencies reflect the focus each takes to its commissioning function (see Box 8.1). Social services emphasize the centrality of the service user. Health services place strategic emphasis on the process, however at practice-based commissioning (PBC) level the focus is on consultation, greater choice and direct involvement in designing individual patient-centred care packages (DH 2007). As commissioning has developed, following the reorganization of the NHS in England, and the introduction of clinical commissioning groups (CCGs) in 2013, there has been greater focus on service users, patient choice and clinical involvement.

Box 8.1 Definitions of commissioning

Health-care definition: 'Commissioning is a strategic and proactive process of identifying the healthcare needs of a given population and prioritising services to meet the needs within the resources available. Commissioning embraces patient choice and voice' (DH 2006; Wade *et al.* 2006).

Social services definition: 'Commissioning is the process of specifying, securing and monitoring services to meet individuals' needs at strategic level. This applies to all services, whether they are provided by the local authority (LA) or by the private or voluntary sectors' (Social Services Inspectorate & Audit Commission).

King's Fund and Nuffield Trust definition: 'Commissioning is the process of measuring health needs of a population, assessing which services are needed to meet these needs and then purchasing the appropriate services on behalf of patients. The term refers to multiple activities performed by a number of professionals. Clinical commissioning refers to a range of attempts to give clinicians a central role in some or all of these activities' (Naylor *et al.* 2013a).

Why commissioning?

When the NHS was founded Britain was a different place than it is today. Immediately after the Second World War the Welfare State was welcomed and revered. Paradoxically the health service and benefits introduced by the post-war Labour government have challenged subsequent governments' finances to the extent that various methods have been explored to limit health-care services' expenditure. Originally the thrust of state control was top-down, but over 60 years the move has been in the opposite direction with more local control of the limits put on specific health-care services.

Funding for NHS and public services is finite, and how it is allocated needs prudent management to ensure appropriate service procurement. The demands on services have increased substantially: life expectancy is increasing, the population is expanding and people are living longer due to improvements in care and treatment across the lifespan, better management of long-term conditions, and the impact of preventative and health improvement strategies. Lifestyle issues, for example, smoking, alcohol consumption and obesity, have altered demand, and the public's expectation of instant access, best treatment and recovery add to the strains on resources. Clearly commissioning has an important role to play in contemporary health and social care, established to ensure that needs are assessed, priorities identified, and services designed, implemented and evaluated to achieve improvements in the population's health. Commissioning also tackles inequalities by means of evidence-based approaches to improve health and well-being.

Commissioning was formally established in the NHS in 1991 following the Community Care Act 1990. The Conservative government of the day first introduced the purchaser–provider split and forms of commissioning based on health authorities and general practice (GP) fundholding. Not all GP practices participated, with many smaller practices remaining outside the arrangements. Other practices combined into consortia and, with increased purchasing power, created a division between themselves and non-participating practices leading to, what many considered to be, two-tiered GP services. Further changes took place in 1994 when the total purchasing pilot scheme was introduced, enabling GP practices to commission a full range of services for their patients.

The 'New Labour' government in 1997 abolished GP fundholding, retained the purchaser–provider split, and primary care groups were superseded by primary care trusts (PCTs). Practice-based commissioning was introduced in 2004. Again general practices were able to choose whether they became part of the 'new system'. Indicative budgets were allocated and efficiency savings could be used to develop new services. This was another controversial step because it resulted in differences between services at GP practices that were inside or outside the system. A King's Fund survey revealed the majority of GPs and practice managers supported PBC's potential to improve patient care. However, GPs also acknowledged that they lacked skills, resources and capacity to become effective commissioners (Wood and Curry 2009). Universal coverage of the population only became a reality with the advent of CCGs in April 2013.

How services are commissioned in England from 2013

Established in April 2013, the result of major legislative change in the Health and Social Care Act 2012, the majority of NHS services are now commissioned through CCGs, where most of the NHS budget is held. Unlike previous commissioning arrangements, it is mandatory that all GP practices participate, thus providing universal coverage for the first time since the introduction of commissioning.

Responsibilities have been transferred from PCTs across three organizations to the local authority which now has responsibility for public health budgets; the newly established Public Health England (PHE) is responsible for commissioning primary care and CCGs. These changes were set out in the Conservative/Liberal Democrat Coalition government's White Paper, *Healthy Lives, Healthy People* (DH 2010b). Health and well-being boards (HWBs) have been established whose function includes overseeing and coordinating commissioners, and commissioning support units will provide support services to commissioning bodies.

Table 8.1 summarizes the current commissioning arrangements in England, their budgets and scope of responsibilities. Note that functions are not exhaustive and may overlap between the three main commissioning bodies and the commissioning board (CB). Local differences may occur resulting in some joint commissioning of services between CCGs and LAs, for example, smoking cessation, sexual health and drugs/alcohol services. Coordination of services may be undertaken at strategic

Table 8.1 Commissioning budgets and responsibilities in England from April 2013

Clinical commissioning groups – for secondary care and community services Budget: £65 billion	The local population: urgent and emergency care; out of hours; elective hospital care; community health services; maternity and new-born; children's healthcare, learning disability and mental health services; NHS continuing care; infertility services
Local authorities – 152 – plus budget for social care, housing, education and other services Budget: £2.7 billion	Public health advice to CCGs on: commissioning of services to the local population. Public health services for children including school nursing, health visiting and family nursing partnership (from April 2015); contraception over and above GP contract; sexual health; mental health promotion and prevention. Physical activity; obesity programmes; drugs and alcohol misuse services; stop smoking services; nutrition initiatives; NHS health checks; health at work initiatives; dental public health; accidental injury prevention including falls services, seasonal mortality reduction
NHS England area teams – for primary care and specialized services Budget £25 billion	Prevention services, health improvement and support for local authorities. Social marketing and behaviour change campaigns Infectious diseases including current functions of the Health Protection Agency (HPA) Public oversight of prevention and control, including co-ordination of outbreak management Emergency preparedness and response including pandemic influenza preparedness Health intelligence and information on health improvement and health protection (with local authorities), including many existing functions of public health observatories, cancer registries, National Cancer Intelligence Network, HPA and National Treatment Agency for Substance Misusers; National Drug Treatment Monitoring System
NHS Commissioning Board (CB)	National commission responsibility. Specialized and highly specialized services. Immunization programmes. National screening programmes. Antenatal and newborn screening. Health services (excluding emergency care) and public health services, prisons and other custodial settings. Health services (excluding emergency care services) for the armed forces personnel and families. Pharmaceutical services; primary ophthalmic services; all dental services; sexual assault services

Source: Adapted from Naylor et al. (2013c) and NHS Commissioning Board (2012)

level with budgets allocated by the NHS CB. Very specialized and expensive services will be managed strategically to ensure equal distribution of resources. More detailed information can be found in the references accompanying this chapter.

Future development of CCGs and commissioning of local services

Commissioning NHS services has been in a constant state of change for over 25 years with pivotal variations occurring as governments come and go. There is evidence now that the system is becoming more sophisticated or, some might say, overwhelmingly complicated. The recent changes are seen to be transformational as they are accompanied by legislative change and major NHS organizational restructuring implemented over a relatively short time. Despite the rhetoric from opposition parties any reversal in health-care strategy would be difficult, but inevitably new models will continue to emerge. The role of clinicians has changed in this new commissioning landscape as the latter is more collaborative and less hierarchical than previous arrangements, according to Curry's research (Curry *et al.* 2013; Naylor *et al.* 2013a).

What are the priorities for commissioners?

As a result of research undertaken by Naylor *et al.* (2013a), ten priorities were suggested to support the transformation of health-care services in England. The aims are designed to address the growing burden of disease and escalating costs of medical technology. Broadly these include chronic disease management, empowering of patients, developing a population public health approach to commissioning with a more integrated approach, and models of care.

Ten priorities for commissioners (Naylor *et al.* 2013b)

- Active support for self-management.
- Primary prevention.
- Secondary prevention.
- Managing ambulatory care sensitive (ACS) conditions.
- Improving the management of patients with both mental and physical health needs.
- Care coordination through integrated health and social care teams.
- Improving primary care management of end-of-life care.
- Medicines management.
- Managing elective activity – referral quality.
- Managing urgent and emergency activity.

The focus of the priorities for commissioners is threefold: health outcomes, patient experience and cost savings.

Thinking point

The King's Fund research proposed ten priorities to support transformation of health-care services in England. Taking ONE priority as it relates to your field of practice, in your opinion, what would be the best way of commissioning services to improve health outcomes, patient experience and cost savings? Give reasons for your thoughts. Please read and refer to the document: Ten priorities for commissioners (Naylor *et al.* 2013b).

Outcomes-based commissioning

The drive for improving health outcomes in England is based on three outcomes frameworks: NHS Outcomes, Public Health, and Adult Social Care Outcomes Framework, all of which set out strategic performance targets and domains, and are revised annually. Subsequently, NICE has developed performance indicators, based on the outcomes frameworks, on which to measure CCG, LA and PHE performance. There is commitment to improving alignment between each framework, for example, including improving quality of life for people with dementia and improving people's experience of integrated care and addressing loneliness and isolation.

Specific outcomes for health improvement, according to *The Public Health Outcomes Framework for England, 2013–2016* (DH 2013a), are structured around two high-level outcomes and four outcome domains which are intended to be exclusive activities. Domain outcomes include improving the wider determinants of health, health improvement, health protection, health-care/public health and preventing premature mortality (Figure 8.1). The NHS CB will work with CCGs to commission services and quality standards to achieve these outcomes.

The *Adult Social Care Outcomes Framework 2013/14* (ASCOF) (DH 2012) is based on four domains with associated outcome measures. The aims are to address the needs of an ageing population, provide personalized and preventative care, early intervention and support to remain independent (or retain independence), promote quality of life and positive experiences of care.

- Domain 1: Enhancing quality of life for people with care and support needs.
- Domain 2: Delaying and reducing the need for care and support.
- Domain 3: Ensuring that people have a positive experience of care.
- Domain 4: Safeguarding adults whose circumstances make them vulnerable and protecting from avoidable harm.

Joint models of commissioning and integrated services

Inherent in the Health and Social Care Act 2012 is the requirement for local authorities and CCGs to work together to identify the health and well-being needs of local communities and to agree joint strategies to improve health and well-being

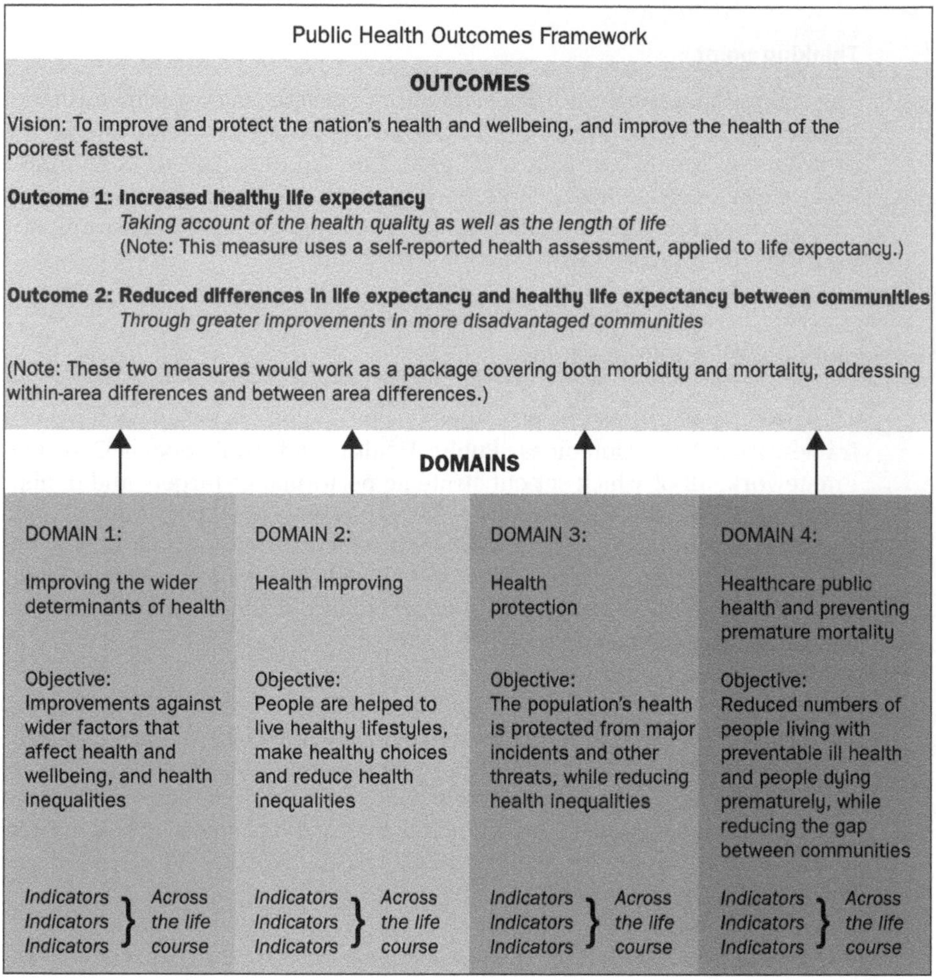

Public Health Outcomes Framework

OUTCOMES

Vision: To improve and protect the nation's health and wellbeing, and improve the health of the poorest fastest.

Outcome 1: Increased healthy life expectancy
Taking account of the health quality as well as the length of life
(Note: This measure uses a self-reported health assessment, applied to life expectancy.)

Outcome 2: Reduced differences in life expectancy and healthy life expectancy between communities
Through greater improvements in more disadvantaged communities

(Note: These two measures would work as a package covering both morbidity and mortality, addressing within-area differences and between area differences.)

DOMAINS

DOMAIN 1:	DOMAIN 2:	DOMAIN 3:	DOMAIN 4:
Improving the wider determinants of health	Health Improving	Health protection	Healthcare public health and preventing premature mortality
Objective: Improvements against wider factors that affect health and wellbeing, and health inequalities	Objective: People are helped to live healthy lifestyles, make healthy choices and reduce health inequalities	Objective: The population's health is protected from major incidents and other threats, while reducing health inequalities	Objective: Reduced numbers of people living with preventable ill health and people dying prematurely, while reducing the gap between communities
Indicators ⎫ Across Indicators ⎬ the life Indicators ⎭ course	Indicators ⎫ Across Indicators ⎬ the life Indicators ⎭ course	Indicators ⎫ Across Indicators ⎬ the life Indicators ⎭ course	Indicators ⎫ Across Indicators ⎬ the life Indicators ⎭ course

Figure 8.1 Public Health Outcomes Framework 2013–2016
DH (2013a).

outcomes and reduce health inequalities. To do this statutory organizations and a range of local partners must work collaboratively through the health and well-being boards (HWBs) to establish community engagement and understanding of community needs to commission the most appropriate services.

The concept of joint commissioning is well established: central to policy making for several decades. Almost two decades ago, the Department of Health (1995) defined joint commissioning as 'the process in which two or more commissioning agencies act together to coordinate their commissioning, taking joint responsibility for translating strategy into action'. This recognized the reality and the need for statutory and voluntary agencies to work together to achieve the best possible outcomes for service users, patients or residents. The definition retains currency with the emphasis on joint responsibility and making things happen. Indeed successive governments have produced policy guidance aimed at greater partnership working, collaboration and planning both at strategic and local level to achieve results on an ever increasing scale. In the new NHS this has never been more relevant and is now enshrined in legislation.

Joint commissioning, necessary to improve the effectiveness and efficiency of local health and social care delivery, has evolved as the result of the way in which health and social care services were established. At the inception of the NHS they were separate entities which resulted in fragmented services. Health services continue to be provided, free at point of delivery, through taxation and direct government funding; social care services delivery is funded through local government and by means testing of the individuals receiving services to assess their financial contribution, if any.

One of the first White Papers produced by the coalition government in 2010, *Equity and Excellence, Liberating the NHS* (DH 2010a), heralded major legislative changes for reorganization of health and social care which incorporated new commissioning arrangements with emphasis placed on joint commissioning: CCG, LA and PHE. New providers and agencies such as social enterprises have been encouraged. What is not clear, however, is the effectiveness of such joint commissioning arrangements as evidenced in the systematic review undertaken in 2012 by Newman *et al.* Their examination of the evidence base for commissioning, in health, education and social care and the impact of joint commissioning arrangements on future commissioning, concluded that the following are important:

- consideration given to the development of positive relationships between commissioners
- in situations of collective resources there need to be clear responsibilities and legal structures
- matching geographical boundaries
- clear communication and information systems between stakeholders.

Newman and colleagues remind us that the new arrangements are indeed opportunities for much needed research but this means that evaluative strategies should be integral to any future joint commissioning proposals.

Models and the process of commissioning

Models enable the practitioner to visualize commissioning through a series of stages. Wilson and Baldwin (2009) undertook a review of commissioning models and processes and designed a model that encapsulated the stages into a logical sequence (Figure 8.2).

Service users

Placed at the centre of the model is the service user whose involvement is not merely to meet a duty but to bring about 'better service outcomes'. Service users can be involved throughout the commissioning cycle.

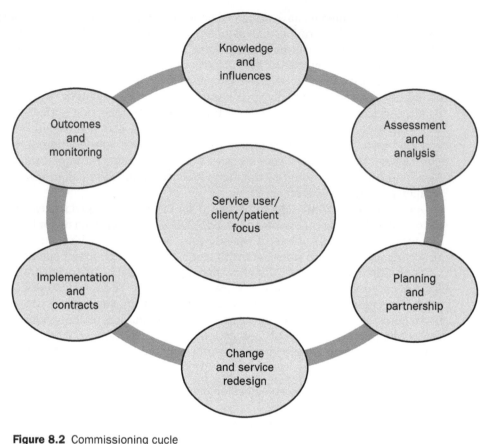

Figure 8.2 Commissioning cycle
Source: Wilson and Baldwin (2009).

Knowledge and influences

Commissioners draw on and intelligently apply a repertoire of skills, knowledge and experience: appraisal and decision-making skills, due diligence to steward-ship and governance of resources. They proactively acquire, use and share knowledge in all stages of the cycle: knowledge gained from, for example, policy directives, legislation, the Department of Health and service users. Commissioners are influenced by professional, legal, fiscal, research, political, management and lay sources of knowledge, and need understanding of the working methods of each, for example, research methods, change management and legal statutes.

Assessment and analysis

Joint strategic needs assessment (JSNA), a statutory duty and the building block of commissioning, demands rigorous application of analytical methods/tools.

Commissioners analyse the population's health and social care needs and reflect on current services to secure care that is fit for purpose, cost-effective and cost-efficient. They base decisions on detailed assessment and data interpretation relating to current and future populations' needs. Commissioners analyse the shortcomings in services, which inform priorities for equity, fair user access and allocation of resources.

Planning and partnership

Collaborative working is essential to commissioning contemporary integrated health and social care services that are responsive to needs and preferences, facilitate empowerment and social inclusion, and contribute to the best use of collective resources. Commissioners and partners develop programmes, either novel or revised, relevant to various provider organizations and agencies that contribute to improving the lives of populations, and maximize outcomes that reflect the values and principles of contemporary society.

Change and service redesign

Demographic changes influence the nature of services required by populations. Economic and political climates influence commissioners' decisions, for example, major transformational reorganization in care services. Commissioners face service redesign resulting from altered cost–benefit analyses, poor performance, business or financial difficulties of provider organizations or sudden crises, and changing population demands. Changes cause disruption that can impact on the workforce as roles are revised or abolished, and impact on service users also.

Implementation and contracts

Contracts explicitly state agreements between service providers and commissioners to meet the health and social care needs of specific populations. Contracts express objectives to meet needs, and articulate service specifications and quality standards to be achieved. Contracts influence and inform the outcomes and monitoring elements of commissioning and operationalize the principles of fairness and openness, giving transparency to the quality and standards expected.

Inherent is procurement, whereby private, independent, voluntary and statutory organization suppliers are identified. Economics and politics demand procurement provides value for money, is evidence based and meets needs efficiently and effectively.

Outcomes and monitoring

Reflecting commissioners' aspirations, outcomes need to be measureable to determine the success of commissioned services. Intrinsic is the ongoing process of monitoring to inform commissioners of the effectiveness of outcomes, the service-users' satisfaction, use of resources, providers' business processes, and value for money.

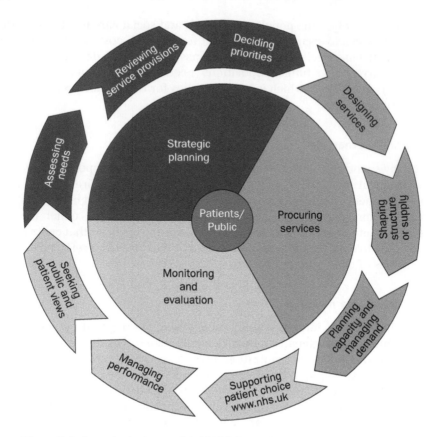

Figure 8.3 Commissioning model: NHS Information Centre commissioning cycle
Source: NHS Information Centre.

Health services commissioning: NHS Information Centre commissioning cycle

This model, developed to support world-class commissioning, conceptualizes three central commissioning components, strategic planning, procuring services, and monitoring and evaluation, and specifies commissioning activities. Patients and public, as above, are depicted at the centre of commissioning (Figure 8.3).

Commissioning model: Institute of Public Care (IPC) joint model for public care

This generic, popular, model is represented as a four-quadrant application of the cycle relevant to public care commissioning such as health care, education, social care (Figure 8.4). The Scottish Social Work Services used this model to guide strategic commissioning and it is the basis on which the recent publication, *Commissioning for Health and Social Care* (Institute of Public Care 2014), explores evidence-based commissioning.

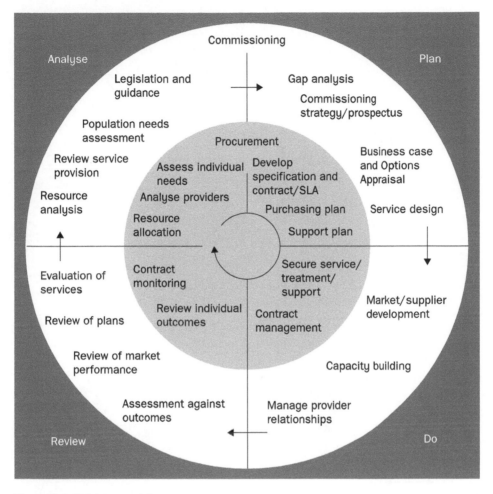

Figure 8.4 IPC joint model
Source: Welsh Assembly Government (2010).

The four quadrants encompass key performance management exercises that commissioners apply to commissioning activities – Analysing, Planning, Doing and Reviewing. The circles link commissioning and procurement. The outer circle, commissioning, drives the inner circle, procurement/purchasing and contracting activities. Together, they inform the commissioning strategy.

National Audit Office (NAO) model of commissioning and the third sector

The NAO's model (Figure 8.5) aims to help public sector commissioners to get 'better value for money from third sector organizations' (TSOs) (NAO 2010). The focus is effective financial relationships with TSOs and recognition that decommissioning is a natural part of commissioning.

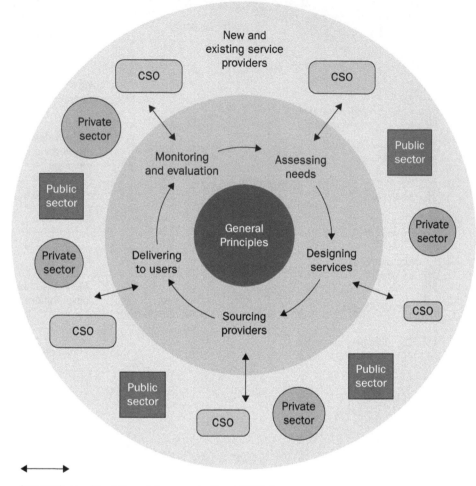

Interactions with civil society organizations (CSOs)

Figure 8.5 A model of the commissioning environment, process and interactions with third sector organizations

Source: National Audit Office (2010).

The model highlights the elements where good relationships with TSOs have significant impact on achieving good value for money.

ABC model

A generic outcomes-based model founded on evidence obtained from the outcomes literature, ABC depicts commissioning linearly; information in each step influences and informs subsequent steps. Steps reflect the commissioning models explained above but the cornerstone of the ABC model is outcomes.

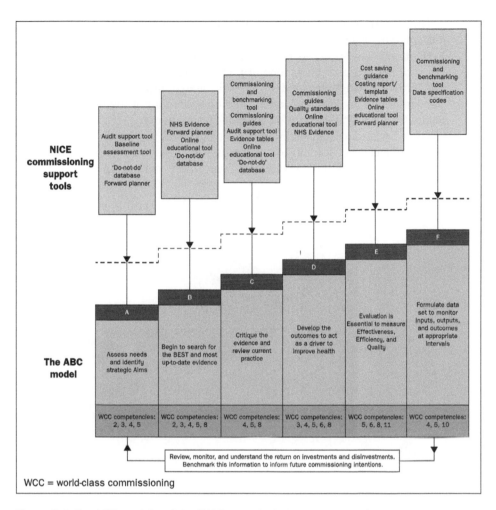

Figure 8.6 The ABC model and the NICE commissioning support tools

Source: Callaghan and Perigo (2010); Callaghan (2011).

The model (see Figure 8.6) enables commissioners to justify their decisions, based on quality, standards, and contemporary evidence. It combines the commissioning cycle, national commissioning competencies, evaluation, evidence-based care and 'matrix working' to effect desired outcomes.

Education commissioning

Health Education England (HEE) has responsibility for strategic workforce planning. Local education and training boards (LETBs) with local workforce and education groups (WEGs) agree local commissioning and education plans based on NHS workforce strategic development needs.

They work with local stakeholders and education providers to establish anticipated professional workforce requirements for future service delivery. Education commissioning, guided by the priority needs of patients in response to, for example, the Francis enquiry (DH 2013b), ensures compassionate and committed nursing care, and strong NHS leadership. The workforce must reflect the demographic changes forecast and take account of the requirements of NHS, Social Care and Public Health Outcomes frameworks.

The education commissioning cycle (Figure 8.7) includes: workforce planning and intelligence gathering; data analysis and assessment of need; stakeholder consultation; planning; investment plan and contracting; and review and evaluation.

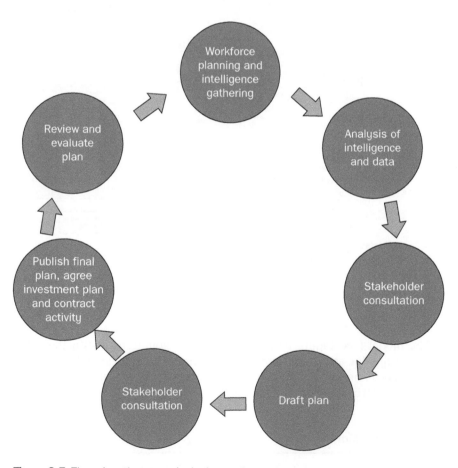

Figure 8.7 The education commissioning cycle
Source: NWLETB (2012).

Summary of the commissioning models

The models above have represented the activities required of commissioners.

Thinking point

From what you have read about commissioning models: What, in your opinion, are the merits and demerits of each model? What are your thoughts on where policy needs to go from now to reduce inequalities in health? Give reasons for your opinions.

Case study: Commissioning in education and workforce development – some examples of commissioning and redesigning the workforce in England

To meet changing needs of society due to population expansion, changing health status and continuing high levels of deprivation the workforce must be adequate in number with a balance of skills and ability to meet changing demands. Partly due to an ageing workforce, the number of health visitors working in the community had declined to an all-time low in 2010/11 in England and Wales. The Health Visitor Implementation Plan 2011–2015 A Call to Action (DH 2011) set out to expand the health visiting service by training an extra 4200 health visitors between 2012 and 2015 and encouraging health visitors no longer working in the service to return to practice.

The vision was to create a new model of service delivery to meet the changing and growing demands of families and communities and to implement the Healthy Child Programme (HCP) which would shape the new service specification. This impacted on higher education providers to expand provision to accommodate an unprecedented increase in health visiting commissions and to tailor a new curriculum to meet the new service model. Additional practice placements and mentors had to be identified by community service providers as well as training and updating of the existing workforce.

As part of the overall plan, early implementation sites were identified where the new service model would be rolled out and evaluated.

Applying the commissioning cycle to Health Visitor Implementation Plan

Workforce planning and intelligence gathering. Data collected on the health visiting workforce in 2011–12 to determine current baseline service provision by each region.

Analysis of intelligence and data. Data analysed to determine the shortfall of health visitors, per region and local area. Application of formula determined the shortfall based on a model of projected average caseloads and local deprivation scores.

Stakeholder consultation. Strategic Health Authority (SHA) consultation with local employers: primary care trusts, higher education providers. The workforce

(continued)

consulted throughout England by the Community Practitioners and Health Visitors Association (CPHVA), RCN and other health-care unions.

Draft plan. Draft plan prepared identifying training and recruitment needs and estimated costs.

Stakeholder consultation. Further consultation on draft plan. Confirmation of projected training and recruitment requirements by local area/PCT/CCGs.

Publish final plan, agree investment plan and contract activity. Final commissioned numbers by local trust/area – three-year plan 2012/2015 (DH 2011) and *National Health Visiting Service Specification 2014/15* (NHS England 2014).

Review and evaluate plan. Included in the *National Health Visiting Service Specification 2014/15* (NHS England 2014) is a provider performance framework which aims to measure the following outcomes:

- Health Visitor (HV) growth/capacity
- HV service delivery
- breastfeeding
- early identification of families at risk
- safeguarding
- annual random audit of referrals.

For detailed information on this outline case study please see:

Department of Health (2011) *Health Visitor Implementation Plan 2011–2015. A Call to Action.* London: DH.

NHS England (2014) *National Health Visiting Service Specification 2014/15.* Redditch: NHS England.

Commissioners' responsibility for meeting health and social care needs requires fiscal management. Resources, by their nature, are finite and need to be deployed to their best effect. Health and social care needs could easily outstrip resources, therefore stewardship is essential for successful commissioning.

Tools such as programme budgeting and marginal analysis (Morris *et al.* 2012) enable commissioners to utilize resources to best effect: maximizing health and well-being.

Programme budgeting and marginal analysis

Programme budgeting and marginal analysis (PBMA) (Brambleby *et al.* 2010) involves two separate, but related, activities starting from existing services and understanding how resources are currently spent, then examining ways of changing the resource allocation, that is, marginal changes in services. Using this tool, commissioners ask themselves if there was an increase in resources what would be their best use to ensure the greatest increase in benefit. Conversely, if resources were reduced, how and which cuts should be followed to safeguard benefit to the programme, that is, ensuring minimum loss of benefit.

Central is the concept of cost-effectiveness – in terms of 'margins'. Appraising the most cost-effective means of spending finite resources, marginal analysis, avoids the trap of the law of diminishing returns. Instead, lower-priority services are traded for services providing higher value. Thus the impact of health and social care resources on the needs of the population is maximized.

In a dynamic climate, spending ever-changing resources (that is, more or fewer resources) to their best effect is critical if objectives are to be met within given resources. This analytical tool can help decision makers, the commissioners, to meet needs assessment and needs addressment (www.healthknowledge.org, accessed 10 Apr. 2014).

Some concepts and definitions to aid understanding of healthcare economics

It is vital to identify what to include when estimating the total cost of a health intervention programme or service development need, for example, immunization programme or health visiting service. Costs can be divided into direct costs of providing a programme and costs that may be avoided as a result of the programme. Costs to patients and families, such as travel, waiting times and lost productivity, may be substantial and adversely affect vaccine uptake, outpatient or clinic attendances. A third category is future costs or savings resulting from the impact of an intervention or new service. Health impact assessments (HIAs) may be undertaken to determine potential effect and may reveal unanticipated consequences. If a societal view is adopted then every cost and potential savings should be included.

Type of evaluation

It is important to justify the type(s) of economic evaluation chosen as different types of analysis serve different purposes (see Table 8.2). For example cost utility analysis (CUA) is the preferred option to facilitate comparisons both among vaccines and among health-care interventions more generally. The outcomes are expressed in a combined measure of morbidity and mortality (for example, quality adjusted life years – QALYs – or disability adjusted life years – DALYs). Using a range of outcome measures will increase the potential utility of the analysis (WHO 2008).

Commissioning: UK and international comparisons

The ways in which health and social care services are run and commissioned in England, Scotland, Northern Ireland and Wales are beginning to look very different as a result of devolution, and the way in which data are collected and presented makes comparisons between services difficult. England has undergone more radical change by introducing new structures and models of commissioning compared with the other countries. The public health challenges faced by each country remain comparable with similar strategies aimed at reducing inequalities and increasing well-being.

Table 8.2 Economic evaluation

Cost minimization analysis	Simplest form of economic evaluation Assumes that the outcomes or effectiveness of each intervention are equal in order to make a direct cost comparison If evidence of equivalence is available then the most efficient intervention is the least costly alternative	Involves the assessment of two or more interventions with identical outcomes to determine which is the cheapest way of delivering the same outcome. For example, if two rotavirus vaccines have equivalent levels of effectiveness against severe gastroenteritis, cost minimization analysis would identify which of the two vaccines was the least costly
Cost–benefit analysis	All the benefits of interventions can be related to their costs Considered to be the gold standard of economic evaluation Provides an analysis of whether the benefits outweigh the costs (i.e. the absolute benefit of a programme) The monetary valuation of intangible benefits are difficult to analyse, e.g. the value of life	Expresses health outcomes in terms of monetary units. This type of analysis enables comparisons between vaccines or other interventions in the health sector or in other sectors, such as education, in order to identify which generates the greatest return on investment. The need to measure outcomes in monetary units limits the use of this type of analysis in determining health policy.
Cost-effectiveness analysis	The cost-effectiveness of immunization provides a comparison of costs and outcomes and is measured in units, e.g. life years saved, cases successfully treated or cases prevented	Cost-effectiveness analysis measures the outcomes of approaches. For example, if the outcome of interest was a reduction in childhood pneumonia, cost-effectiveness analysis might compare vaccines against Haemophilus influenzae type b (Hib) and pneumococcal diseases in order to determine which averted a case of pneumonia most cheaply

	The cost-effectiveness of immunization impacts on the following: reduces morbidity reduces number of hospitalized cases/mortality reduces direct and indirect medical costs improves outcomes for children, the elderly and risk groups (Allwin and Doerr 2002)	Cost-effectiveness analysis also enables comparisons to be made between vaccines and other health-care interventions that seek to address the same condition, such as rotavirus vaccination and management of childhood diarrhoea using zinc
Cost-utility analysis	Is similar to cost-effectiveness analysis, CUA being seen as an extension of CEA (WHO 2008) Differs in the measurement of outcomes Combines mortality and morbidity data into a single measure, e.g. QALY The QALY is a measurement of the quality of life gained by treatment weighted or adjusted by increases in the quality of life Allows comparison of the relative efficiency of health-care related interventions for different conditions One of the most commonly used measures in economic evaluations	The outcomes are then expressed in terms of measures such as QALYs or DALYs For example, it might be useful to compare vaccines against rotavirus and Hib in terms of which averts a DALY most cheaply However, it also enables comparisons between different health sector interventions, such as interventions to control HIV/AIDS, TB and malaria In practice, there has been a blurring of the distinction between CEA and CUA, with the latter being seen as an extension of the former (WHO 2008)

Source: Drummond et al. (1997); WHO (2008).

Scotland

In Scotland, national commissioning is undertaken for specialist services that are very expensive to maintain and includes the diagnosis and treatment of rare conditions where local or regional commissioning is not appropriate. In 2011 the majority of Scotland's 5.3 million population was located across the central belt, with smaller/remote communities in the highlands and islands. The system is designed to ensure equity of access for Scottish residents, secure best possible clinical outcomes, avoid duplication of services and promote a cost-effective environment. The National Services Division (NSD) of NHS Scotland commissions a full range of screening services for, and on the advice of, the UK national screening committee. In addition the NSD commissions some clinical networks to promote standards of patient care through integration and collaboration. Functioning of commissioned services is continuously reviewed and subject to an annual process of performance management. A comprehensive list of these and specialist services can be found on their website. The NSD also pays for Scottish access to some prescribed services through NHS England which are assessed on an individual basis. (http://www.nsd.scot.nhs.uk)

http://www.nsd.scot.nhs.uk/services/specialised/index.html (link to website for above)

Wales

Health and social care in Wales are organized as separate entities. NHS Wales underwent major restructuring in 2009. Arising from the Welsh Assembly Government's (WAG 2007) 'One Wales' strategy, since 2009 the NHS in Wales comprises seven LHBs with responsibility for delivering all NHS health-care services within a geographical boundary. Funded by the Welsh government, the LHBs are responsible for primary, secondary and tertiary health-care delivery.

Three NHS Trusts were created: the Welsh Ambulance Services Trust responsible for emergency services, Velindre NHS Trust with responsibility for specialist services in cancer care and a range of national support services, for example, blood transfusion, and Public Health Wales. These changes were effected with a view to improve health outcomes and health-care delivery between the NHS and its partners. Committed to the NHS created by Bevan some 60 years earlier, the WAG pledged to eliminate private hospital provision or private finance initiatives. Community health councils (CHCs), the statutory lay bodies that represent the interests of the public giving people an independent voice, were retained by the WAG although reduced in number to seven in 2009, geographically mirroring the LHBs.

With regard to social care, recent legislation (March 2014) was passed by the WAG aimed at making social services sustainable and making access to care equal wherever people live in Wales. The legislation aims to simplify the laws regulating social care and ensure councils assess carers' needs.

Northern Ireland

In 2011 a major review of the health and social care services in Northern Ireland was undertaken based on a model for integrated health and social care which would provide a vision for future services. This was in response to pressures on health and social care from an increasing and ageing population, poorer health, growth in chronic conditions, and instability in the health and social care system. Individuals and their homes are at the centre of the care system with access to integrated locally commissioned health and social care provision. The Northern Ireland model integrates planned, emergency and specialist care services, along with a shift of care and resources from hospital settings into the community. See the review of Health and Social Care in Ireland, *Transforming your Care* (HSCI 2011), and the King's Fund report authored by Ham *et al.* (2013) on integrated care.

The way in which health care is organized in different countries of the world is largely determined by the model of health-care funding. The UK health-care system is based on the Beveridge model, funded through taxation and national insurance. The population is entitled to receive health care free at the point of use accessed through primary care services. Other countries based on the Beveridge model are defined by the amount of government control and include Spain, New Zealand, most of Scandinavia, Hong Kong and Cuba. New Zealand, for example, introduced a purchaser–provider split into its system in 1993, and studies suggest that there have been many challenges especially around contracting and resulting from reorganizations, but services have been able to focus on care provision and the quality of care with the introduction of more competition.

Other models such as the Bismark model found in Germany, France, Belgium, the Netherlands, Japan, Switzerland and parts of Latin America are based on a 'not for profit' insurance system.

The national health insurance model has elements of both Beveridge and Bismark models, using private sector providers and payment through government-run insurance systems that every person pays into, as for example in Canada, Taiwan and South Korea.

The out-of-pocket model is typical of low-income countries where those who can afford to pay can obtain health-care and treatment. Those who cannot pay may resort to traditional medicine. Many such countries also benefit from different types of funding, including international funding programmes, charities and NGO funding, but they may be time limited or intermittent and only benefit those in close proximity to them (Reigelman 2011).

Conclusion

The commissioning system in England seems to be unique. The concept of commissioning for health improvement and well-being has been explored in this chapter. Commissioning has been considered in the context of the NHS and its developments. The principles and policies on which commissioning is founded have been examined and the roles of commissioners and stakeholders analysed, in the main, from a UK perspective. Commissioners of public services work strategically, and locally, to effect health improvement and well-being. Examination of principles and models can lure one into reifying the concept of commissioning, which potentially endangers its purpose: to enhance service delivery. In other words, commissioning is a means to an end. It is not, and must not become an end in itself, otherwise it is rendered nothing more than impotent and will jeopardize any attempts at providing evidence-based public health and social care services.

From your reading of the chapter, of wider resources and engagement with the suggested thinking points, it is hoped that you are inspired to further examine the issues facing commissioners. This is essential because commissioning in England is in a state of development and refinement.

Thinking point

Commissioners face a number of challenges when trying to influence, educate and procure evidence-based health and social care services. Given everything you have read in this chapter, how do you think commissioning, applied to your field of practice, will look in three to five years' time? In your opinion, what role do research, user groups and health economics have in developing effective commissioning?

Find an opportunity (it may be possible to shadow a commissioning team) to explore the commissioning of services in your local area: what are the local priorities, what systems are in place to provide a comprehensive system of commissioning? For example does the theory of commissioning match the reality?

References

Allwin, R. and Doerr, H. (2002) The 'influenza vaccine' – benefit, risk, costs, *Medical Microbiology and Immunology*, 191(3–4), 183–5.

Brambleby, P., Jackson, A. and Knight, K. (2010) *Programme Budgeting And Marginal Analysis*. Available from www.healthknowledge.org (accessed 4 Apr. 2014).

Callaghan, S. (2011) *The 'ABC' Approach to Commissioning for Outcomes*. NHS National Institute for Health and Clinical Excellence Shared Learning Database. Available at www.nice.org.uk/usingguidance/sharedlearningimplementingniceguidance/examplesofimplementation/eximpresults.jsp?o=384 (accessed 1 Apr. 2014).

Callaghan, S. and Perigio, E. (2010) *ABC Commissioning for Outcomes Model: Can It Be Used for Any Service?* Available at www.eguidelines.co.uk/eguidelinesmain/gip/vol_14/jan_11/callaghan_commissioning_jan11.php (accessed 1 Apr. 2014).

Curry, N., Goodwin, N., Naylor, C. and Robertson, R. (2008) *Practice-Based Commissioning. Reinvigorate, Replace or Abandon?* London: King's Fund. Available at www.kingsfund.org.uk/publications/practice-based-commissioning (accessed 9 Apr. 2014).

Department of Health (DH) (1995) *Practical Guidance on Joint Commissioning for Project Leaders*. London: HMSO.

Department of Health (DH) (2006) *Health Reform in England: Update and Commissioning Framework*. London: DH.

Department of Health (DH) (2007) *Commissioning Framework for Health and Well-being: Health and Social Care Working in Partnership*. London: DH.

Department of Health (DH) (2010a) *Equity and Excellence: Liberating the NHS*. London: DH.

Department of Health (DH) (2010b) *Healthy Lives, Healthy People: Our Strategy for Public Health in England*. London: DH.

Department of Health (DH) (2011) *Health Visitor Implementation Plan 2011-2015. A Call to Action*. London: DH.

Department of Health (DH) (2012) *The Adult Social Care Outcomes Framework 2013/14 (ASCOF)*. London: DH.

Department of Health (DH) (2013a) *The Public Health Outcomes Framework for England, 2013-2016*. London: DH.

Department of Health. (2013b) *Hard Truths: The Journey to Putting Patients First. Volume One of the Government Response to the Mid Staffordshire NHS Foundation Trust Public Inquiry.* London: DH.

Drummond, M.F., O'Brien, B., Stoddart, G.L. and Torrance, G.W. (1997) *Methods for the Economic Evaluation of Health Care Programmes*, 2nd edn. Oxford: Oxford University Press.

Ham, C., Heenan, D., Longley, M. and Steel, D.R. (2013) *Integrated Care in Nothern Ireland, Scotland and Wales: Lesson for England.* London: King's Fund.

Health and Social Care in Ireland (HSCI) (2011) *Transforming your Care: A Review of Health and Social Care in Ireland.* Available at www.dhsspsni.gov.uk/transforming-your-care-review-of-hsc-ni-final-report.pdf (accessed 4 May 2014).

Institute of Public Care (IPC) (2014). *Commissioning for Health and Social Care.* London: Sage.

Morris, S., Devlin, N., Parkin, D. and Spencer, A. (2012) *Economic Analysis in Healthcare*, 2nd edn. Chichester: Wiley & Sons.

National Audit Office (NAO) (2010) *Successful Commissioning.* Available at www.nao.org.uk/successful-commissioning/ (accessed 4 Apr. 2014).

National Health Service (NHS) Information Centre (2010) Commissioning Cycle, available from http://webarchive.nationalarchives.gov.uk/20100402134053/ic.nhs.uk/commissioning (accessed 19 September 2014).

National Health Service (NHS) (2012) *Design of the NHS Commissioning Board.* Leeds: NHS.

National Health Service (NHS) England (2014) *National Health Visiting Service Specification 2014/15.* Redditch: NHS England.

Naylor, C., Curry, N., Holder, H., Ross, S., Marshall, L. and Tait, E. (2013a) *Clinical Commissioning Groups.* London: King's Fund and Nuffield Trust.

Naylor, C., Imison, C., Addicott, R., Buck, D., Harrison, N., Ross, S., Sonola, L., Tian, T. and Curry, N. (2013b) *Transforming our Healthcare System. Ten Priorities for Commissioners.* London: King's Fund. Available at www.kingsfund.org.uk/projects/gp-commissioning/ten-priorities-for-commissioners (accessed 17 Oct. 2013).

Naylor, C., Shilpa, R., Curry, N., Holder, H., Marshall, L. and Tait, E. (2013c) *Clinical Commissioning: Supporting Improvement in General Practice?* London: King's Fund and Nuffield Trust.

Newman, M., Bangpan, M., Kalra, N., Mays, N., Kwan, I. and Roberts, T. (2012) Commissioning in health, education and social care: models, research bibliography and in-depth review of joint commissioning between health and social care agencies, EPPI-Centre Report No 2007, September, EPPI-Centre, Social Science, London.

North West Local Education and Training Board (NWLETB) (2012) Workforce Development and Education Commissioning Strategy 2013/2014 to 2015/16. Available from https://www.ewin.nhs.uk/resources/item/677/workforce-development-and-education-commissioning-strategy-201314-to-201516 (accessed 22 September 2014). Reigelman, R. (2011) *Global Community Health.* London: Jones and Bartlett.

Social Services Inspectorate & Audit Commission (2003) *Making Ends Meet: A Website for Managing the Money in Social Services.* Electronic document. Available at www.joint-reviews.gov.uk/money/Commissioning/2-contents.html (accessed 15 Aug. 2007).

Wade, E., Smith, J, Peck, E. and Freeman, T. (2006) *Commissioning in the Reformed NHS: Policy into Practice.* Birmingham: University of Birmingham, Health Services Management Centre NHS Alliance.

Welsh Assembly Government (WAG) (2007) *One Wales: A Progressive Agenda for the Government of Wales: An Agreement between the Labour and Plaid Cymru Groups in the National Assembly.* Cardiff: WAG.

Welsh Assembly Government (WAG) (2010) Commissioning Framework Guidance and Good Practice. Cardiff: WAG. Available from http://ipc.brookes.ac.uk/publications/index.php?absid=643 (accessed on 22 September 2014).

Welsh Assembly Government (WAG) (2011). *Sustainable Social Services for Wales: A Framework for Action.* Cardiff: WAG.

Wilson, F. and Baldwin, M.A. (2009) Commissioning for public health, in F. Wilson and A. Mabhala (eds) *Key Concepts in Public Health.* London: Sage.

Wood, J. and Curry, N. (2009) *PBC Two Years On. Moving Forward and Making a Difference?* London: Kings Fund.

World Health Organization (WHO) (2008) *WHO Guide for Standardization of Economic Evaluations of Immunization Programmes.* Geneva: WHO.

Evaluating outcomes following health improvement and well-being interventions

Dr Janine Talley

Introduction

The improvement of health and well-being and the reduction of inequalities are currently high on policy and discourse agendas nationally and internationally. This is manifest for example in the UK government vision to 'improve the health of the poorest, fastest', through key policies such as *Healthy Lives, Healthy People* (Department of Health 2010a: 64). Flowing from such aspirations and policies are a wide range of initiatives aiming to improve health and well-being and reduce inequalities. Associated with these is an increased need for evidence that these activities are successful, and the view that evaluation is an essential and integral element of working for health and well-being (Ovretveit 2003).

Evaluation of health and well-being interventions has not always been considered or undertaken, often being seen as too complex, costly, difficult or irrelevant. However, it is important for many reasons. Chelimsky (1997) classically identified three purposes evaluation serves: accountability, development and knowledge. The first of these, accountability, is determining whether an intervention achieves its intended outcomes to inform and satisfy stakeholders such as funders, managers and intended beneficiaries. In the current economic climate value for money is a particular priority. The second, development, is providing information to make improvements in practices, organizations and programmes. The third relates to gaining deeper knowledge and understanding, for example about processes or participants. In addition, evaluation plays a role in participation and empowerment, most significantly in providing opportunities for increasing participation and empowerment of stakeholders such as intended beneficiaries (Hills 2004).

Evaluation is closely related to, but distinguishable from, more traditional research (Nutbeam and Bauman 2006). It draws on paradigms, principles and practices of research and related methodology (Kellogg Foundation 2004), and involves consideration of what counts as knowledge and evidence and how they should be generated. These issues are influenced by philosophies, values and other factors. As health and well-being encompass a wide range of activities and founding disciplines, evaluation is influenced by many fields and approaches, including sciences such as epidemiology, social sciences, social policy and anthropology. Underpinning paradigms and approaches include positivist and phenomenological, quantitative and qualitative (Ovretveit 2002). What matters to whom will vary, being different for policy makers concerned with achieving policy objectives and managing financial resources than for community project leaders aiming to empower their community or lay people concerned with what makes life feel better for them. Ovretveit (2003) includes useful frameworks, described as perspectives or lenses, that provide ways through the complexity, linking key issues of why, what, who and how. These are experimental – focused on effects; economic – focused on resource issues; developmental – focused on processes; and managerial – focused on accountability and performance. Developing these ideas he describes five evaluation approaches: experimental, economic, social research, action and managerial (Ovretveit 2002).

Of particular importance to current perspectives and policies is the relationship between evaluation and empowerment. If participation and empowerment of individuals and communities to improve their own health and well-being is desired for practical, philosophical and ethical reasons (WHO 1998; Hills 2004), then approaches to evaluation which support and enable this are crucial. Evaluation has traditionally been approached objectively, as a functional, top-down activity, done to people rather than with and by them. In contrast, participatory methods can be used (Hills 2004), including approaches variously called empowerment, participatory, emancipatory, illuminative and action research. Fundamental questions about what evaluation is for, what counts as success, who does evaluation and how are considered. Key principles include a bottom-up approach, recognizing participants as decision makers of what is most important, as owners and shapers of evaluations, and as researchers and co-producers of knowledge. They may give greater prominence to subjective perspectives and flexible approaches, including methodologies where learning about change feeds back into the intervention, via cycles of action and reflection. Drawing on some of these principles, Ovretveit (2002: 5) has developed his action evaluation approach which is

> carried out for one user group using their value criteria and provides them with data to make more informed decisions. The evaluator works with the evaluation user to clarify the decisions which the user has to make which can be informed by the evaluation. It is collaborative, usually gathers people's subjective perceptions and is carried out in a short time and provides actionable data for the evaluation users.

Goal-free evaluation (Scriven 1996) (in contrast to goal-driven evaluation) is an approach which similarly emphasizes an intervention meeting the needs of its target beneficiaries, rather than the goals and intentions of other stakeholders; it focuses on actual rather than intended outcomes, and employs needs assessment to judge the quality and fitness of the programme to client needs. Goal-free evaluation increases the likelihood that unanticipated side effects (positive or negative) will be identified and useful context specific information will be gained.

If an intervention is essentially an action which results in a change (Ovretveit 2003), then at the core of interventions and evaluations are basic assumptions of

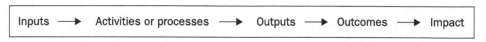

Figure 9.1 Basic logic diagram for health and well-being interventions

some form of cause and effect relationship – a link between something we do and something that happens as a result: for example, we develop policies to change the health status of different groups to reduce inequalities, or provide educational literature to individuals to encourage uptake of a screening programme. A logic model (Rogers 2005) offers a useful visual representation of the general theory of interventions – the way in which interventions such as policies, programmes and projects are understood to link to particular results. A basic example of a logic diagram using accepted terminology for elements of the process is illustrated in Figure 9.1.

So, an intervention will involve use of resources or inputs such as money and time to undertake activities or processes, with the aim of producing an output (a service or product). Outcomes are the changes that result from the work, whether wanted or unwanted, expected or unexpected. Impacts are the effects of the intervention at higher or broader levels, in the longer term, after a range of outcomes have been achieved, and often affect a wider user group than the original target.

The nature and aim of interventions to improve health and well-being have been influenced by developments in thinking about quality of life, how health and well-being can be defined, and what can and should be done to make improvements. Outcomes in health and well-being can be very varied, operate at individual, local and national levels, and be biological, personal or social. They may be objective or subjective, absolute or relative. For example, the relative outcome of reducing inequalities is a major focus for current policy internationally (WHO 2006) and in the UK (Department of Health 2010b). In order to focus effort and resources, key goals for action may be developed. For example, Table 9.1 shows these for health and well-being in England (Department of Health 2010b).

Table 9.1 Key domains for health and well-being outcomes in England

Health protection and resilience	Protecting the population's health from major emergencies and remain resilient to harm
Tackling the wider determinants of health	Tackling factors which affect health and well-being and health inequalities
Health improvement	Helping people to live healthy lifestyles, make healthy choices and reduce health inequalities
Prevention of ill health	Reducing the number of people living with preventable ill health and reduce health inequalities
Healthy life expectancy and preventable mortality	Preventing people from dying prematurely and reduce health inequalities

Source: Department of Health (2010b).

Interventions undertaken to achieve health and well-being goals are very wide in scope and take place at many levels, from international and national to smaller-scale projects and activities in communities and other settings. They also take place at the one-to-one level, and encompass activities ranging from therapeutic to preventative to structural. The current economic and social climate has been a particularly significant driver to focusing on interventions which are both evidence and outcome (or results) based (Department of Health 2009, 2010b).

At its most basic, evaluation consists of defining evaluation questions, identifying measures on which to base collection and analysis of data, and reporting on and using findings. To successfully fulfil its role, evaluation should be built into an intervention at the planning stage, be carefully designed and support all stages of an activity. There are many models and frameworks available to guide planning and evaluation of health-related interventions. Table 9.2 shows a framework developed by Wimbush and Watson (2000) based on common elements of a number of other respected frameworks. The table shows how evaluation can inform and support the stages of an intervention.

In designing interventions and their evaluations, consideration needs to be given to a range of factors including what the intervention aims to achieve (which may be different for different stakeholders), which design will produce the most powerful and appropriate evidence of effects, what is practical in terms of human and financial resources, and ethical issues. Criteria for success may include effectiveness, appropriateness, acceptability, equity and efficiency (Bowling 2002). A key consideration in high-quality evaluation is validity; the extent to which the study assesses what it is attempting to assess. This includes internal validity, which is the rigour with which all aspects of the study are completed, as well as the quality of interpretation where for example causal inferences are being made. It also includes external validity, which is the extent to which the results can be generalized or transferred to other situations. Fink (2004) provides a useful review of threats to internal and external validity.

There is an extensive range of possible designs for evaluation studies, based on comparisons of variables before and after, against standards and objectives, or against other places, situations or interventions (Ovretveit 2002). Designs fall essentially into three main categories: experimental (randomized controlled), quasi-experimental (non-randomized controlled) and observational (Fink 2004). The choice of evaluation design (or structure) will determine the confidence with which observed effects can be attributed to interventions. Until recently, design and methodology in health work has been heavily influenced by the biomedical model and the dominance of health improvement by biomedical interventions, with outcomes measured in terms of reductions in mortality and morbidity. This has drawn on underpinning principles and assumptions of science, including the premise of linear cause and effect relationships and the importance of using scientific experimental methodology to provide the strongest evidence of causal relationships. The primacy of this conceptual framework has led to widespread reference to the randomized controlled trial (RCT) as among the highest standard experimental method for generating evidence and supporting evidence-based practice; Chelimsky (1997) refers to the RCT as the gold standard of evaluation approaches. This is reflected in guidelines such as those produced by the National

Table 9.2 Health Education Board for Scotland evaluation framework

Stage	Evaluation focus	Evaluation questions
Planning	Learning from other evaluations of effectiveness; option appraisal	What are likely to be the best ways of addressing a need or problem with a group or setting?
Design and pilot	Feasibility of proposed approach; 'theory of change'	Is the proposed programme feasible and acceptable? What outcomes can be realistically achieved in what time period? How and why will/does it work? How should the programme be adapted to maximize effectiveness?
Implementation – early start-up	Delivery and quality assurance; monitoring and review systems; baselines	Are we on track? Are there any problems that need to be addressed? What action needs to be taken to improve practice or performance?
Implementation – establishment	Implementation process; reach; programme impacts/results	How is the project working? Is it being implemented as intended? To what extent is the target population being reached? To what extent are programme objectives/impacts being achieved? At what cost?
Implementation – fully operational	Intermediate outcomes/ effectiveness	To what extent were intermediate outcomes achieved? How were these achieved? In which groups/settings are the greatest benefits shown?
Dissemination	Replicability of outcomes; generalizability of theory	Can the programme be transferred to another setting or population and achieve the same outcomes?

Source: Wimbush and Watson (2000).

Institute for Care and Clinical Excellence (NICE) for the ranking of evidence of effectiveness (NICE 2005), summarized below.

- systematic review and meta-analysis
- RCTs
- cohort studies
- case control studies
- cross-sectional surveys
- case reports
- expert opinion.

The RCT has classically been defined as 'A carefully and ethically designed experiment which includes the provision of adequate and appropriate controls by a process of randomisation, so that precisely framed questions may be answered' (Bradford-Hill 1965: 107–11). The RCT methodology involves the random allocation of participants to two groups, one of which receives the intervention and one of which does not (the control group). The approach aims to even out factors other than the intervention (confounding factors) which may contribute to outcomes; and to reduce bias, so that causal inferences can be made about the intervention. The basic structure of the RCT design is shown in Figure 9.2.

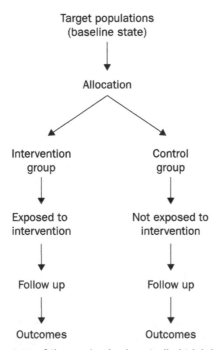

Figure 9.2 Basic structure of the randomized controlled trial design

Source: Kelly (2008).

The illustration shows an example of a concurrent controls design in which the groups are studied at the same time. RCTs of this sort are widespread and can be found most commonly in medical interventions such as drug trials (MRC 2008). Trials may involve the control group also having an intervention, for example, a placebo or an intervention already used. Variations on the basic RCT approach offer possibilities for managing particular circumstances. For example, where it is impossible to allocate individuals to intervention and control groups, a cluster randomized design (or group randomized, place randomized or community intervention trial) can be used. In this case groups rather than individuals are randomized. MacDonald *et al.* (2001: 42) describe how this might be used for an educational intervention for tobacco use prevention:

> [A]n evaluation team could select a group of similar schools, then randomly assign some schools to receive a tobacco-use prevention curriculum and other schools to serve as control schools. All schools have the same chance of being selected as an intervention or control school. Because of the 'random assignment,' you reduce the chances that the control and intervention schools vary in any way that could influence differences in program outcomes. This allows you to attribute change in outcomes to your program. For example, if the students in the intervention schools delayed smoking onset longer than students in the control schools, you could attribute the success to your program.

An example of the methodology's application to an intervention to reduce inequalities in the UK is described by Mackenbach and Gunning-Schepers (1997). In this the effect of providing free milk on growth rates of disadvantaged schoolchildren was determined by assessing the effects on height and weight. Outcomes were measured after two years for a group of 250 children given daily milk or nothing, with results suggesting that the intervention produced small improvements in growth rates.

The randomized stepped wedge design (MRC 2008) is an experimental method useful where it is undesirable for any group not to receive the intervention, for example, where there is already some evidence that it is beneficial and not offering it would be unethical. The intervention is undertaken with individuals or groups over a number of time periods, so that all receive the intervention randomly but at different times. Along similar lines, a wait-list control study design (Fink 2004) is where one group receives the intervention first and, if it appears to be effective, participants on the wait-list receive it. Participants are randomly assigned to the experimental and wait-list groups. Other designs use individual preferences or post-randomization consent to enable allocation to intervention and control groups (MRC 2008).

In non-randomized controlled trials (also termed quasi-experiments), the principle of having a control group for comparisons remains, but is achieved through predetermination of the groups without random assignment. The aim is to achieve comparability or equivalence of intervention and control groups (Fink 2004). The study groups are opportunistically populated by virtue of people volunteering or being available due to circumstances of geography or timing. Variables such as social class, age and sex might therefore not be balanced at the start of an intervention, and potentially could confound results (Fink 2004). To address this attempts can be made to achieve equivalence; for example, through matching, where pairs or clusters of participants comparable to one another in respect of important variables are selected. So an evaluator comparing feelings of well-being in those who undertake physical activity and those who do not could select pairs of people, one of whom does physical activity and one who does not, but both being matched as far as possible on other variables such as age, sex and medical history. Other ways to proceed without randomization involve working over a timescale and using individuals or groups as their own controls; for example, looking at changes from one time to another, or assessing a change in a trend in relation to the timing of an intervention.

Arguments have been put forward for greater use of experimental methodology in a wide range of health and well-being work (Oakley 1998; MRC 2008). However, RCTs and experimental designs have become a focus for contention and debate (WHO 1998; Rosen *et al.* 2006). Tones and Tilford (1994: 59) summarize some of the key issues:

> In practical terms it can be difficult to plan and implement fully controlled experimental studies of health education activities. The use of laboratory type conditions can be both artificial and inappropriate and where interventions have been tested in such artificial situations we have to ask questions about the generalisability of findings to the real world. Even when experimental studies in health education have taken place in normal practice settings the outcomes which result from the extra efforts which typically go into an evaluated study may be an unrealistic guide to what can be achieved in routine practice. Finally, while experiments can establish statistical significance, it may be more important to focus on practical significance.

Some have argued that RCTs should be one method among many and should not have higher standing, since the best method is the one most fit for purpose. The privileging of methods based on science which emphasize objectivity and quantitative outcomes is of concern in areas of work where subjectivity, empowerment and other factors are more important. The reality is that in many situations it is not practical, appropriate or desirable to use experimental designs to assess the relationship between an intervention and outcomes (Ovretveit 2002).

Observational or descriptive designs may be most practicable or suitable in many circumstances. These do not involve controlling for confounding factors. Cohort, case-control and cross-sectional studies are three common types of design in this category. A cohort design involves following a group of people who have something in common over time; for example, Reynolds *et al.* (2007) describe how the effects of a school-based, early childhood intervention on adult health and well-being were evaluated by following low-income families over a period of 19 years and assessing outcomes in terms of educational attainment, criminal behaviour, economic status, health status, behaviour and mental health. Case-control designs are traditionally used in research to explore causes of mortality and morbidity. The principle involves looking at the history of two groups of people, one subject to the phenomenon or situation of interest and the other not, to compare variables that may provide explanations in terms of relative risk. Khlat (1997) shows how this type of study can be used in a programme evaluation. So for a breast-screening programme, the ratio of the death rates from breast cancer in screened and unscreened individuals is calculated to provide information on relative risk. Cross-sectional (or survey) evaluation designs provide a portrait of the outcome for a group or groups at a particular point in time. Heron *et al.* (1999), for example, describe a study to evaluate the effectiveness of stress management training workshops in a workplace setting which compared groups of workshop attendees and non-attendees. Interventions may also combine a range of designs.

Where the outcome of interest relates to addressing inequalities, this needs to be taken into account in evaluation design. Whitehead (2007) notes that often interventions do not evaluate for differential impact on different socio-economic groups, only for average impact across the whole population. She recommends that work on inequalities assesses differential impact by socio-economic status, as well as other variables such as gender and ethnicity. When evaluating health inequalities the focus can be on addressing absolute or relative outcomes, which can range from improving the position of the worst off, through closing the gaps between the extremes of the distribution, to addressing the association across the whole population (Graham 2003, 2004; Marmot 2010). Each of these has implications for evaluation. For relative changes the outcome of interest may be expressed as probabilities, rates and odds (Plewis 2009). Mackenbach and Gunning-Schepers (1997) discuss practical aspects of evaluating interventions to reduce inequalities, including study designs which nest differences between groups into broader recognizable designs.

As new ideas emerge, these influence approaches to evaluation. The life course approach (Mayer 2009), for example, highlights the importance of considering outcomes in the long term, emphasizing trajectories and trends and how these may be changed. An ecological understanding of health and the circumstances in which interventions take place has also been influential. Systems thinking and complexity science have significantly contributed to developments in this area. Interventions may be highly complex in a range of different ways (MRC 2008). There may be many contributions to the outcome scenario from different projects, organizations and sectors, acting independently or interdependently. Interventions may therefore have a range of possible outcomes or variations across a population, and it can be difficult to determine which intervention or combination of interventions is significant. This has led to other approaches based on different underpinning ideas about cause-and-effect relationships and the importance of context. Complexity science acknowledges that interventions in complex systems are likely to have diverse, far-reaching, and non-linear effects (Shiell *et al.* 2008).

Theory-based approaches to evaluation offer alternatives in complex circumstances, where plausible logical models or theories of change are developed to link an intervention and its components to expected outcomes. Evidence can be used to underpin each link in the model. Significantly, they can offer means to show how activities may lead to medium- and long-term outcomes. These ideas can enable the development of frameworks to guide the planning, implementation and consideration of the results of the evaluation. Theory-based and related evaluation methods include theories of change (Weiss 1972; Chen and Rossi 1983; Chen 1990; Connell *et al.* 1995; Funnel 1997; Weiss 1997; Owen and Rodgers 1999;

Judge and Bauld 2001); programme theory evaluation (Rogers 2008); realistic evaluation (Pawson and Tilley 1997); and contribution analysis (Mayne 2008). Contribution analysis adds to the field by including a focus on the exploration of plausible alternative explanations for outcomes, such as other programmes, trends (economic or social) or behavioural factors unrelated to the programme. Contribution analysis involves six key steps (Eirich and Morrison 2011):

Step 1:   Set out the attribution problem to be addressed.
Step 2:   Develop a theory of change and risks to it.
Step 3:   Gather the existing evidence on the theory of change.
Step 4:   Assemble and assess the contribution story, and challenges to it.
Step 5:   Seek out additional evidence.
Step 6:   Revise and strengthen the contribution story.

Tilley (2000) argues that consideration should be given not just to the outcome but to the circumstances that produced it, and why and how it was achieved, so that valuable information can be obtained on the reproducibility and generalizability of the findings.

Outcomes frameworks are being developed for different sectors and aspects of health and well-being, for use in developing, planning and evaluating interventions. These include frameworks for complex health and well-being interventions which employ theory-based approaches and a range of tools such as outcomes triangles, logic models and results chains. Figure 9.3 is an example of the stages of developing an intervention framework.

An outcomes triangle gives an overview of how activities contribute to different levels of outcome, such as service outcomes, intermediate outcomes and overarching strategic outcomes. Figure 9.4 shows an outcome triangle for mental health developed by NHS Scotland.

A logic model such as the one in Figure 9.5 shows the main links between activities and outcomes, and how these contribute to the achievement of intermediate and overarching strategic outcomes. The assumptions and outcomes of such models are evidenced (indicated by numbered links in the diagram). Local, national and international evidence sources can be used (for example, research studies, evaluations, surveys and case studies).

Indicators

For each outcome in an intervention there needs to be one or more indicators, which can be defined as a 'quantitative or qualitative factor or variable that provides a simple and reliable means to measure achievement, to reflect the changes connected to an intervention, or to help assess the performance' (Development Assistance Committee 2002: 25). Indicators provide a basis for collecting evidence. An example of how an indicator links to an outcome and evidence (data sources) is shown in Table 9.3.

International, national and local outcomes and related indicator sets are already available or being developed by organizations such as WHO and the UK

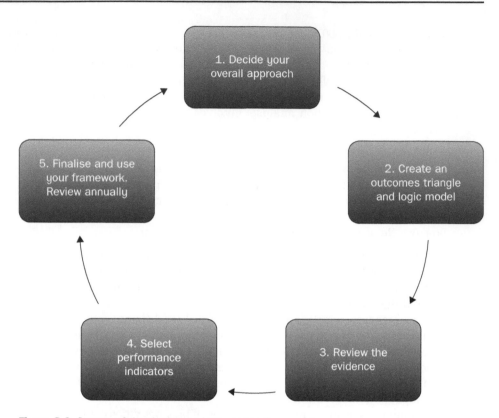

Figure 9.3 Stages of developing an intervention framework
Source: Local Government Improvement and Development (2011).

Department of Health, for work in improving health and well-being. Indicators may be direct, such as numbers of immunizations performed, or may be indirect or proxy, such as mortality as a proxy for health. Indicators suitable for evaluating work to reduce inequalities have also been developed (Hamer *et al.* 2003; Marmot 2010). Figure 9.6 shows examples of those being used in practice for establishing baseline data (London Health Observatory 2011).

Data gathering

Having defined indicators for success, the evaluation process next involves gathering data to provide evidence of change. Consideration needs to be given to what, when and how this is done, and the comparison being made. Essentially data is required to compare the situation before and after the intervention, and if relevant, between any other individuals or groups being used for comparison. Relevant data may be derived from primary (collected specifically for the purpose of the study) or secondary (collected for another purpose, but applicable to the

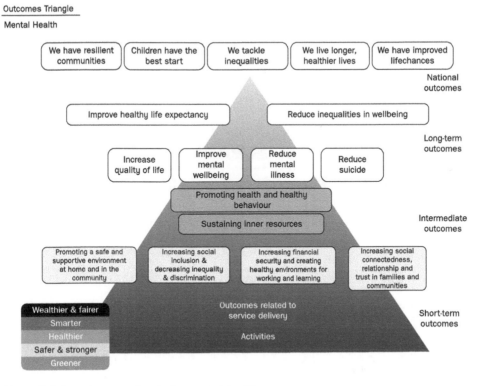

Outcomes Triangle

Mental Health

Figure 9.4 An outcomes triangle for mental health

Source: NHS Health Scotland (2012a). Reproduced with kind permission from NHS Health Scotland (www. healthscotland.com).

intervention) sources. Whether data generation is part of the evaluation process depends on the nature of the intervention and target group, the indicator in question and the quality required, as well as the time and resources available. In some cases suitable national or local data is already available through activities such as official registrations and notifications, censuses and surveys, or through other projects and programmes. For example, figures for mortality, morbidity, employment and educational attainment can be accessed from national data-sets.

Measuring health, well-being, social class and other constructs requires their definition and operationalization. This can be complex if there are no universally accepted definitions or measurement tools, which is the case for health and well-being. These constructs can be measured in a range of ways using a range of dimensions. Traditionally, objective measures have been based on a medical model of health, with health as the absence of death and disease using the proxies of mortality and morbidity. Measures based on these include the quality adjusted life year (QALY) and disability adjusted life year (DALY). On a national level until recently, income and wealth as measured by gross domestic product (GDP) has been used as an objective measure of health and well-being on the assumption that these are positively correlated. However, in recognition that these measures and

Logic model 5–Increasing financial security and creating mentally healthy environment for working and learning.

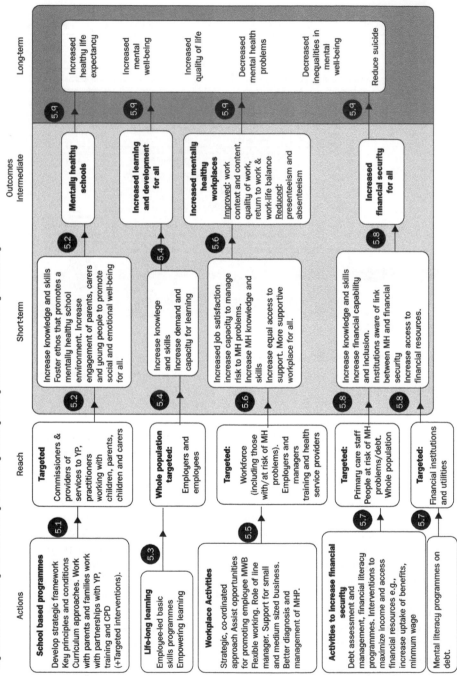

Figure 9.5 Logic model for mental health

Source: NHS Health Scotland (2012b). Reproduced with kind permission from NHS Health Scotland (www.healthscotland.com).

Table 9.3 Example of linking outcomes, indicators and evidence

Outcomes	Indicators	Evidence/data sources
Increased awareness of, and exposure to, messages about the hazards of environmental tobacco smoke	Percentage of adults who recall the content of an environmental tobacco smoke media campaign (which includes brochures, posters, presentations)	State surveys

Source: adapted from: MacDonald *et al.* (2001)

- Male life expectancy
- Female life expectancy
- Slope index of inequality (SII) for male life expectancy
- Slope index of inequality (SII) for female life expectancy
- Slope index of inequality (SII) for male disability-free life expectancy
- Slope index of inequality (SII) for female disability-free life expectancy
- Children achieving a good level of development at age 5
- Young people who are not in education, employment or training (NEET)
- People in households in receipt of means-tested benefits
- Slope index of inequality for people in households in receipt of means-tested benefits

---

Figure 9.6 Examples of health inequality indicators

their underpinning assumptions are limited, considerable work has taken place to develop more appropriate, extensive and sophisticated definitions and measures of health and well-being, most notably at national level through the Office for National Statistics' Measuring National Well-being (MNW) Programme which was launched in November 2010 (Department of Health 2011).

In addition to objective measures relating to external factors considered necessary for a good quality of life such as adequate income, housing and education, subjective measures relating to how people feel, engage with their environment, and survive and thrive in the challenges of life are important. So, for example, a subjective indicator would measure how people feel about their level of income, rather than their actual level of income (Lambeth First 2011). Well-being measures may also be indirect, for example by capturing how people spend their time in different activities they are involved with; this might measure how often people do voluntary work. Health and well-being may thus encompass mental, physical and social aspects of life and include concepts such as happiness, resilience, and the assets and resources (capital) that underpin living.

Where it is necessary to generate data, appropriate methods and tools need to be chosen or developed, taking into account that there are many good tools and approaches already available, and it can be time consuming and costly to develop bespoke methods and tools for an intervention. The data required may be qualitative or quantitative and methods such as surveys, questionnaires, interviews, focus groups, community consultation events and documentary analysis may be used. Measures may be as simple as a single-item question such as 'Thinking about your own life and personal circumstances, how satisfied are you with your life as a whole?' (University of Sheffield 2012), through to tools with many dimensions such as that in Figure 9.7 (Lambeth First 2011).

There are many instruments available for measuring health and well-being focusing on specific dimensions (such as mental health), groups (such as children) or settings (such as workplaces). For example, the Warwick-Edinburgh Mental Well-being Scale (WEMWBS; NHS Health Scotland 2006) (Figure 9.8) has been developed to measure mental well-being.

When considering inequality outcomes, demographic data will also need to be collected alongside health and well-being data in order to assess changes. Munoz-Arroyo and Sutton (2007) review inequality measures, including their applicability to different circumstances and audiences.

Methods and tools for measurement need to be considered in terms of their fitness for purpose. Two key elements of this are reliability and validity. Reliability refers to how consistent a measuring device is. A measurement is said to be reliable or consistent if it produces similar results if used again in similar circumstances. For example, a measurement of psychological well-being giving the same values when applied several times to the same individual at a point in time would be considered reliable. Validity refers to whether a tool measures or examines what it claims to measure or examine, for example, establishing that a tool to measure psychological well-being actually measures this and not something else. There are many reliable and well validated instruments available relevant to work in improving health and well-being.

- How they feel about themselves (personal feelings), e.g. How happy are you?
- To what extent do you feel a sense of meaning and purpose in your life?
- Do you feel able to influence things in your individual life, local environment or wider society?
- Do you feel you are dealt with fairly and confident that your interests are acknowledged?
- How they function at a personal level (personal functioning)
- What activities do you engage in, including those aspects of your life linked to enterprising activity and creativity?
- How would you assess your skills and educational attainment?
- How motivated are you?
- To what extent do you feel in control, especially in work or financial terms?
- How they feel in relation to those around them (social feelings)
- Do you feel a sense of belonging to a community or place?
- What is your experience of your neighbourhood, your friendships and support networks?
- How they function in a social context (social functioning)
- How do you relate to others, and how involved are you in social activities such as volunteering, work, hobbies, community groups?
- How valued do you feel at work?
- To what extent do you actively contribute to civil society, or vote?
- How much do you put back into the local community?

Figure 9.7 Lambeth First multi-dimensional well-being assessment tool

When looking at outcomes for an intervention consideration needs to be given to the scale of the work and whether it is possible or desirable to look at the whole population of interest or just samples. If samples, these must be of a suitable size and composition so that conclusions can be extrapolated to the wider intervention.

Below are some statements about feelings and thoughts

Please tick the box that best describes your experience of each over the last 2 weeks

STATEMENTS	None of the time	Rarely	Some of the time	Often	All of the time
I've been feeling optimistic about the future	1	2	3	4	5
I've been feeling useful	1	2	3	4	5
I've been feeling relaxed	1	2	3	4	5
I've been feeling interested in other people	1	2	3	4	5
I've had evergy to spare	1	2	3	4	5
I've been dealing with problems well	1	2	3	4	5
I've been thinking clearly	1	2	3	4	5
I've been feeling good about myself	1	2	3	4	5
I've been feeling close to other people	1	2	3	4	5
I've been feeling confident	1	2	3	4	5
I've been able to make up my own mind about things	1	2	3	4	5
I've been feeling loved	1	2	3	4	5
I've been interested in new things	1	2	3	4	5
I've been feeling cheerful	1	2	3	4	5

Figure 9.8 The Warwick-Edinburgh Mental Well-being Scale

Source: NHS Health Scotland (2006). © NHS Health Scotland, University of Warwick and University of Edinburgh, 2006, all rights reserved.

Approaches combining methods

A range of tools which combine methods have been developed to provide information on the effects of interventions on and within communities, particularly programmes addressing health inequalities. These include health impact assessments and health equity audits (Quigley *et al*. 2004). Methods such as the latter have been built into health service planning and delivery in the UK (NICE 2003). Approaches have been developed which specifically aim to overcome practical difficulties of evaluation and make it easier to do for a wider range of stakeholders. These include Ovretveit's (2002) action evaluation approach mentioned earlier in this chapter and the RE-AIM framework developed by Glasgow *et al*. (2006).

The RE-AIM framework provides an evaluation methodology useful for complex multi-level activities such as those incorporating policy, environmental and individual interventions. This framework focuses on the five main dimensions of reach, efficacy, adoption, implementation and maintenance, on the premise that these interact to determine the overall outcome of an intervention. The consideration of maintenance or sustainability (extent to which a programme is sustained over time) is a valuable element of this model.

The purposes of RE-AIM are to:

- broaden the criteria used to evaluate programmes to include context and external validity
- evaluate issues relevant to programme adoption, implementation and sustainability
- help close the gap between research studies and practice by informing design of interventions, providing guides for adoptees, and suggesting standard reporting criteria.

Evaluation case study – The Target Well-being initiative

The Target Well-being (TWB) initiative (http://www.targetwell-being.org.uk/sites/default/files/TWB_full_report_03.10.pdf) is a project funded by the UK Big Lottery fund which aims to improve well-being and encourage healthier lifestyles in the North West of England. The initiative focuses specifically on reducing inequalities through activities targeted on areas of greatest need and deprivation, particularly the key areas of increasing physical activity, encouraging healthy eating and improving mental well-being. Key subthemes within these are:

1 Mental well-being. This comprises improving the mental health and well-being of vulnerable and marginalized young people, adults and older people:

1a People benefiting from improved self-management.
1b People benefiting from increased job control.
1c Increased sense of belonging within their community.
1d Increased self-esteem.

(continued)

2 Physical activity. This comprises increased and sustained physical activity levels through physical activity and lifestyle interventions, leading to reductions in obesity levels and improved physical fitness:

2a Increased cycling and walking.

2b Increased use of open space for physical activity.

2c More active daily lifestyles.

3 Healthy eating. This comprises increasing healthy eating patterns and reducing body fat profile by improving access to healthy eating programmes:

3a Increased number of people involved in food growing.

3b Increased availability of healthy food.

3c Improved levels of food preparation and cooking skills.

The TWB initiative takes an outcomes-based approach, and aims to reduce inequalities through two population level and ten area-based programmes. The population level activity focuses on prison and older people's care settings. The ten local programmes are each made up of a number of projects, totalling 90 in all, delivered by 67 local organizations and benefiting over 55,000 people. Examples of projects include the promotion of cycling to school for children, chair-based exercise for people over 50, healthy cooking sessions for families, and mental health projects centred around worklessness.

This initiative exemplifies how many interventions may be taking place that all contribute to a set of key outcomes. The range of outcomes each project might contribute to has been assessed, and the ways in which interventions may interconnect have been recognized. For example,

'[I]n the healthy eating projects, three projects will interconnect to bring fresh produce and healthy eating to Manchester's most deprived communities. For the purposes of the TWB evaluation it was important to consider how projects would contribute to the portfolio's outcomes based on the specific activities that they deliver. Each project is expected to contribute to a primary or priority theme but secondary benefits might also be expected to follow. For example, an allotment project would contribute to outcomes 3a, 3b [and] 3c above but could also contribute to outcomes 1c and 2c from mental well-being and physical activity themes.

The main elements of evaluation include:

1 The collection and analysis of regional level outcome data.

2 The analysis of key indicators in target areas over time.

3 The collection and analysis of regional level process data.

4 Support to individual projects to identify their own indicators and means of measuring them.

5 Baseline mapping of areas on key indicators and tracking over the lifetime of the project.

Data sources include local and regional data already available, as well as bespoke tools to generate both quantitative and qualitative data. Central to this are welcome and exit questionnaires to generate pre- and post-intervention scores for a range of elements related to the outcomes. Outcomes cover cognitive, affective and behavioural dimensions as well as measures such as height and weight. The questionnaires draw on established and academically validated tools such as the Health Survey for England, the Short Warwick and Edinburgh Mental Well-being Survey, and well-being and life satisfaction questions. Other tools include focus groups. The evaluation also aims to include beneficiary and stakeholder participation, and makes use of reach analysis to provide evidence that the initiative is successfully reaching intended beneficiaries.

References

Bowling, A. (2002) *Research Methods in Health: Investigating Health and Health Services*, 2nd edn. Available at www.mcgraw-hill.co.uk/openup/chapters/0335206433.pdf (accessed 27 Mar. 2014).

Bradford-Hill, A. (1965) Heberden oration: reflections on the controlled trial, *Annals of Rheumatic Diseases*, 25: 107–113.

Chelimsky, E. (1997) Thoughts for a new evaluation society, *Evaluation*, 3(1): 97–118.

Chen, H.T. (1990) *Theory-Driven Evaluations*. Thousand Oaks, CA: Sage.

Chen, H. and Rossi, P. (1983) Evaluating with sense: the theory-driven approach, *Evaluation Review*, 7(3): 283–302.

Connell, J.P., Kubisch, A.C., Schorr, L.B. and Weiss, C.H. (1995) *New Approaches to Evaluating Community Initiatives: Concepts, Methods and Contexts*. Washington, DC: Aspen Institute.

Department of Health (2009) *World Class Commissioning – An Introduction*. Available at www.dh.gov.uk/en/Publicationsandstatistics/Publications/PublicationsPolicyAndGuidance/DH_107079 (accessed 12 Feb. 2011).

Department of Health (2010a) *Healthy Lives, Healthy People: Our Strategy for Public Health in England*. Available at www.dh.gov.uk/en/Publicationsandstatistics/Publications/Publications PolicyAndGuidance/DH_121941 (accessed 12 Feb. 2011).

Department of Health (2010b) *Healthy Lives, Healthy People: Transparency in Outcomes. Proposals for a Public Health Outcomes Framework*. Available at www.dh.gov.uk/dr_consum_dh/groups/dh_digitalassets/@dh/@en/documents/digitalasset/dh_123113.pdf (accessed 12 Feb. 2011).

Department of Health (2011) *No Health Without Mental Health: A Cross-Government Mental Health Outcomes Strategy for People of All Ages*. Available at www.dh.gov.uk/prod_consum_dh/groups/dh_digitalassets/documents/digitalasset/dh_124058.pdf (accessed 15 May 2014).

Development Assistance Committee (2002) *Glossary of Terms in Evaluation and Results-Based Management*. Paris. Available at www.oecd.org/dataoecd/29/21/2754804.pdf (accessed 27 Mar. 2014).

Eirich, F. and Morrison, A. (2011) Contribution analysis, in Anonymous, *A Service Improvement Evaluation Framework Detailed Evaluation Short Guide*. Edinburgh: Joint Improvement Team. Available at www.jitscotland.org.uk/search/ (accessed Feb. 2014).

Fink, A. (2004) *Evaluation Fundamentals: Insights into the Outcomes, Effectiveness, and Quality of Health Programs*, 2nd edn. London: Sage.

Funnell, S. (1997) Program logic: an adaptable tool, *Evaluation News and Comment*, 6(1): 5–17.

Glasgow, R., Klesges, L., Dzewaltowski, D., Estabrooks, P. and Vogt, T. (2006) Evaluating the impact of health promotion programs: using the RE-AIM framework to form summary measures for decision making involving complex issues, *Health Education and Research*, 21(5): 688–94.

Graham, H. (2003) Building an inter-disciplinary science of health inequalities: the example of life-course research, *Social Science & Medicine*, 55(11): 2005–16.

Graham, H. (2004) Tackling inequalities in health in England: remedying health disadvantages, narrowing health gaps or reducing health gradients? *Journal of Social Policy*, 33(1): 115–31.

Hamer, L., Jacobson, B., Flowers, J. and Johnstone, F. (2003) *Health Equity Audit Made Simple: A Briefing for Primary Care Trusts and Local Strategic Partnerships*. London: Health Development Agency. Available at www.nice.org.uk/niceMedia/documents/equityauditfinal. pdf (accessed 27 Mar. 2014).

Heron, R., McKeown, S., Tomenson, J. and Teasdale, E. (1999) Study to evaluate the effectiveness of stress management workshops on response to general and occupational measures of stress, *Occupational Medicine*, 49(7): 451–67.

Hills, D. (2004) *Evaluation of Community-level Interventions for Health Improvement: A Review of Experience in the UK*. London: Health Development Agency.

Judge, K. and Bauld, L. (2001) Strong theory, flexible methods: evaluating complex community-based initiatives, *Critical Public Health*, 11(1): 19–38.

Kellogg Foundation (2004) *W. K. Kellogg Foundation Evaluation Handbook*. Battle Creek, MI: W.K. Kellogg Foundation.

Kelly, M. (2008) The value of a strong trials infrastructure in supporting evidence based medicine, PowerPoint slides presentation at HM Treasury, Raising standards in UK policy evaluation: 'Learning from the last 10 years'. Available at www.civilservice.gov.uk/wp-content/uploads/2011/09/ Policy_evaluation_value_of_strong_trials_mkelly_tcm6-36805.pdf (accessed 27 Mar. 2014).

Khlat, M. (1997) 'Contribution of the case-control method to health program evaluation', in M. Khlat (ed.) *Demographic Evaluation of Health Programmes*, Paris: CICRED.

Lambeth First (2011) *Measuring Well-being in Lambeth, A Guide for Practitioners*. Available at www.lambethfirst.org.uk/public.getfile.cfm?type—ultiplefile&fid (accessed 26 March 2012).

Local Government Improvement and Development (2011) *How do I Create my Own Framework?* Available at www.idea.gov.uk/idk/core/page.do?pageId=21652857 (accessed 27 Mar. 2014).

London Health Observatory (2011) *Marmot Indicators for Local Authorities in England, 2012.* Available at www.lho.org.uk/LHO_TOPICS/NATIONAL_LEAD_AREAS/MARMOT/ MARMOTINDICATORS.ASPX (accessed 15 May 2014, page last updated 11 Feb. 2011).

MacDonald, G., Starr, G., Schooley, M., Yee, S.L., Klimowski, K. and Turner, K. (2001) *Introduction to Program Evaluation for Comprehensive Tobacco Control Programs*. Atlanta, GA: Centers for Disease Control and Prevention. Available at www.cdc.gov/tobacco/tobacco_control_ programs/surveillance_evaluation/evaluation_manual/pdfs/evaluation.pdf (accessed 27 Mar. 2014).

Mackenbach, J. and Gunning-Schepers, L. (1997) How should interventions to reduce inequalities in health be evaluated? *Journal of Epidemiology and Community Health*, 51(4): 359–64.

Marmot, M. (2010) *Fair Society, Healthy Lives: Strategic Review of Health Inequalities in England post 2010*. Available at www.marmotreview.org (accessed 27 Mar. 2014).

Mayer, K. (2009) New directions in life course research, *Annual Review of Sociology*, 35: 413–33.

Mayne, J. (2008) *Contribution Analysis: An Approach to Exploring Cause and Effect, ILAC Brief 16*, Rome, Institutional Learning and Change (ILAC) Initiative.

Medical Research Council [MRC] (2008) *Developing and Evaluating Complex Health Interventions: New Guidance*. Available at www.mrc.ac.uk/complexinterventionsguidance (accessed 15 May 2014).

Munoz-Arroyo, R. and Sutton, M. (2007) *Measuring Socio-Economic Inequalities in Health: A Practical Guide*. Edinburgh: Scot PHO, Public Health Information for Scotland. Available at www.scotpho.org.uk/downloads/scotphoreports/scotpho071009_measuringinequalities_rep. pdf (accessed 15 May 2014).

National Institute for Care and Clinical Excellence (NICE) (2003) *Health Equity Audit Made Simple: A Briefing for Primary Care Trusts and Local Strategic Partnerships*. Available at www.nice.org.uk/niceMedia/documents/equityauditfinal.pdf (accessed 23 Mar. 2012).

National Institute for Care and Clinical Excellence (NICE) (2005) *Reviewing and Grading the Evidence* (2004 version, updated March 2005). London: National Institute for Clinical Excellence.

NHS Health Scotland (2006) *The Warwick-Edinburgh Mental Well-being Scale (WEMWBS)*. Available at: www.healthscotland.com/documents/1467.aspx (accessed 23 Mar. 2012).

NHS Health Scotland (2012a) *Outcomes Triangle Mental Health*. Available at www.healthscotland.com/OFHI/MentalHealth/content/MHOutcomes_triangle.html (accessed 27 Mar. 2014).

NHS Health Scotland (2012b) *Logic model 5 – Increasing Financial Security and Creating Mentally Healthy Environment for Working and Learning*. Available at www.healthscotland.com/OFHI/MentalHealth/logicmodels/MH_LM5.html (accessed 27 Mar. 2014).

Nutbeam, D. and Bauman, A. (2006) *Evaluation in a Nutshell: A Practical Guide to the Evaluation of Health Promotion Programs*. Sydney: McGraw-Hill.

Oakley, A. (1998) Experimentation and social interventions: a forgotten but important history, *British Medical Journal*, 317(31). Available at www.bmj.com/content/317/7167/1239.full.pdf (accessed 27 Mar. 2014).

Ovretveit, J. (2002) *Action Evaluation of Health Programmes and Changes: A Handbook for a User-focused Approach*. Oxford: Radcliffe.

Ovretveit, J. (2003) *Evaluating Health Interventions*. Maidenhead: Open University Press.

Owen, J. and Rogers, P. (1999) *Program Evaluation: Forms and Approaches*, 2nd edn. St Leonards: Allen and Unwin.

Pawson, R. and Tilley, N. (1997) *Realistic Evaluation*. London: Sage.

Plewis, I. (2009) Health inequalities: evaluating causal effects on the social gradient. Unpublished paper.

Quigley, R., Cavanagh, S., Harrison, D. and Taylor, L. (2004) *Clarifying Health Impact Assessment, Integrated Impact Assessment and Health Needs Assessment*. London: Health Development Agency. Available at www.apho.org.uk/resource/view.aspx?RID=44782 (accessed 15 May 2014).

Reynolds, A., Temple, J., Ou, S., Robertson, D., Mersky, J., Topitzes, J. and Niles, M. (2007) Effects of a school-based, early childhood intervention on adult health and well-being: a 19-year follow-up of low-income families, *Archives of Pediatrics and Adolescent Medicine*, 161(8): 730–9.

Rogers, P. (2005) 'Logic models', in S. Mathison (ed.) *Encyclopedia of Evaluation*. Beverly Hills, CA: Sage.

Rogers, P. (2008) Using programme theory to evaluate complicated and complex aspects of interventions. *Evaluation*, 14(1): 29–48.

Rosen, L., Manor, O., Engelhard, D. and Zucker, D. (2006) In defense of the randomized controlled trial for health promotion research, *American Journal of Public Health*, 96(7): 1181–6. Available at www.ncbi.nlm.nih.gov/pmc/articles/PMC1483860/ (accessed 27 Mar. 2014).

Scriven, M. (1996). Formative, summative, and goal-free evaluation, *International Encyclopedia of Educational Research*, 2nd edn. Oxford: Pergamon.

Shiell, A., Hawe, P. and Gold, L. (2008) Complex interventions or complex systems? Implications for health economic evaluation. *British Medical Journal*, 336(7656): 1281–3.

Tilley N. (2000) Realistic evaluation: an overview. Paper presented at the founding conference of the Danish Evaluation Society, September. Available at www.evidence-basedmanagement.com/research_practice/articles/nick_tilley.pdf (accessed 17 Aug. 2011).

Tones, K. and Tilford, S. (1994) *Health Education: Effectiveness, Efficiency and Equity*. London: Chapman and Hall.

University of Sheffield (2012) *Well-being Measures*. Available at www.sheffield.ac.uk/cwipp/measurement (accessed 23 Mar. 2012).

Weiss, C. (1972) *Evaluation Research – Methods for Assessing Program Effectiveness*. Eaglewood Cliffs, NJ: Prentice Hall.

Weiss, C. (1997) *Evaluation*. Eaglewood Cliffs, NJ: Prentice Hall.

Whitehead, M. (2007) A typology of actions to tackle social inequalities in health, *Journal of Epidemiology and Community Health*, 61(6): 473–8.

Wimbush, E. and Watson, J. (2000) An evaluation framework for health promotion: theory, quality and effectiveness, *Evaluation*, 6(3): 301–21.

World Health Organization (WHO) (1998) *Health Promotion Evaluation –Recommendations to Policy-makers. Report of the WHO European Working Group on Health Promotion Evaluation.* Copenhagen: WHO.

World Health Organization (WHO) (2006) *Engaging for Health. 11th General Programme of Work, 2006-2015. A Global Health Agenda.* Available at http://apps.who.int/iris/handle/10665/69379 (accessed 15 May 2014).

10 Skills and activities for improving health and well-being

Allison Thorpe

Introduction

Previous chapters have given a broad overview of the health and well-being agenda, locally, nationally and globally. As they describe, the scale and scope of the challenge is undoubtedly enormous, requiring input from across the whole of society, not just the health system, if sustainable progress is to be made. But how confident can we afford to be that this input is appropriately skilled? And where do we need to put in additional support?

Globally, there have been considerable changes in public health practice and regulation since the turn of the century. In England, from 1999, when *Saving Lives* (Department of Health 1999) gave formal support to the creation of the multidisciplinary specialist practitioner, to the present day, when the locus of many public health operations has been re-situated in local authorities, the structures and professional contexts for practice have all changed fundamentally. In effect, the composition of the workforce has been widened and the agenda and forums for practice redefined, drawing in personnel working in the health and social care sectors, but also increasingly town planners, local authority officers, volunteers and community workers . . . and the list goes on.

England is not alone in adopting this approach. Recognition of the broad scope of health improvement practice, and the contribution to improving health and well-being that public health skills and activities can make at every level of the workforce, can be traced in many other countries, and in cross-country policies. The new European Health Policy Framework, Health 2020,[1] for example, has strengthening people-centred health systems and public health capacity as one of its four priority areas for action.

Informed citizens, conscientious businesses, independent agencies and expert bodies are increasingly recognized as having a role to play in securing health and well-being improvement, but this is not always recognized as being a core role for every sector. And access to knowledge, skills, training opportunities and evidence-based support is neither uniform nor universal. But could it be prioritized?

In this chapter, we consider what skills and competences are required to improve health and well-being, introduce some of the approaches to describing skills and competences, and reflect on the contribution we as professionals can make to driving forward skills development in order to promote population health and well-being. Inevitably, in a short chapter, we are not able to cover all of the skills and activities which are influential in improving health and well-being but, through signposting, readers are directed to other resources where further more detailed information can be found.

Summary of key aims and learning objectives

Drawing on national and international literature, this chapter:

*   reflects on the context
*   provides a broad oversight of the generic and professional skills base for improving health and well-being
*   encourages reflection on how these skills can be applied in different settings
*   signposts resources for readers wishing to explore the skills and competencies for health and well-being in more depth.

This chapter focuses on the core, foundational competences shared by people working within the field of health and well-being improvement. In addition to these competences, there are also technical-, functional- and discipline-specific competences; that is, skills and abilities specific to a particular aspect or practice role. These technical competences are beyond the scope of this chapter.

Improving professional practice: the competency approach

Previous chapters have highlighted the mounting evidence of the gap separating the rich and the poor between and within countries. Maintaining and improving the health of populations, and reducing the experience of health inequalities and health inequities, requires concerted action across the three domains of public health, building healthy policy, creating supportive environments, strengthening community action and reorienting organizational activity in a range of settings. Workforce development and capacity-building strategies have an important role to play in achieving this.

Competence frameworks are increasingly used in workforce development as a way to increase transparency about the knowledge, skills, attitudes and behaviours expected of a workforce. They act as a structured set of common reference points, describing the core skills, competences and attributes required to promote and support high-quality practice, and are often characterized by a focus on the results or outcomes of activity, rather than solely on the ability to perform a task.

In recent years one could be forgiven for thinking there has been something of an outbreak of such frameworks in the health professions and health arenas. A quick Google search asking for competency frameworks and public health returned some 8,250,000 returns in 0.4 seconds. An initial search through the first 30 pages demonstrated that these frameworks were generally either uni-disciplinary or reflected on single subject areas such as alcohol, and focused on professional roles in relation to the subject area. A more systematic European Review of Competence Frameworks[2] in use across the European Union (Trace

Project undated) demonstrated that despite the apparently great diversity in the scope, detail and usage of the frameworks it identified, in general terms the approaches taken to describing competence development reflected a limited number of themes (see Table 10.1)

One of the fundamental problems, however, is understanding what exactly the frameworks are trying to describe – professional roles, services specifications, or skills and attributes of the workforce – with some lists of competences being more reflective of the descriptions and specifications of services, rather than the competences to be expected of the professionals expected to perform these services (Birt 2011). Navigating this complex landscape can be confusing and lead to conflicting understanding of what skills and competences are required to support and enhance population health and well-being.

Even the fundamentals are not always clear. While in broad terms, the academic literature tends to agree that a 'competence' is a standard, reflecting an individual's capacity to perform a job's responsibilities ('she is a good statistician'), and 'competency' is more contextualized, focusing on the broad range of skills which underpin performance in a particular situation, quite often the concepts of competency and competence are used interchangeably in the frameworks.

The concept of core competencies implies that there is, or should be, a set of knowledge, skills and attitudes which constitute a common baseline for all people working in the area covered by the competency framework. Yet, at the time of writing and despite the proliferation of activity, there is no single set of commonly agreed competences which encapsulate the skills and attributes required for delivery of effective health and well-being services. Infrastructural differences between and within countries, lack of clear definitions and shared understanding of roles, responsibilities, boundaries and interrelationships between sectors, have resulted in the development of multiple (often geographically specific and uni-disciplinary) competency lists and frameworks, many of which have broad relevance to skills which could improve health and well-being, and many of which, recognizing the relevance of other frameworks, cross-refer. (See Table 10.2 for examples.)

Table 10.1 Competence frameworks: approaches to competence development and assessment

Development	Based on the acquisition of knowledge
	Based on task analysis
	Based on competence analysis
	A combination of the above
Assessment	Knowledge-based tests or examinations
	Practical tests (that may be based on a task or competence-based indicators)
	Production of evidence of competence against standards or indicators (for example by building a paper-based or electronic portfolio)
	A combination of the above

Table 10.2 Examples of competency frameworks

Framework	Scope	Website
National Occupational Standards for Public Health	These standards have been designed to be used across service, organizational and individual levels across all sectors to develop services, plan workforces, guide practice and the management of people, and form the basis of education, training and qualifications	www.wales.nhs.uk/sitesplus/ documents/888/EnglishNOS.pdf
Public Health Skills and Knowledge Framework	Skills and knowledge are split across the four core areas of public health practice, which anyone working in the field of public health will need to have, as well as the five specific areas of practice within which individual practitioners will develop and work	www.phorcast.org.uk/page. php?page_id=313
The Australian Health Promotion National Competency Framework	This is a set of health promotion core competencies for health promotion practitioners, organisations, employers and educators. It identifies competencies for health promotion at beginner practitioner levels	http://research.uow.edu.au/content/ groups/public/@web/@criphn/ documents/doc/uow101717.pdf
CompHP	Designed for use by practitioners whose main role and function is health promotion, and who have a graduate qualification in health promotion or a related discipline. The standards will also be useful to those working in other professional areas whose role substantially includes health promotion; employers, professional associations and trade unions with a remit for health promotion practitioners; and in the development of education and training programmes supporting health promotion practice	www.iuhpe.org/images/PROJECTS/ ACCREDITATION/CompHP_standards_ handbook_final.pdf
National Occupational Standards (NOS) for Social Marketing	The NOS for social marketing provide a comprehensive functional map of social marketing. They describe the outcomes required from the functions, but do not restrict the ways in which the functions are carried out	www.ukstandards.co.uk/nos-search/Pages/ SearchResults.aspx?k=All%20 NOS&r=organisation%3D%22Council%20 for%20Administration%22%20 suite%3D%22Social%20Marketing%22

(Continued)

Table 10.2 Examples of competency frameworks (*Continued*)

Framework	Scope	Website
Core Competencies for Public Health Practice	Designed for public health professionals at three different levels: Tier 1 (entry level), Tier 2 (supervisors and managers), and Tier 3 (senior managers and CEOs). The Core Competencies are a set of skills desirable for the broad practice of public health, reflecting the characteristics that staff of public health organizations may want to possess as they work to protect and promote health in the community	www.phf.org/resourcestools/Pages/Core_Public_Health_Competencies.aspx
Prevention and Lifestyle Behaviour Change Competency Framework	This is essentially a commissioning-led framework for workforce change. It describes the competences required by the workforce to enable them to develop their skills in addressing the health and well-being needs of the local population	http://chain.ulcc.ac.uk/chain/documents/competenceframeworkintro.pdf

In effect, the overlaps between the agendas of public health, health promotion, health education, social marketing, social epidemiology and health strategy (to name but a few) have created a situation whereby one could be forgiven for thinking that the best approach to defining the skills and competences for health improvement and well-being is 'pick and mix'.

But there are areas of agreement. For example, while the frameworks and lists are neither uniform in their approach to competence development and assessment, nor standard in their application of role definitions and outcomes, generally the rationale for their development has reflected on a common set of goals:

- development of quality assurance systems for practice, education and training
- underpinning future developments in health and well-being training and course development
- continuing professional development of (sometimes specified, sometimes ill defined) workforces
- supporting accreditation and development of professional standards, consolidating (health improvement and well-being, or other specified activity) as a specialized field of practice.

These areas of agreement are not restricted to the purposes of the competency framework. On the contrary, by reading across the frameworks, it is apparent that there are a number of areas of practice where, despite differences in language and terminology, some common foundational knowledge and skill sets are being advocated. Key to the notion of core competencies is that they transcend the boundaries of the specific disciplines working within the field of health and well-being, and reflect the common knowledge, skills and abilities of all professionals working to improve the population's health. They should also be independent of programme or topic areas so that they reflect a coherent baseline to support practice in this area.

Core health and well-being sciences and knowledge

As successive reports by the Marmot Review teams (Commission on Social Determinants of Health 2008; Marmot 2010, 2011; Marmot and World Health Organization 2010) have reiterated, health and well-being practice and advocacy need to go beyond health care, putting health on the agenda for all sectors, ensuring that the health consequences of decisions and broader responsibilities for health and well-being are recognized, so that we are able to tackle the wider determinants of health and well-being and really get to the 'causes of the causes' of ill health, including mental ill health. Only in this way will we address the health equity gap, and make progress towards sustainable population health and well-being. To achieve this we need transformational change in the way we deliver health and well-being services – particularly preventive services.

Throughout the competence frameworks, reference was commonly made to a series of high-level concepts and principles as being influential in guiding and

Table 10.3 Core knowledge domains underpinning health and well-being practice

1   Awareness of the concepts, principles and values of health promotion as defined by
     the Ottawa Charter for Health Promotion (WHO 1986) and subsequent charters
2   Understanding of the concepts of health equity, social justice and health as a human
     right
3   Awareness of the determinants of health and their implications for effective practice
4   Understanding of social and cultural diversity
5   Awareness of models and approaches to support health promotion, behaviour change,
     empowerment, participation and equity
6   Awareness of the broader health and social care infrastructure and context for action
7   Policy analysis techniques to identify the scope, impact, strengths, weaknesses and
     implications of proposed policy developments

informing practice. In effect, this suggests that these domains of knowledge may
be the cornerstones for health and well-being practice, irrespective of discipline
(see Table 10.3).

Programme planning, implementation and evaluation

Programme planning is commonly cited in the competence frameworks as an
essential organizational practice for health improvement and well-being. While the
balance of activities covered in the frameworks varies, in general terms, effective
programme planning for health and well-being draws on a variety of consistent
skills and competences:

- specialist skills such as research skills, population and situational needs
  analysis, knowledge and understanding of current models and approaches
  which support health improvement action, and evaluation
- more generic project management skills, such as setting realistic goals and
  achievable objectives, resource allocation planning and quality assurance of
  service delivery, risk management skills, contingency and resilience planning,
  and evaluation skills
- communication skills, for instance, team building, negotiation, partnership
  working and stakeholder management.

Globally, rising demands for health care, limited resources, and increasing
inequalities and inequities in health outcomes and access to health services are
common problems. Surveillance of the population, monitoring trends, analysing
causes and identifying population health needs are vital skills, enabling practitioners, managers and policy makers to effectively and efficiently identify and
address current and evolving health challenges, identifying those in greatest need
and enabling resources to be targeted to maximize the opportunities for health
improvement.

Thinking point

Look at Table 10.4. The skills in column one are commonly associated with needs assessment as part of the programme planning process in the competence frameworks. Thinking about your personal practice, complete the table. (The examples given in the boxes are to stimulate your thinking only.)

Evaluation needs to be built into the planning process for health and well-being projects. The ability to design appropriate evaluation strategies that incorporate process, impact and outcome measures is essential to inform the development of effective interventions both now and in the future.

Supporting and enabling change through partnerships, collaborative action and advocacy

Working across sectors is a critical part of the health and well-being agenda. Collaboration may seem like a simple word, but it hides a complex process, spanning a range of activities from networking, to coordination, through cooperation and collaboration to an end point which can be full integration of activities. It can be as simple as exchanging information, or refer to redesigning services, or to sharing resources, risks, responsibilities and rewards. However, one of the key skills in collaborative working is knowing who you need to work with, why you are working with them, and when you need to bring them on board. Facilitating the development and sustainability of networks and partnerships for action requires an appreciation of how members with different sectoral interests are engaging in the proposed collaborative activities.

Case study

You have recently accepted a new role working with your local council. One of your key tasks is a project which is developing/designing services for older people with the aim of promoting their health and well-being, and of reducing their use of the Accident and Emergency department. A small sum of money has been allocated to invest in start-up costs, but the local health and social care system will be expected to generate all further investments from service redesign initiatives, development of existing roles, and full engagement of local voluntary and statutory sectors. Using the sample table (Table 10.5), think about who you might need to work with on your project. In completing the table, think about the relative power and interests of each of your proposed stakeholders, the multiple hats stakeholders may wear, and the networks to which they may belong.

Advocacy can mean many things, but in general for the broader health and well-being agenda, it refers to taking action to influence social, political and economic systems or services, to bring about change which will impact positively on the

Table 10.4 Needs assessment: knowledge, skills, and demonstrations of competence

Competence	What skills do you think are associated with this competence?	What background knowledge would you need to do this effectively?	How do you demonstrate this competence	Who else might do this?	Which organizations might require these skills
Identifying the health status of populations and their related determinants of health and illness	Ability to obtain, review and interpret data	Awareness of data and information sources Understanding of health inequalities	Searching the Internet for published reports and information on local health indicators	Members of the public Researchers Project officers	Local authorities GP surgeries
Assessing the health status of populations and their related determinants of health and illness	Statistical analysis Qualitative research methods Ability to work with groups and communities	Understanding of range of assessment methods and approaches	Conducting health impact assessments		
Identify priorities for health promotion action based on best available evidence and available resources	Partnership building and negotiation Critical appraisal skills				

Table 10.5 Effective collaborative working: identifying and managing your stakeholders

Stakeholder group	Nature of interest in project	Potential impact on project (why are you working with them?)	What communications channels can you use?	When do you need to bring them on board
Older people reference group	Target audience	High, if services are not acceptable to audience, programme will fail	Focus groups	From outset

health and well-being of groups of people. In 1920, in his treatise on how to decide what is to be told to stakeholders in designing and planning public health programmes, Winslow said:

> Our facts should be fact . . . Our facts should be important . . . and the facts we teach should be comprehensible to the man in the street, and not merely to the statistician, physician, or sanitarian . . . our facts should be emotionally accept-able. If we are to attain results, it is essential not only to catch the interest of the hearer but to arouse in him a desire to attain the aim set forth. (Winslow 1920: 183)

This remains, for me, a foundational truth for health improvement and well-being advocacy; effective advocacy is not just about giving out information. It relies on having identified a clearly defined issue or challenge, realistic goals and objectives, and a defined target audience. Advocacy messages need to define the issue, suggest solutions and motivate action, by describing not just what needs to be done, but by whom. In addition, advocates need to have identified and prioritized their channels of communication, and ensured that resources are in place both to support the advocacy activity and to ensure that responses to the activity are able to achieve the desired outcome. After all, as Winslow (1920: 183) said, it is important that: 'Our facts should be usable. . . . It is useless to urge an adult to go to his physician for a health examination unless there is some reasonable probability that when he goes he will get one.' Add in planning, monitoring and evaluation, and the complexity of the skill set associated with effective advocacy becomes clear.

Communication

Public health communication has been defined as 'the scientific development, strategic dissemination, and critical evaluation of relevant, accurate, accessible, and understandable health information communicated to and from intended audiences to advance the health of the public' (Bernhardt 2004). In the field of health and well-being, this dimension of practice involves an interchange of ideas, opinions and information, addressing numerous dimensions of communication, including: internal and external exchanges; written, verbal, non-verbal and listening skills; computer literacy; providing appropriate information to different audiences; working with the media; and social marketing techniques.

Skills for international working

As other chapters in this book have demonstrated, we are living through a time of global transition, with impressive gains in life expectancy and declining fertility rates, and enormous changes in the profiles of diseases and causes of death. While the scope, scale and speed of change is not shared equally across every country, increasingly the quality of health and well-being training means that many of our skills are transferable to other settings. However, while many of the generic skills and activities may be transferrable, operationalizing these skills within a dynamic political and cultural context can be challenging. The effective utilization of skills and knowledge can be derailed by infrastructural shortcomings, lack of resources available on the ground, and even failure to recognize or respond adequately to cultural norms and practices.

Thinking point: Skills mapping

Take your favourite health journal. Pick a paper of your choice from the contents page. Read it, then populate Table 10.6. One example has been completed to aid you with this task.

However, as previously discussed, success in improving health and well-being relies not only on the exercise of professional skills and competencies, but also on broader societal engagement.

Broadening access to skills and competences

In recent decades, there has been increased recognition that professional roles alone are unlikely to be able to deliver sustainable population health improvement. This has been accompanied by a push towards broadening access to public health knowledge and skills as a method of improving population health and well-being. Documents such as the Wanless papers (HM Treasury 2002), which first introduced the concept of the 'fully engaged scenario' in the UK and, more recently, the European Union's Health 2020 (European Commission 2012), have made a compelling case for embedding health improvement skills into both the specialized and generic workforces, lending strength to arguments for the fusion of service and workforce redesign, putting capacity, capability and workforce flexibility at the centre of attempts to increase productivity, by making sure that everyone has the fundamental skills and knowledge to make every contact count. Such documents provide an impetus for action – but what they cannot do is adequately capture the fundamental skills and knowledge which will be required at each level of the workforce to realize these dreams.

A number of projects have been set up which have aimed to support broader workforce skills development. In England, projects such as Making Every Contact Count (MECC)[9] offer an opportunity to equip the broader workforce to act as ambassadors for healthy lifestyles, and to increase the capacity for the delivery of health improvement and the prevention of poor health. This project supports people from a diverse range of organizations to develop and exercise appropriate skills to have conversations based on behaviour change methodologies (ranging from brief advice, to more advanced behaviour change techniques), empowering people to make healthier lifestyle choices and signposting people to services where appropriate. The programme has been active in a number of areas and settings, supporting diverse groups to develop the skills and confidence to discuss health issues opportunistically with their contacts. Examples of groups who have undertaken MECC training include the fire service, the voluntary sector, midwives and community support workers.

Table 10.6 Applying generic skills in international arenas

Paper topic area	Geographical location	Evidence of skills in paper	Evidence of knowledge base in paper	What different skills/knowledge would have been required if this research had been carried out in USA, Africa, Caribbean
Developing a programme to improve teenage nutrition	UK	Health needs assessment Behavioural change techniques	Health promotion models Health settings approaches	Understanding of local determinants of health and health inequalities Understanding of social and cultural diversity in area Knowledge of local policies, strategies and health and social infrastructures

Accreditation of skills and competencies: an evolving agenda

Health tends to be an area which is subject to intense regulation, with an array of institutions, laws and rules in place to protect the population from poor performance and professional misconduct and assure the provision of high quality services.

At the time of writing, the processes for accrediting skills and competence development in health and well-being varies greatly by country and by discipline, reflecting differences between countries in the educational, practice, political and resource situations, and their approach to competency frameworks and skills mapping.

Various forms of accreditation exist. (All websites in the following list were accessed on 23 March 2014.)

1 Occupational accreditation:

   (a) Statutory regulation for individual specialists, for instance as offered by the Faculty of Public Health (www.fph.org.uk) for medically qualified public health specialists.
   (b) Voluntary registration for individual specialists and practitioners, such as offered by the UKPHR (for non-medically qualified specialists, and, on a pilot basis, for public health practitioners) (www.ukphr.org).

2 Organizational accreditation:

   (a) For educational providers as Schools of Public Health (for example, see CEPH Schools of Public Health accreditation criteria at www.ceph.org).
   (b) For service deliverers as providers of health and well-being services (see, for instance, www.phaboard.org/accreditation-process/guide-to-national-public-health-accreditation/ for public health departmental accreditation processes).

3 Output accreditation:

   (a) Programme accreditation for educational providers (such as www.aphea.net and www.ceph.org) for Master of Public Health (MPH) accreditation.
   (b) Course accreditation (see the Royal Society for Public Health – RSPH – for examples of course accreditation, available at www.rsph.org.uk/en/products-and-services/accreditation/training-programme-accreditation/programme-directory/index.cfm)

Despite the differences in focus, the systems share a commitment to rigorous, independent and continuous assessment.

Conclusion

As this chapter has demonstrated, the breadth and evolving spheres of practice of the health and well-being workforce have informed the growth of a complex and multi-tiered landscape for skills development for health and well-being activities. Numerous formal and informal frameworks exist which function at different levels, from the individual to organizational and provider levels.

While a number of systematic lists have been developed which aim to describe the core skills, competences and attributes required for delivery of health improvement outcomes, there are significant differences in the way the lists have been framed. In this context, the potential breadth of the professional role in relation to health and well-being skills development is extraordinary – driving progress in our own spheres of expertise, while also providing support and input to build capacity in other related occupations and spheres of practice, to optimize their impact and ours. In effect, not only do we have to exercise our own knowledge and skills appropriately, and share this experience with peers and colleagues, but we also have a key role in delivering, supporting and developing skills and activities for improving population health and well-being in other workforce groupings and across traditional boundaries.

Consolidation/thinking points

- What do you understand by the term 'competency'? What do you think are the strengths and weaknesses of this approach to skills development?
- In the light of your reading of this book, who do you think should be the key target audience(s) for health and well-being skills development? Can you make a prioritized list, based on your professional practice, of occupational groupings where further support to build targeted skills and knowledge of health improvement and well-being could impact positively on the population's health and well-being? What role could you play in supporting skills enhancement in these groups?
- What skills and competences do you think could/should be seen as (a) core, (b) specialist and (c) fundamental across all workforces? How can you support others to achieve these skills and competences?

Please now revisit your case study. In doing so reflect on the information you have read in the second part of this chapter. Would you now change any of the factors you identified earlier?

Notes

1 See www.euro.who.int/en/health-topics/health-policy/health-2020-the-european-policy-for-health-and-well-being/about-health-2020 (accessed 23 Mar. 2014).
2 Not health specific.
3 See   www.midlandsandeast.nhs.uk/OurAmbitions/Everycontactcounts.aspx (accessed 23 Mar. 2014).

References

Bernhardt, J.M. (2004) Communication at the core of effective public health, *American Journal of Public Health*, 94(12): 2051–3.

Birt, C.F.A. (2011) The developing role of systems of competences in public health education and practice, *Public Health Review*, 33(1), 134–47.

Commission on Social Determinants of Health (2008) *Closing the Gap in a Generation: Health Equity through Action on the Social Determinants of Health: Final Report: Executive Summary.* Geneva: World Health Organization.

Department of Health (1999) *Saving Lives: Our Healthier Nation White Paper and Reducing Health Inequalities: An Action Report.* London: DH.

European Commission (2012) Social investment packages commission staff documents: Investing in health, *Action Plan for EU Health Workforce.* Available at http://ec.europa.eu/health/strategy/docs/swd_investing_in_health.pdf (accessed 23 Mar. 2014).

HM Treasury (2002) *Securing Our Future Health: Taking a Long-Term View.* Available at www.hm-treasury.gov.uk/consult_wanless_final.htm (accessed 7 Nov. 2013).

Marmot, M. (2010) *Fair Society, Healthy Lives: The Marmot Review.* London: UCL Institute of Health Equity.

Marmot, M. (2011) *Health Inequalities: A Challenge for Local Authorities.* London: UCL Institute of Health Equity.

Marmot, M. and World Health Organization (2010) *Interim First Report on Social Determinants of Health and the Health Divide in the WHO European Region: Executive Summary: European Social Determinants and Health Divide Review.* Copenhagen: WHO Regional Office for Europe.

Trace Project (undated) *Tranparent Competences in Europe: Overview of European Competency Frameworks:* 12. Available at http://see-trace.eu/ (accessed 23 Mar. 2014).

Winslow, C.E.A. (1920) The untilled field of public health, *Modern Medicine*, 2(1): 183–5.

World Health Organization (WHO) (1986) *Ottawa Charter for Health Promotion.* Geneva: WHO.

Index

HEALTH PROMOTION THEORY
Second Edition

Liza Cragg, Maggie Davies and Wendy Macdowall

9780335263202 (Paperback)
October 2013

eBook also available

Part of the *Understanding Public Health* series, this book offers students and practitioners an accessible exploration of the origins and development of health promotion. It highlights the philosophical, ethical and political debates that influence health promotion today while also explaining the theories, frameworks and methodologies that help us understand public health problems and develop effective health promotion responses.

Key features:

- Offers more in-depth coverage of key determinants of health and how these interact with health promotion
- Revised structure to allow more depth of coverage of health promotion theory
- Updated material and case examples that reflect contemporary health promotion challenges

www.openup.co.uk

OPEN UNIVERSITY PRESS
McGraw - Hill Education

HEALTH PROMOTION FOR PEOPLE WITH INTELLECTUAL AND DEVELOPMENTAL DISABILITIES

Laurence Taggart and Wendy Cousins (Eds)

January 2014
9780335246946 *(Paperback)*

eBook also available

People with learning disabilities are affected by significantly more health problems than the general population and are much more likely to have significant health risks. Yet evidence suggests they are not receiving the same level of health education and health promotion opportunities as other members of society.

This important, interdisciplinary book is aimed at increasing professional awareness of the importance of health promotion activities for people with intellectual and developmental disabilities. Written by an international board of experts, it is a thorough and comprehensive guide for students, professionals and carers.

The book considers a variety of challenges faced by those with intellectual disabilities, from physical illnesses such as diabetes, epilepsy and sexual health issues, through to issues such as addiction, mental health and ageing.

www.openup.co.uk

OPEN UNIVERSITY PRESS
McGraw - Hill Education